A CALL
FROM
PURGATORY

A CALL FROM PURGATORY

–A Paranormal Memoir–

KRISTEN HALDER

Published by Kristen Halder

ISBN: 978-1-7377409-0-2

Editor: Lia Ottaviano

Cover design, illustration & interior formatting:
Mark Thomas / Coverness.com

Special thanks to my dear friend, Ed Carlton,
who pushed me to write this book.

Also, many thanks to my parents, sister, and my love, Hunter,
for their endless support in my writing journey.

CHAPTER ONE:
INTRODUCTION

I f, a few years ago, someone told me the things I knew about myself today, I would have said that they were insane. I still sometimes can't wrap my head around everything that has happened and never expected for my spiritual journey to unfold in the unique way that it did.

I was born on January 28th, 1997, in Charlotte, North Carolina. From the time I was a baby, I had the ability to see ghosts. Mom didn't realize I could do it at first, but in time she picked up on the unusual things going on with me. I would stare at nothing or follow something with my eyes and start crying or laughing. Dad was more skeptical of the paranormal, but Mom couldn't help but notice the paranormal activity in our house after I was born. Lights would turn on by themselves, toilets would flush, my animated toys would start singing on their own—all of the stereotypical signs of a haunting.

Restless in my crib, I would stare at the same corner of my room, screaming, "The lights!" My small hands would grab onto Mom in a panic. Babysitters and grandparents would mention the strange occurrences to my parents after watching me, explaining the eerie feeling they would get as my eyes followed something in a void space. In the beginning, my family didn't understand the odd happenings in the house, my behavior, or what was causing it. The things I saw scared me when I was barely talking, but as I got a few years older, I loved being able to see the spirits surrounding me.

The ghosts often had no features or faces—they were black or white silhouettes, depending on how light or dense their energy was. There were others I could see vividly. I could see what clothes they were wearing, and what they would have looked like in the physical world. Using my Barbie pencil, I sketched daily pictures for my parents so they could see what I saw. I still have the drawing of a man I saw at four years old on our staircase. He looked like he was from the 1800s, dressed in a jacket that I described as "button ribbon button." His head was topped with a long, white, curly wig that I described as paper towel rolls. Another one of my drawings presented a figure similar to Abraham Lincoln, complete with a top hat and cane.

Children are very intuitive and open, free from the self-doubt and second guessing we experience as adults. Having psychic senses often comes naturally to children because they block nothing out, and I was lucky enough to be one of those kids. Although I loved my gift, when I turned eight, my family and I moved to a new home and my ability faded. It was a scary feeling not to see spirits anymore, like diving in a dark ocean without goggles. Although I was blind to their presence, I could still feel them. After losing my ability, hardly any paranormal activity took place in the new house, and my paranormal life became a distant memory.

The one thing that kept me anchored to that part of me was a spirit that never left. I always felt it was a man and have always referred to him as "my ghost." This ghost's energy has clung to me ever since I can remember—I don't even know what it feels like to be alone. As eerie as it may sound, his presence has always been a comfort to me. But as time went on, I distanced myself further and further from my former supernatural reality.

Looking back on my day-to-day experiences as a child and reflecting upon them in my present reality made it all seem like a figment of my imagination. In time I looked up ways to regain my sixth sense, and even tried sleeping in front of a mirror for a while but found no luck. When I realized that my ability wasn't coming back, I didn't think much else of it, and slowly let it go.

At the age of fourteen, my family that was once so tight knit fell apart as my parents divorced. Mom, my sister Kylie, and I moved out of our second house and into my third. I struggled with making peace about the new arrangement, wondering why we couldn't stay together as a family. With a hard time accepting the split, I tried everything under the sun to convince my parents to stay together but my life would never be the same.

Some people notice dimes or pennies everywhere they go, often known as signs from someone in Heaven. As for me, I received hearts, especially at my lowest points and during this time. In morose times, I would see a heart in the tissue I'd used to wipe away my tears. During a difficult day, I would find a heart imprint in the carpet, or I would look down at my feet and see a heart-shaped object that hadn't been there before. I always felt the spirit that put hearts at my feet was someone who was watching out for me, someone who witnessed my pain and wanted to offer support.

That year I started my freshman year of high school. Everything felt unfamiliar: a new school, a new house, and a new family structure. My sense of humor had always kept my spirits up, but it became exaggerated after the change. My obnoxious personality that I thought my peers found funny now makes me cringe. I was never a social student and wasn't one to take part in clubs, only participating in drama, choir, and tennis through my high school career.

I didn't smoke, drink, or go to parties— I kept to myself. To my own surprise, my reputation landed me the title of class clown in my senior year. I'm not sure how I got a superlative with my small group of friends, my two best being Allison and Beverly, who I'd known since elementary school.

During high school, the three of us were inseparable. Every day after school we walked to my house, stopping at the grocery store at the top of the hill for snacks to enjoy during our binge-fest of poorly-made horror movies. At sixteen, we discovered lucid dreaming and astral projection, but never ended up being able to do it after many failed attempts. My friends tried it for the fun, but I found myself taking it very seriously. I spent months practicing but was never successful in achieving a projection. But my first visitation back to supernaturalism re-awoke something in me, and odd things began happening again.

It was a summer day before senior year. Allison and I were watching TV in the basement, pausing it when we heard footsteps upstairs. Dad lived out of state, so there was no way that it was him. Mom was at work, and Kylie was away at college. We looked at each other, frightened that somebody had broken in. What sounded like heavy work boots plodded slowly above us as we listened in a panic. Like two 17-year-old girls would do, we grabbed a pair of scissors, hid, and called 9-1-1.

As I made my way down the hall to let the officer in, I noticed that the door was untampered with, unopened, and locked. The officer stepped in cautiously as I told him what we heard and the direction the footsteps had headed. We waited anxiously by the door as the officer checked out every corner of the house. Fifteen minutes later, he walked back towards us with his guard down. In his southern drawl, he assured us, "Well, ladies, all clear. Don't hesitate to call us back if you hear it again." I apologized for having him come all the way out. As he left the two of us stood puzzled, knowing we both heard the same thing.

Two days later I was home alone, downstairs and watching TV. The heavy work boots came back, walking slowly across the floor above me. I took matters into my own hands and grabbed my weapon. Scissors in hand, I nervously searched under every bed and in every closet, only to find nothing.

For the next few weeks, the presence I normally felt became stronger. Walking by myself I would feel compelled to check behind me, certain someone was there. The activity would pick up when Allison and Beverly were over, and I was glad they witnessed it, too, so I knew it wasn't my imagination. They knew of my paranormal experiences growing up and were aware of the ghostly presence that lingered with me, jokingly blaming him when weird things occurred.

American Horror Story, the dark love story between an edgy, depressed teen and the ghost of a killer who died in 1994, Tate Langdon, was our current obsession. The recent hauntings reminded us of the ghost, Tate, so we found it kind of fun when the radio would turn on by itself. It was 2014, summer break was ending, and soon we'd be starting senior year. The TV room in the basement of my house was filled with piano playing, laughing, and Face Timing our boyfriends as we drank for one of our first times. The night rolled on as we enjoyed being dumb together for the last weekend of summer break.

By 1a.m., the three of us had passed out on the couch to the closing credits of *Back to the Future*. We planned on getting breakfast in the morning and hanging out until late afternoon. 8:30 a.m. rolled around and I woke up to see Allison already awake and on her phone. "Good morning, Allerson." I smiled as I reached for my phone. My phone light flashed to the left side of the couch and I noticed that Beverly wasn't there. I grumbled, "Where's Bev?" "She's probably in the bathroom," Allison said from behind her phone. My phone lit up as I unlocked it to a screen full of notifications. "Oh, Bev texted me. A lot." I said, concentrating on the screen.

The first text bubble read, *"DUDE, YOU/YOUR HOUSE IS HAUNTED. I literally had my dad come get me at 4 in the morning because I was sitting on your porch. Crying. There's no way I can go back into your house."*

"What? How would it be so bad where she had to leave?" I asked, flashing the screen to Allison. With hidden excitement I texted back, *"Omg did you see my ghost? And did he look like Evan Peters in any way? Was it a guy or a girl?"* Three bouncing dots indicated that she was typing. *"Neither."*

My stomach dropped and face flushed as I jumped off of the couch to turn on the lights in our pitch-black, windowless room. Frantically, we tried calling Beverly, but were greeted with her voicemail box each time. *"Sorry guys, I can't even talk right now. I can text you about it."* With furrowed brows I tried to comprehend her explanation. Around 4 a.m., Beverly had woken up at random. She opened her eyes to see a demonic-looking figure standing over me and watching me as I slept. The tall, thin, black figure with an alien-shaped head and hunched back loomed over me, the processes of its spine sticking out.

Beverly watched, frozen, as the figure turned to her. Its large, piercing white eyes with black pinpoint pupils locked onto her as it dropped to the floor. The figure scurried up to her ear, whispering in a hateful tone, "Why are you even friends with her? Leave her alone!" It spewed out phrases in a different language, and Beverly darted off the couch and upstairs through the front door. It was then that I realized the seriousness of this, and that it wasn't fun anymore. Allison and I hurried out of the TV room and into the brightness of my bedroom, word-vomiting theories about how the demon has been following me to eventually possess me.

I felt naive, and terrified to be in my own house. My "ghost" was now something that I wanted nothing to do with. I was scared knowing that I'd been in its presence for as long as I had. Beverly agreed to a meet up, but it could not be at my house, nor hers. My hand shook as I unlocked my car door and Allison and I sat quietly inside. As we pulled out of the driveway, we noticed the song on the radio, the message in the lyrics implying, "With you is my favorite place." Fumbling for the button, I switched it over. From then on, the lyrics of the song "Rather Be" were unsettling to me.

*

The three of us met at a park table. Looking upon Beverly's frightened face, I realized that there was no way she was making this up. She wore a detached expression, and her eyes were swollen from crying. She attempted to explain what she saw, but she couldn't get the words out without bursting into tears. I knew I was responsible for her trauma and I felt terrible about it.

That night none of us could sleep. During the next day, I stayed in the brightness of my living room. I'd stop myself from nodding off, too paranoid to close my eyes. Allison suggested that we sleep over at her house so that we didn't all feel alone, and I was surprised that either one of them wanted to be around me. That night as I packed my bag, I worried about leaving mom home alone. At the same time, I worried about keeping this presence in our house, or bringing it to Allison's, as though I was a walking infection. The three of us spent the night talking about what had happened, agreeing that we shouldn't share it and make ourselves look attention hungry.

The next morning, I called mom to check on her. During our talk, I learned that a few hours after I had left the night before, as she was going to bed, the whole house shook—she swore it. From that point on, I didn't want to leave her home alone again, and slept with all of my lights on. My boyfriend Cameron and I planned on a date night to get my mind off of everything. It was early in our relationship and I was at first hesitant to tell him this bizarre story. In the late afternoon, he kept me company as we watched an old 80's classic in the TV room. Before long I announced I was going to take a quick shower and noticed his expression change. Timidly, he got up to follow me into the bathroom.

I chuckled, "I'll only be five minutes, why don't you just watch TV till I get back?"

"No, I'm good," he shrugged, "I'll just hang out with you." I knew he was trying to play off how spooked he was and gave him a smirk. "I don't wanna be in the TV room by myself after all that. Shit freaks me out." Cameron saying that brought me some relief. "He actually believes us," I thought.

I reassured him as he followed me to my bedroom, unsettled as I took out a T-shirt and shorts to change into after my shower. I threw the clothes onto the couch in the TV room and left for the bathroom to draw the water with Cameron still following close behind. Together, we walked back into the TV room to grab my clothes. I stopped as I noticed only my shorts were there. "Cameron. Where'd you put my shirt?"

He shot me a look. "What? I was with you; I didn't take it."

Growing irritated after minutes of debate, I snapped, "This isn't cute, it's annoying. Just give me my shirt back, the water's running."

"I didn't do anything to your shirt, Kris!" Frustrated, he helped me look around.

"My shorts and everything are here, and I swear I picked a shirt out, it was my delorean one." I said, stumped. After five minutes of looking, we gave up.

Walking back into the bathroom, I discovered my shirt waiting for me neatly folded next to the sink. Cameron's voice quieted. "Bro, what the fuck," he whispered. Knowing neither one of us put the shirt there and that it was balled up when I threw it on the couch was enough to make Cameron to sit on my bathroom floor while I showered.

Anxious to leave, Cameron made conversation about dinner as we walked to the car. As he lowered himself into the seat, the car door slammed on his head *by itself.* It wasn't that the door wasn't opened enough—it closed with force. He looked at me with worry as I sat speechless. The thought of this entity attacking my friends and possibly my family troubled me to my core. We remained quiet for the ride, drowning out the silence with Cameron's music.

Weeks passed. Soon, my mom, Kylie, and I would be leaving for a cruise. We all needed a getaway, but I was scared of bringing the evil with us. Mom suggested I wear a cross necklace for protection. Luckily, I had at least ten cross necklaces that my Godmother sent me throughout the years. From then on, a dainty silver cross laid over my chest. Every day, the chain would break one way or another, but I didn't let it stop me from wearing it.

Before leaving for vacation, a mutual friend, Liam, agreed to meet with us about the situation and to give us some insight. Being a religious leader, he shared stories with us about the people he had helped. The people in his stories had all taken on interests in dark matters and lost their way, falling under the temptation of the devil. He explained how TV and dabbling with "voodoo" are gateways to drawing in bad entities. Feeling irresponsible and full of guilt, I agreed to let go of my interests in the paranormal.

Liam advised me to start being closer to God, to put a cross in my room to repel the evil out of my space. At the end of our meeting, Liam said a prayer to banish this evil presence. I pretended to feel better, but I could sense that the presence was still there. After opening my eyes from the prayer, I was shocked to look down and see a single heart-shaped leaf by my foot. It taunted me as it laid on the ground, and I realized that it was this demonic entity that had been leaving the hearts all along.

I was determined not to give the demon any satisfaction, shutting out any thoughts of it when they'd pop in. As vacation came and went, things seemed to go back to normal. As we got ready for the last dinner of the trip, Kylie and I sat in front of the mirror, curling our hair, when we heard something hit the wall. I walked over to where the noise had come from. I looked down to see that next to the baseboard was my jewelry that had been sitting on the bed at least three feet away from us. Kylie and I exchanged looks, engulfed in the sinking feeling that the demon wasn't gone.

I once read that by ignoring a spirit or entity only entices them to be more persistent. All I wanted was to push this evil away, but I knew that doing so would make it act out. I had no clue what its plan was, and that terrified me. I wondered what this all meant for me. I was worried, but mostly for my loved ones.

I kept the demon at a distance, not breathing a word about it. On any day that I slipped and brought it up, I would feel it come back. A light would flicker, something would fall off of a shelf, or the TV would turn on by itself. I tried not to give it attention, knowing entities have only as much power as you give them. Feeling it come in, I'd sing a religious song just like Liam had taught me, and it would go away. Every night I'd say a prayer, keeping my fish tank and lamp on.

It always lingered. I'd feel its presence the strongest when I was in my car alone late at night. By myself in a box of darkness, I was completely vulnerable. Nervousness and anxiety would creep up my stomach as I felt someone directly behind me, watching. The feeling would sometimes be so strong that I would have to turn on the lights in my car and roll down the windows to let in even the light from the moon as I said a prayer. I lived like that for months, finding that once I stopped paying attention, the signs also stopped. But the presence never went away.

About a year passed since the night that Beverly had fled my house in terror, and she never slept over again. We'd still hang out from time to time, but it was never like before. Our friendship slowly fizzled as time went on. The demon still followed her, encouraging her distance from me. Although we remained distant, I still considered her my best friend.

Without a word Cameron blocked me on social media, cutting me off without explanation. The situation put me in a three-month funk. It was like someone had died. It might sound dramatic, but losing my first boyfriend was devastating at 18. I didn't have the support of Allison and Beverly as they were changing, too. But once I overcame the loss of my relationships, I had a wonderful time meeting new people, and transitioned into a much stronger version of myself.

In 2017, after two years, Cameron and I reconnected. I had faith that we had both grown up since then and I took him back. In the fall of that year, I was catapulted into another trying transition in my life when mom's boyfriend of three years, Brad, took his life. Devastated over his death, we leaned on each other in grief. That same day, the lamp by mom's bed began flickering and both of the clocks in her room stopped working, along with every watch she owned except for the one that Brad had given her. We felt that he could be sending signs from the afterlife. It was the only solace that Mom found during her time of darkness and was yet another nudge toward my paranormal path.

Within two weeks we lost our family dog. It crippled me to see Mom so sad. *Supernatural* had become my favorite show months back, and it was one of the many tools that led me to becoming more open minded to things beyond our understanding. As irrelevant as a show may seem, the universe has subtle ways of guiding us to where we need to be.

With an open mind, I suggested seeing a psychic medium to help us connect with Brad, just like I had seen happen in the show. Although hesitant at first, this possibility rekindled a bit of hope in Mom. I would settle for nobody short of five-star reviews, trustworthiness, and legitimacy. We came across Martha, a local medium who had been doing this for over ten years. She had the best reputation, with five out of five stars from everybody who had left a review. We decided to take a chance and see for ourselves.

The day of the reading we hurried out of the door in anticipation. I felt nothing but excitement and faith that this would be a wonderful, healing experience for Mom. She stayed quiet during the drive, nervous and on edge. In an attempt to distract her from her nerves, I made small talk, which didn't help. I started to doubt if this was a good idea, worrying about how much worse she would feel if it didn't work out. "Just remember, don't give her any hints so you'll know if she's for real or not," I advised.

With a mixture of excitement and uncertainty, we stepped into a quiet, serene office. The room was glowing from the salt lamps, crystals, and welcoming plush couches. Martha put our minds at ease with her quirky personality as we picked our seats. After pushing her glasses to her nose, she gripped onto her sketch pad, "So, first off, I'll explain to you how my readings work. I may get messages or symbols that don't make sense right now but might down the road, because the messages meant for you will come through one way or another. What I do is I clear out my own energy and call in my spirit guides and angels, as well as yours and your loved ones, to relay the messages. Spirit will tell you what you need to hear. You don't get to choose like a pizza menu. All right?" Just the thought of angels being real pushed me to the edge of my seat.

As Martha began the Lord's prayer, I observed the feeling in the room. We have always been led to believe that mediums are doing the Devil's work. The warmth, the wonder, and the light that I was experiencing in that moment felt opposite of everything I had heard speculated about psychics.

Martha's eyes remained closed as she shaded in a yellow space on a blank page. "I'm picking up on a male presence, a lot of depression and possible suicide." She said it as if it was no big deal while we sat there, shocked at her abilities. "Alcoholic... and I just heard a gunshot." With teary eyes I looked over at Mom, whose face was in her hands as Martha described Brad, from his sense of humor right down to his lead foot. "He's pointing to a golden watch on his wrist, what does that mean to you? There was also another death very close to his, I'm getting a couple of weeks. He says, 'I'm with the dog.' Did you two own a dog together? There's another dog that's being shown to me, a little black and white one, Sparky? Lucky? Some dog name like that?"

Mom and I looked at each other. "Our dog just passed away, but she was an all-black cocker spaniel. Her name was Miley," I sniffled.

Martha closed her eyes again, "Huh, well, I'll let that go for now. Let's see what else...Kristen, correct? I know you're here for your mom, but there is a very dominant male figure around you. Also, a guardian energy, Michael? I believe it's Archangel Michael." I sat speechless, taken aback and honored. As I expressed my gratitude for his presence, Martha cut in to ask if I wore a specific necklace all of the time.

"My boyfriend's necklace that he gave to me?" I suggested, to break the silence.

"No, no." She replied.

I offered the silver cross that I wore to ward off the demon. "That's not the one, this is a saint's pendant. It looks like a tiny oval, flat and gold, there's a little cross in it." All of a sudden, it dawned on me. I couldn't believe it. I had that exact necklace that she'd just described to a T. I'd only worn it once to church a few years back, which is why I almost forgot I had it.

"Brad's telling you to wear it every day and to wear a chain that won't break!" I took the advice with caution and fear, like I *had* to wear it. "Don't let that message scare you, the purpose of the necklace is to strengthen your Godly connection. This isn't about a demon, there is no demon around you…" I breathed with a sigh of relief. Since then, the pendant has been around my neck every single day.

Martha exhaled. "I keep channeling that spirit around you, not demonic like you thought. It's a male. Why do I keep seeing a J in your aura field? Like, what's with the J?" Curiously, I leaned forward as Martha continued sketching. "He won't tell me his name. Guess it's top secret." She chuckled. "I'm getting the image of Betty Boop. It's either a hint at a letter in the first or last name, or did someone really like Betty Boop?" I looked over at Mom for an answer. "I've written down a few names that have been floating around with him. I don't feel like he's referring to his own name, I believe he's referring to other people. You have a lot going on so I'm just everywhere. I got David, Patrick, Ted, and Robert."

My mind spun as I tried to think of who we knew that had passed, but none of the four names rang a bell. "Well, let's leave the names for now. This man wasn't close to his mom in life…but they're closer now that she's passed on, too." Martha pondered. She was stuck on the month of May, a Taurus or Gemini sign, unsure if the April or May time frame meant a birthday or a future significant move.

Martha explained as "J" showed her walls full of beer signs and a guitar collection that belonged to a man that may be named Kenny. "I'm getting a Vietnam War vibe. Maybe he was into the Grateful Dead or Rolling Stones. He's bringing up number sixty-seven, maybe the year 1967." With nothing resonating, I wrote it off as her being inaccurate.

I listened in awe with my chin on my hand as Martha explained how the soul system works. She slowly rebuilt my awareness with each fact she relayed. Learning of past lives and reincarnation during this exchange was fundamental in the opening of my third eye, the energetic point between the eyebrows that holds psychic awareness. I always thought that the afterlife was just black and white. You live, die, go to heaven and stay there, or don't and become a ghost. The way that she explained it, we are all souls on a journey evolving into the best version of ourselves. To do this, we go through multiple lifetimes or reincarnation. We do this to learn the lessons necessary to progress until we become one with God, in the brightest light possible.

Reincarnation is similar to school, and school is life on earth. The soul is in heaven for a time while planning out the next incarnation. When it's time, the soul comes back to earth to learn the lessons it needs to achieve soul maturity, and it keeps recycling into different bodies and forms until it has understood every lesson. We travel in soul clusters throughout our different lives, and the souls bonded closest to us are often a part of the majority of our experiences on earth.

We don't always stay the same gender, and we may not always maintain the same relationship with each person in our soul tribe every lifetime. This is because we need to experience every way of living in order to grow. For example, whoever your parent is in this lifetime may have been your child in another. Whoever your wife is now may be your sister, or even your brother next time. Although we are reborn as different genders and races, the soul origin has no gender or defining factor as we are all made from light.

Sometimes we are paired with someone we hate. We don't realize that these people are necessary to teach us the lesson that we have to learn. When the soul learns all of the lessons and fulfills all of the karmas, there is no more need for it to come back into another lifetime, and it remains a spiritual being.

Martha explained that everyone is born with intuitive or psychic gifts, but most aren't aware of it. All it takes to connect with that part of ourselves is opening up to it and focusing on it. We can set an intention to grow our abilities by practicing meditation, and Martha was encouraging me to do just that. I wished I could pay for five more hours to listen to all of her wisdom. The session not only helped Mom immensely, but it opened up a door for me, and I couldn't wait to start meditating. I felt that connecting with Martha's energy boosted my own awareness, and I began setting aside ten minutes of "me" time each day to meditate so that I could see ghosts again.

I found myself wanting to learn more and wished that I had learned everything sooner. It was then that Diane Foster, a childhood friend of Mom's, found her through social media. Mom and Diane caught up through messaging, and Diane shared that she had her own practice as an energy healer, or Reiki practitioner. A Reiki healer uses their abilities to channel energy to heal a person physically and emotionally by removing energetic clutter. They do this by tapping into the patient's energy to locate a blockage in the body or aura field. Using their abilities, they send positive, healing energy to that area. Aside from Reiki, Diane could read into soul DNA and past lives. I didn't know what most of that meant but booked a session with her immediately. I found it to be an amazing coincidence that Mom and Diane re-connected during this time of our third-eye expansion.

During my energy session, I could feel the tip of a large iceberg beginning to reveal itself. Through Diane's messages I uncovered pieces of my soul's origins, dating back as far as 500 BC. Diane saw my aura as shades of red and amber like the fall, my favorite season. She told me of Archangel Michael's presence without me sharing with her what Martha had said. Visions flashed to her of my lives, one taking place in the ice age, and one of me helping in the production of the Nazca Lines of Peru.

She was able to validate that one of the forms my soul inhabited was in fact a real person, the first High Priestess of Avalon. A high priestess was a messenger and a leader of a religion, or spiritual movement. Her focuses were on intuition, higher knowledge, working with energies of spirit, and empowering the psychic power of females.

The following vision was one of a vast open field; a medieval knight was riding horseback. As the knight approached, they lifted up their helmet to reveal my face underneath. The vision represented my warrior-type soul, a "knight in shining armor," and foretold a journey that was to come in my near future. Diane felt it was something to do with my own hidden psychic mediumship, and that I was going to do something with it "that is not normally done." It would arrive quickly, and I had to be sure to take care of my vessel in preparation and during.

That session left me feeling curious and empowered and changed the way I looked at myself. I Googled "High Priestess of Avalon" and found an image of a tarot card with her on it. It showed her standing in front of a castle window, stirring a potion. In every picture, she's accompanied by a black cat that reminded me of mine, Jack, but also a black crow that I didn't yet know the significance of. She has dark hair, blue eyes, and facial features similar to my own. On her forehead rests a crescent moon, identical to a scar I have on the back of my right calf. As I looked at the pictures, something in me felt the connection, too, just as Diane had said.

Though I was eager to share my excitement, I found that I often had to stop myself short. I worried that Cameron or my family wouldn't understand. I restricted myself from talking about my gifts and abilities and instead focused on developing them in private. I meditated about five minutes a day so that I could see spirits again and gradually worked my way towards a longer time. At first when I closed my eyes, I would see only black, as many people do when their eyes are closed. In time, this vision progressed into waves of light, moving like a lava lamp.

The very first visual I saw was a white dot that separated vertically into two dots, forming a body. A skull appeared in place of the head. I looked at the skull as it began to melt, dripping as the vision faded away. Then, all of a sudden, those two vertical dots appeared again, this time forming a person. Every day that I meditated from then on, I would see a shadow of this same man, standing in the distance. I disregarded this vision's significance. I had no clue who or what that shadow would become.

CHAPTER TWO:
WHEN ONE DOOR CLOSES,
ANOTHER ONE OPENS

I open my eyes from my weekly meditation and stretch my legs after having had them crossed for ten minutes. Regaining awareness, I get up and touch the space between my eyebrows, feeling a slight tingle on my third eye. The TV sounds from across the hall and reminds me that Kylie's in the next room.

I stride towards her door to ask if she would like to watch a horror movie with me, like we always used to do. Before approaching I hesitate, remembering what Liam told me those three years ago about my interests. They are a gateway to evil things and can re-introduce the darkness into my space. I reconsider since its spooky season.

I approach, standing closely to the crack of Kylie's door, and whisper in a Scottish dialect for her to join me in the TV room.

Rain patters on the roof as I huddle under my blanket and search the movie list for new releases. We scroll for what seems like forever and nothing catches our eye. I peak over my phone. "Well, maybe we should just watch normal TV since we're striking out."

"What about this one, Kris? It's about that famous serial killer, when he was in high school," Kylie says.

I look up to the screen. "Oooh, let's watch the trailer."

I try to think of what I know about this killer. I arrive at nothing except a memory of an American Horror Story scene that he was in. I turn my attention back to the TV as the preview loads. A teenager looks out of the bus window through aviator glasses. I laugh. "Is that supposed to be him? That's the actor from Disney Channel."

"I guess. I don't know what the killer's supposed to look like," Kylie replies.

"Me either, but I think he had the glasses." I continue to watch, intrigued. The preview depicts a sinister adolescent as he caresses bones in his hand. "I'm just like anybody else," he says in the dim lighting of a passenger seat. The title screen flashes, then the screen fades black.

Kylie and I look at each other for approval. "Yas, let's do it!" we agree. We try every available streaming platform to play the movie, only to end up staring at a loading screen every time. I pucker my lower lip. "That sucks, I actually really wanted to watch that." After looking at other options, we find something else. For weeks I feel a pull to watch that movie and I try to play it every few days, unsure why I'm so driven, just as unsure as to why it never seems to be able to load.

It's now February, and I have yet to give up on this damn movie. The smell of fresh cut grass seeps in through the window, I inhale its nostalgic scent. "Don't do it today," a voice inside of me insists. I resist, staring at the remote. "I can't not try." I think to myself. I grab it, embarrassed by how many times I've attempted this, and for what?

I click through the keyboard that appears on the screen, spelling out the movie's name. I watch as the circle spins around and around, taunting me with its incompetent results. Finally, one result loads. I select the title and a black screen fades in, accompanied by music. "Hell yeah!" I exclaim. "Kye! Come here!" A school bus rolls over a hilly road as I pause the movie. Kylie steps in to ask what for. I turn around and smirk. "I got it to load finally." We load up with snacks, find our spots on the couch, and prepare to watch.

The film takes place during the killer's teenage years. It chronicles his troubles at home; his parent's constant fighting. His younger brother is put on a pedestal while the parents blindly ignore their quiet teen, leaving him to his own devices. It also depicts his troubles at school, his challenges with bullying as he tries to find his place as an outcast. He is a loner, spending most of his time dissecting and studying dead animals to satisfy his own morbid interest. Towards the last half of the movie, his parents have a messy divorce, fighting for custody over only his brother. At this time, he discovers his feelings of violence and homosexuality, adding to his confusion. Day in and day out, alarming thoughts that frighten the teen cloud his mind, so he turns to alcohol in hopes of ridding himself of the thoughts, often getting drunk during his 8 a.m. classes. In class and in the hallways, he flails on the floor to get the laughs and the attention that he is missing at home. On the day of his graduation he comes home to an empty house with no power, finding that he has been abandoned by his family. His violent urges intensify as his fears of abandonment are triggered, and the movie ends with the beginning of the first murder.

The credits roll, playing a slow, 70's song. "That was actually really depressing," I chuckle. "Yeah, I kinda feel for him," Kylie replies. I sit in silence; the story has taken me by surprise. We originally just wanted to see blood and guts. I struggle, wondering if I feel bad for the actual killer, or the pitiful, lonely character from the movie. I pull out my phone to see what the real guy looks like. His mug shot appears; a blonde man with blue eyes, a blank expression, and the signature glasses. I continue scrolling down to his description. As I read about him taking the lives of 17 men, my sympathy dissipates. I lock my phone and set it down.

The next sun rises and sets. As I lounge in my fuzzy socks and large hoodie, Allison texts, saying that she's at the door. I jump off of my couch and greet her with excitement when she walks in. As we drink our favorite cheap red blend and catch up, I feel sentimental being with my best friend of 11 years. After a bottle of wine and a couple of hours, the movie that Kylie and I watched last night comes up. "Omg, let's watch it," Allison says, wide-eyed.

I give her the wide-eyed look back. "I would honestly love to see it again." Watching it for a second time, I pick up on details that I missed from the first. Looking at the life of this killer before his downfall creates a strange and conflicting sympathy in me for him. It's as if my pull to watch the movie mutated, turning into a want to know more about this person. For the next few days I research him. Initially, I was expecting to watch the interviews and see this scary and brutal character, but that's not what I observe.

Seeing the story of this killer is the first time I've consider that these "horrible monsters" are not all monsters; some are really wounded people. There's often much more to a person's story than we care to see, and it's easy to write off someone as evil. There is no excuse for hurting another human being the way he did, but I realize stories like his are important to be aware of. His story encourages me to be more compassionate towards others, and to consider the hurt that forms "bad people" into who they are.

*

I look at the shamrock-decorated page of my 2018 calendar. It's now been three months of looking daily for work with zero luck since my nannying job ended. Boredom grows in my mind, making me stir-crazy. I press submit on my fifth job application of the day and shut the screen of my laptop. I toss the computer to my side and reach for my phone.

On the floor, I sit cross-legged and close my eyes for a meditation. I've tried to stay patient in gaining abilities but have yet to see anything and have begun to lose hope. Three minutes into my meditation, my phone hums twice, notifying me of a text from Cameron. *Do you still wanna come over?* A smile spreads across my face. I throw on comfy clothes and head for my car.

*

Cameron takes a bite of his sandwich as he stares at the screen, scrolling through the list of his favorite shows. "Can I pick this time?" I ask with a timid smile, slowly pulling the controller from his hand. As I type in the letters of the movie I've been talking about, Cameron throws back his head in protest.

"Shhh," I say as I continue typing. "It's a good movie, and you promised you'd watch it with me." He flashes me a look and continues eating. I feel nervous as the opening credits appear on the screen. The bus rolls in with the main character looking out of the window. "Why's he making that face?" Cameron laughs.

Mid-movie I peek over for a look of approval on Cameron's face, and a buzzing comes from my phone. I don't recognize the number and press pause on the movie to answer. A southern man introduces himself as the doctor from the chiropractic clinic position that I was interested in. I look over to Cameron in excitement as the doctor offers me an interview. I tell him that I'm available the next day and wait until the movie is over to go to the store for professional attire.

The next day, I drive down Highway 521 towards the clinic, nervous when I notice that I'm only ten minutes away.

I take the key out of the ignition and stare at the building. Stepping out of my little grey car, I adjust my shirt and dress pants as I walk across the parking lot. The doctor's wife comes through the door. Welcoming me with a charismatic smile and a firm handshake, she escorts me into the office and asks me to wait so that she can get a few papers from the other room. Anxiously, I sit in front of the desk as I twiddle my thumbs and observe the room.

The walls are full of plaques and awards the practice has received for its many years of service. Throughout the room there are models of spines, bones, and posters of human anatomy, and my mind goes to the killer. I think about how fascinated he would be to see all of these displays. The door creaks open and I sit up. I hold my posture so that I look fit for a chiropractic job, flashing the doctor a smile as she walks in. "Sorry for the wait! I had to get one of my patients up," she apologizes.

I play with my hands in my lap as she introduces the practice. I make sure to maintain eye contact and a soft expression as she speaks. Five minutes in and we find ourselves talking about almost everything but the job interview. At the end of the interview, she offers me the marketing position which entails me making my own schedule and working from home. I take in a deep breath and thank her for the opportunity and prepare to start on Monday.

I'm over the moon to land such a great position working for such humble people. I think of how stressed I was just a few weeks ago over work. Now, I couldn't be more thankful for the way it all worked out. I'm back on my feet financially and feel that my life once again has direction.

*

I sip on a milkshake across from Cameron and enjoy "Runaround Sue" playing out of the diner's jukebox. "So, Kris, would you wanna move out with me now that you're saving up again?" Cameron asks, reaching for a French fry.

"Aw, I didn't even think about moving out until now... I would love to live with you! I just don't know if I'm ready to leave Mom. She's still in a dark place over Brad, and I would feel horrible leaving her at her lowest time. Plus, her and I are super close." Over the course of thirty minutes and a basket of fries, I agree that finding a place together might be worth considering. I consider that a place to myself while Cameron is at work is the perfect opportunity to crack down on opening my third eye in my own, quiet space. After a lot of convincing from Cameron's end, and a lot of reassurance from my mom, I realize it's time to leave the nest, being that I'm twenty-one years old.

It's April 11th, and we sign a lease at a brand-new apartment complex called The Indigo. I look around at the state-of-the-art features, in awe of the resort-like pool area, complete with fire pits and hanging chairs. As a plus, it's less than five minutes from Mom's house. It is the absolute perfect place, the place that will start a new chapter in my life. With the move in date set for June 1st, we have a lot to prepare for our new home. I don't allow the paperwork or packing to stress me out because of how happy I am about this new beginning.

Cameron and I have fun picking out things for our place and sharing ideas with each other. He scoots over to show me his phone. "Babe, look at these mini bars. It'd be bomb to have one. Which one's better? There's the Sharon bar with wine storage, it's the squarer one. And I like that shelf. But I kinda like this one, the Milwaukee mini bar."

I smirk. "Definitely the second one." I love seeing the difference in Cameron. He's expressing so much ambition and confidence, when normally he doesn't show much drive.

I come home from his house feeling on top of the world. I'm just so happy, and my heart is overflowing with gratitude. There's so much to look forward to, and I'm so fortunate.

I sit back on my bed looking at the empty boxes, eager to start filling them. But somewhere behind my joy lives a sadness, and I start thinking about the killer again. What he said right before he died plays in my mind. "This is the grand finale of a life poorly spent, and the end result is overwhelmingly depressing. How it can help anyone, I have no idea." Those words hit me like bricks. I think of the emptiness with which he carried himself. I think of his blank expression, numb to everything after a life of trauma and disappointment, and how he took others down with him. How he was robbed of the simple joys in life, and how he took those joys from others. How he never had and never will experience happiness the way I am right now. I realize how even now he must remain miserable, suffering in hell. A burning sensation climbs up my throat and into my tear ducts. With a heavy heart I lean forward in a weeping fit. The injustice of the situation envelops me like a suffocating hug and makes me gasp for air.

I don't know what has come over me as my tears flood the palms of my hands. On my knees, I inch closer to my Archangel Michael statue and take a deep breath. "Dear God, I am asking that you send light to wherever his soul may be. If he is in hell, spare him a glimpse of light. Allow him to feel the warmth of love and comfort, even if only for one minute. Allow him the feeling of kindness; let him know what good feels like. Just a moment of relief is all I ask. Thank you, thank you. In God's precious name we pray, amen." I feel timid as I come back into my body. What was all that for? Part of me feels ashamed to ask of kindness for such a soul, but I feel better by doing it. With heavy eyes and a heavy heart I tuck myself under my sheets and click off my table lamp, saving the boxes for tomorrow.

*

I check the calendar: it's only two weeks before move in. As I place each one of my things in the moving box, I feel more and more homesick. There's so much sentimental value in this house after seven years of memories. But thinking of everything that I have to be excited about lifts me out of my funk.

I tie up my hair and move to the next corner of my room. I make my way around my bed, reaching for the pile of folded clothes next to my dresser, and glance down to my giant stuffed dog that sits on the floor. I tilt my head as I notice the dog's left leg is in an odd position, touching the right. My OCD tendencies kick in and I kneel down to move its leg back into place.

I leave the room to get more boxes and come back to the dog's leg touching the other one once again. The stuffed dog sits by itself. Its eyes gaze into the distance and it smiles with its tongue out. With a huff I put its leg back into place and watch for any movement. Throughout the week, I'll play this game with the dog leg at least three more times, putting its leg back to its normal position and returning to find it's moved.

That night, I open my eyes from a deep sleep to the sound of knocking on the wall behind me. *Tap...tap...tap.* I look behind me with one eye squinted open to see my headboard wavering. I get up to turn off the fan, hopeful for a solution, and close my eyes in the sweet silence. Then, the tapping starts again, just after I've dozed off. Maybe I was moving around in my sleep and inadvertently shook the headboard. Groggy, I get up to slide the mattress away from the headboard so that they're not touching. I throw myself back onto my pillow and drift back off. In a haze the next morning I wake up to the same scenario, again at the same time as yesterday. Irritated, I get up to pull out my mattress even further and go back to sleep.

The next morning I wake to silence but with a booming headache. Clicking on my phone, I notice the date as May 21st. "Oh, it's *his* birthday; the killer's," I think to myself. "Dear God, wherever he may be, please send him some peace. Lift him from whatever dark place he might be in, just for a little. Thank you, thank you. In God's precious name we pray, amen."

I have a lunch-and-learn at a local fire department, then I get to see Cameron. As 3:00 comes, I roll down the street of my neighborhood, expecting to see Cameron's car waiting for me by my mailbox. Turning into the driveway, I press on my brakes when I see a black lump in my parking spot. I squint my eyes to look closer and notice that it's a foot-long turtle. I step out to kneel on the pavement. "How'd you get all the way up here, my dude?" I ask. I lightly grip his black shell as I walk him over the grass, through my gated fence, and down the hill to the pond. I set him gently by the shore and watch as he paddles into the murky water. I snap a photo with my phone before I head back.

My eyes light up as I see Cameron's car coming over the hill. After running up for my hug, I grab his hand and lead him through the front door as I tell him about the turtle. I glance over my shoulder at his unenthusiastic expression. "Oh, cool." Cameron mutters as he heads straight to the TV room.

"Can I feed you?" I ask.

His eyes lock onto the TV. "Nah, I'm good," he answers.

"How was work today?" I ask.

His response is as stale as the first. "It was good."

I grab onto his face and chuckle, "Why are you being so short?"

Cameron giggles. "I'm just tired. I've worked a lot this week to save up for our apartment."

Reassured, I snuggle up to him and focus on the TV show. A half hour passes and I wake up from a snooze, noticing Cameron moving my arm off of him to get up. "Sorry, are you going to the bathroom?" I say with a yawn. "No, I'm actually gonna head out." Cameron says plainly. "You're leaving? We haven't seen each other all week, are you sure you can't hang out for a little longer?"

He mumbles as he shuffles towards the door, "I'm just tired, Kris."

As I walk him to the front, I reach up for a hug, "Okay, well, love you. Drive home safe." I watch as he drives off, then shut the door in front of me. I sit on the edge of my bed, thinking about how I'll be able to see him more soon enough. My phone starts buzzing and I pick it up to see Cameron's name flashing across the screen.

My heart flutters as I answer with a goofy hello. Cameron sounds meek. "I'm worried about something and I wanted to call you about it…I just don't know. What would happen if we broke up?"

Taken aback, I stutter, "I mean, anything could happen, but I know that we would handle that situation the best that we could if it came down to it. That wouldn't be until way down the road, but we're going to be fine. You know I'm not going anywhere." I walk in and out of my room, listening intently as he explains his concerns.

"I mean, if we broke up, I would still want to be friends..."

I stay silent as a chill runs down my neck. "That's weird, why are you saying that? This is all really random."

"We don't connect anymore. We're just two different people, Kris."

My stomach turns as I pick up on where this conversation is going. "Wait, what? I think we're the happiest we've ever been! We're just beginning and we have so much ahead of us. We're opposite in a lot of ways, but that's what makes us go together so well. We even have the same birthday. We've always connected." The other end of the line is silent. "Are you wanting to end things?" I ask, fidgeting with the pillow in my lap.

"I don't know," he answers timidly, his voice trailing off.

"Well, if we're going to have *that* talk, I want it to be in person, not over the phone. Should I come over?" I ask him, hoping that he'll clarify that breaking up isn't his intention.

"Yeah, I think you should just come here," he replies.

I hang up, stumbling out of my room like a lost puppy. My hands tremble as I put the key in the ignition. We have less than two weeks until we move into our new apartment. We've already bought everything that we need, except for cups. How could I have had no clue that he was feeling uncertain about our relationship, especially when he was the one pushing me to move in with him?

I pull into the wooded back road driveway to see him standing next to his car. I park in my spot and get out. With tears in my eyes, I look blankly at him. He's making that face that he makes when he's sure about something. I want to approach him the way I always do but he's just standing there, cold and uninviting. We sit next to my car on the pavement for over an hour as I prod him for information about his decision. I try to understand everything: how I missed the signs, what I could have done better. There has to be someone else, but he of course denies it when I ask.

Dumbfounded, I ask, "Well, what are we going to do about the apartment?

It's only two weeks till move-in so I think they might charge us for the first month."

"I mean, I'll still take it and can buy all the stuff from you," he answers.

"Cameron, you can't afford that. You will put yourself in a hole. I know I don't have a say in what you do anymore, but I still care." Saying this feels unreal. I reach up to wipe away my dripping mascara. "I'm going to have the lease cancelled. It was going to be hard enough with our money combined, I can't imagine you paying it by yourself. Why don't you try for that one in town with the balcony? You can make that on your own. I just can't believe I won't be there with you now, this is all so bizarre to me."

Crickets chirp and the wind whispers through the trees, breaking our silence as we sit on the ground. I focus on a dead leaf, ripping it up to occupy my nervous hands. I'm giving him the time to realize that this is crazy and to take it all back. Hesitantly, I dare to say, "Well, I guess there's nothing else. I'll get going." He nods in acknowledgement and I choke back my tears. I hold his hand for the last time. "Just please promise me that you will take care of yourself, and that you'll finally stop smoking. I'm serious. If you need literally anything, all you have to do is call me, okay?" I kiss his hand, leaving a few of my tears on his fist.

Just like that, on May 21st, 2018, I walk away from the person that I love, and what I thought would be my new life. I drive away thinking, "What just happened?" My stomach sinks. I can't do this; I can't handle this. I feel lost, as if my future just fell down a bottomless well, and I wail like a child. My eyes are cherry red as I walk through my garage door. Mom and Kylie reach out their arms to console me, their faces red with anger but their eyes soft with sympathy. "He's not getting your stuff from the storage unit. You paid for all of that, it's yours! Would it not bother him to be around the things that *you* picked out? That's nervy of him to still want to move in," Mom complains.

"I'm going to kill him," chimes Kylie. Their ranting sounds like mumbling as I stand in an overwhelmed haze. In bed that night, I'm afraid to shut my eyes and relive this moment in my dreams.

*

Today I'm taking off of work to return everything from the apartment. I can't keep walking past the boxes at the bottom of my stairs, waiting to be taken to the new place. The *Milwaukee bar* box stands tallest and taunts me with what I almost had. I break down for the fifth time today, trying to erase the idea of that new life. Suddenly, I'm soothed by a sense of strength and dignity. The wave of calm dries my tears and lifts my head high, giving me the idea to clean up this mess. By evening, I've taken care of all returns and cancellations. Now, it's almost as if none of it ever happened.

For the next two days, I'm numb. It's a strange and unfamiliar feeling to be home while feeling like my new home is The Indigo. I don't know where I belong, or to whom. The one person who felt like home doesn't even want me.

After two days I figure it's time to pull myself together and get back to work. I can ease into it by working from home, not having to put on a happy face for anybody. I adjust the pillow behind my back and sit with my laptop. The cursor blinks as I stare at the blank search bar. I sniffle and type, "South Carolina health fairs May 2018." As I hit enter, tears well up in my eyes and my throat begins to tense. I know I'm about to have a moment. Mid-reach for the tissue box, I halt. I stop sniffling as the smell of cigarette smoke fills my nose. I look around in puzzlement for the source. Nobody in my house smokes, and none of Cameron's things have even been in my room.

The smell lingers and I become lightheaded from trying to breathe in enough of the scent to figure out what it is. "It's definitely cigarette smoke," I think. My neighbors don't smoke, but maybe a visitor is smoking in their yard, and the smell is creeping in through our air conditioning somehow.

Throughout the week, I'm hit with the smell of cigarette smoke time and time again. Whether I'm making food in the kitchen or walking on the treadmill, it always catches me off-guard. Kylie is sometimes present when it happens. She doesn't smell it when I do, but she swears she has been smelling it randomly, too. My paranormal interests resurface as I remember hearing that ghosts can manifest scents. I consider that as a possibility, being that there's no other explanation for the smell. I'm touched as I remember that my late grandfather was a smoker and may be visiting me during this hard time. "Hey, Grandpa T," I say, smiling.

The pain of my breakup with Cameron still lingers. I just want everything to go back to the way it was a few days ago, but I know that reality is now non-existent. For about a month, Kylie and I had planned a trip to Charleston to surprise my dad for his birthday on the 26th. Celebrating and acting happy is going to be tough, but I can't disappoint Dad, so I pack my bag to head out in the morning.

That night, I burrow under my covers with no emotion. I dread having a dream about Cameron: one where we're together again, only to wake up and find that has changed. With that in mind, I brace myself as I fall asleep. Instead of dreaming about Cameron, though, I have the most vivid dream that I have ever experienced. I'm completely lucid the whole time and lucid dreaming is something that I haven't been able to do since I was little.

The scene was black and white. As I approached, colors slowly faded in. I appeared in a dimly lit room of an art deco styled apartment that I had never seen before. The only light emanated from diamond-shaped sconces on either side of a black wall. Standing in the living room was a blonde guy with long hair, his back to me. I walked up closer to see that it was the killer from the movie. Wearing a pale-yellow collared shirt and brown corduroy pants, he stood with his shoulders hunched. He was staring at Cameron, who was standing in the room in front of him.

I felt that a presence was actually there, that it wasn't just a projection of my mind. Everything was so real that I felt nervous as I walked up behind the killer. Before I could tap on his shoulder, Cameron began to lunge forward in an effort to attack me, his expression was angry and his fists were clenched. With a powerful yet subtle force, the killer's hands blocked Cameron from reaching me. The dream remained vivid and I lucid as he continued to shield me. As I stood watching from behind, Cameron faded into the background and then out of sight. I locked my eyes onto the back of the killer's silky blonde hair. It's impossible to describe how certain I was that this was a real person in that moment. Shyly, the teen turned with open arms. A sense of comfort and an odd familiarity washed over me as my eyes locked with his. I felt drawn to him as he reluctantly extended his arms to me. Before we could reach each other, I awoke from the dream.

I have experienced visitations from loved ones in dreams before, and this felt the same way. It was too real for it not to have actually been somebody visiting from a different dimension, and I have no doubt that a guardian angel had sent that dream to help me. The dream distracts me, pulling me out of the rut that I had been stuck in. After that, my mind stays on the actor who played the killer instead of on Cameron. The actor appears as a kind soul and a happy person who is ambitious and driven. Seeing the kind of person that he is sets an example for the kind of person I now want to be with.

I thank God for sending me that dream. Because of it, I'm able to enjoy my trip to Charleston to visit my Dad without thinking about the breakup so frequently. After surprising Dad, a group of us go to a beach bar for his birthday. We drink fishbowl after fishbowl and dance for hours, to everything from "Hotline Bling" to "Bohemian Rhapsody." My dream is in the back of my mind the whole time, saving me from thinking of Cameron, and I'm so grateful for it.

CHAPTER THREE
GHOSTLY VIBES

I hold a sense of pride for the strength that I maintain after the breakup. It's a night and day difference from how I handle it now and how I handled it in 2015. Years ago, I let the breakup bring me down and keep me prisoner. I was desperate for closure, and him. This time, it has helped me flourish into the person that I've always wanted to be. Without the toxicity in my life, I feel I can do anything that I set my mind to.

*

I've been fighting off a headache since I woke up and toss back a few ibuprofens with a swig of green tea. With no distractions and more free time on my hands, I close my eyes and quiet my mind. The freedom of this independence has seemed to inspire a deeper connection within me during meditation. I sit in silence as I feel my third eye and body buzzing, as if my soul wants to take off. In front of me and beyond the darkness of my eyelids, I notice the ebb and flow of the "lava lamp," moving visuals transforming into black and white images. I squeeze my eyes tighter in attempt to see clearer.

Through the void is a glowing grey outline of that man standing in the distance, that same man that I noticed back when I started. Is this a figment of my imagination? Should I be afraid? I don't interact, observing him from 30 yards away. A mild tapping on my thigh brings me out of my meditative state. I notice now that I had been feeling this for a few minutes, realizing that my fingers have tapping my thigh one by one, starting from the pinky to the thumb and back. Strange, that's never been one of my quirks before. I close my eyes once again and find that the man hasn't moved, and the image doesn't dissolve like the others.

In each meditation the man is there, presenting himself closer and closer each day. I stay in the zone, fascinated that I can see physical visions in my mind. I sit on the carpeted floor as my back relaxes against the foot of my bed. I lay back, waiting for the possibility of seeing something else, like waiting outside for a glimpse of a shooting star. I'm serene as I stare into the pitch black, listening to humming through my ear buds.

I jump as a face pops up. The image is black and white so I can't catch the color of his hair or clothes but I can see aviator glasses resting in front of his eyes. The man's hair is neatly combed over, his facial features blurry but prominent. I'm confused as I stare at the face of the killer himself. The flash of the image happens quickly, lingering for no more than two seconds. Abruptly, I open my eyes. My mind was clear; I wasn't even thinking of him at the time. Day after day the only thing I see is that man in the distance and the killer's face. Soon enough, I begin getting visions of animals and symbols and I disregard the images that I don't understand. The progression in my visual skills excites me, giving me hope that I'll soon see ghosts again.

It has been almost two months since I first learned about the killer, and I can't seem to get him out of my thoughts, and now my meditations. I find myself itching to learn even more about his life over the passing weeks. After I watch documentary after documentary, movie after movie—everything that is out there—I order a few books online. I read a part from one of the books where the detective's last words to the killer are, "Take care of yourself, and stop smoking." The exact words that I had left Cameron with, and a painful reminder of that evening. I wonder what Cameron's doing, if he's even thought about me at all. Maybe he'll text me soon. Maybe I should text him. I go on social media to see if he's posted anything. In the midst of typing his name, thoughts of the killer invade my mind and suddenly my urge to search for Cameron goes away.

My thoughts wander over to "him" instead and I begin to think about the possibility of some outside force that drove him to commit his heinous acts. From what I've read, his surprisingly gentle nature versus the evil of his crimes just does not add up. Neither does the way that he would turn from a nice, normal guy into somebody unrecognizable. Psychologists studied him intensively during his incarceration and shockingly found him to be legally sane, with no split personality. His neighbors and peers described him as "gentle hearted" and "someone who shared what they had with others," somebody who was "tragically lonely and awkward."

The first murder that he committed took place two weeks after a séance that his classmates held at his house party. It took place just weeks after graduation, when he was left to fend for himself in the family home. Feeling isolated and extremely depressed, he threw parties at the house to fill the silence. During the first party, a few guys suggested that it would be fun to perform a séance and attempt to summon Satan.

Excitedly, the group sat in a circle with joined hands, lights off and a few candles illuminating their space. They called in "the Devil," and the candle flames began to waver. Silence fell among the group when the candles all blew out at once. Everyone, including him, was unsettled, as they could feel the presence of something dark and sinister enter the room. A few of the guests were so creeped out that they left early, and that was the last they saw or heard of him before his crimes became known world-wide. When I learn this, I'm reminded of my demon experience senior year.

Back then, I learned that demons are like parasites, attaching to emotionally damaged people to feed off of their negative energy. They also feed into it, manifesting more negativity as they attract issues and darkness to the vulnerable host. I am a firm believer in demonic entities, having had personal experiences of my own. With the knowledge that I have of darker entities, I know that one could've very well influenced me to take a darker path, had I not been aware of its presence. Evil entities can influence people, and I wonder if that was what happened to him.

Tossing that idea aside, I reach for my phone to look for a workout. I enter the passcode for my phone when a box pops up. "Recommended for you, *The Ghost of a serial killer speaks through a spirit box.*" I gawk in disbelief, seeing the face of the killer in the preview. What are the odds? I bite onto my thumbnail and press play. A guy stumbles over leaves in the wooded backyard of the killer's childhood home, holding up an EVP radio to the camera. "Are you here?" he asks. The radio crackles as he waits for a reply.

Over the muffle of the radio a voice responds, "I'm around."

"Can you tell me about who you killed in this house?" Clicking back and forth, the radio frequency picks up a muffled, "...Maybe."

Not yet convinced I rewind the video, holding the speaker up to my ear. Listening closer, I hear that the mid-western, monotone voice on the radio is a dead-ringer for the killer's.

"Can you say who your victim was here?" the guy asks. A response comes through, "Steve...it hurts." Static muffles over faint words. "Do you see me? Help. Help me," The monotone voice pleads.

I remember reading an article about the movie being filmed in that very house. During a nighttime scene, one of the actors got an eerie feeling and stopped saying his lines. Spooked, he started cursing the killer's name, saying that he didn't feel sorry for him, and calling him a piece of shit. His insults fell silent as all of the power blew out in the house. In the midst of the crew's panic, the actor attempted to take back what he said. The frightened techs scrambled to recover the lights only to find that the backup generator was blown, too. When the actor shouted, "I'm sorry! I'm so sorry!" the power came back on. Between the two experiences, I'm beginning to wonder if the killer is stuck as a ghost in his childhood home.

Despite his horrific reign, his tragedies somehow sadden me. A ghost in limbo is essentially a lost cause when nobody is aware that it needs help, especially when it is someone so hated. The thought of that happening to anybody is terrifying, and I find myself anxious about his current state.

Maybe the way of giving myself peace of mind about him is to help him as well as the souls of the lives he took. The thought of his victims weighs on my heart, and the entire situation begins to burrow itself into my mind. With closed eyes I join my hands together. I pray for Steven and the sixteen other men, extending peace to them. I pray for guidance in what to do for the person responsible. After an "amen," I check the date to put his timeline in perspective. June 18th, 2018, the same date he committed his first murder. If this isn't a coincidence, I don't know what is.

Maybe one day, when I re-obtain my abilities, I can go to his childhood home to help. It will take some time before I develop my skills again and will be awhile before I can reach him. I think of other ways of helping, besides sending prayers. I try to think of what tethers a person to this realm; what makes them unable to pass onto the next.

With an absent family and not one best friend, I can only imagine the sorrow that built up in him over the years. I wonder if I can send him energy telepathically, the way that Diane did over the phone during my Reiki session. I wonder if there is a way to send him the energy of love that he missed out on in life.

The house is quiet, and I'm the only one here. I unlock my phone and search, "Sending Love Energy to Someone." I lean forward as multiple results pop up and scroll down to the comments section to see what people really think. One woman shares that within the same day of sending love to her ex-boyfriend, she received a call from him after not hearing from him in over a year. Another comment was from someone missing their cat for two weeks—the day that she sent the love to the cat, he returned home.

Pulling myself from the rabbit hole of the comments section, I feel encouraged to give it a try. Adjusting my ear buds and sitting myself on the carpet, I press play on the first video I find. I quiet my mind, put my body at ease, and listen for guidance. A soft piano introduces the guided meditation and a man's voice begins to speak. He explains that everything is made of infinite energy, constantly flowing through organisms and objects. The soft voice explains that the heart is the biggest conductor of life energy. When you intentionally focus on it, the energy can be sent to anybody anywhere in the universe, despite the boundaries of time or space.

I follow along as the man instructs me to think of a time that brings in the feeling of pure, unconditional love. I recall a memory from my childhood that gives me warmth and appreciation, and feel it gather in my chest. "Now, think of the person that you would like to send love to." In my mind's eye, I see the killer in his last year of life: dirty blonde hair, golden aviator glasses, and an army green prison uniform. He's sitting on the edge of his couch in his childhood home, defeated, with his head in his hands. The voice in my ears advises that it's time to radiate love out to that person.

I watch as a beam of light travels from my heart to his, channeling an intense flow of energy. The bright pink light cascades around his being and envelopes him in an orb of healing. It dances around his body without judgment, moving with grace and gentleness. The love absorbs his pain and washes away what was once heavy negativity, bringing about a comfort that even I feel.

"Don't doubt that you are doing this correctly. Know that this energy travels instantaneously, and that your person of choice is receiving the energy in this very moment." I watch in my mind's eye as his slumped posture lifts and his face releases its tense expression. A slight smile warms his face as he sits inside the energy of pure love for the first time. Concentrating on the words, something slides down the skin of my cheek. I reach up to feel my face and touch a teardrop.

As the audio fades out, so does the scene. Adrenaline soars throughout my body. My headphones are silent as I soak in the euphoria. Coming back to reality, I feel unsure if what I did really worked. My mind forms a speculation. I remain on the floor and decide that I can devote a little time out of each day to send energy to the killer, who may desperately need it to pull himself from relentless despair.

*

I trace my eye with black, fluffing my lashes with a mascara wand as I get ready for work. I stare into the mirror, focusing on the liner, when suddenly my hand goes limp. I slam my palm on the counter to catch myself from nearly fainting. My head booms with a sudden ache as a wave of nausea washes over me. The pain in my head vibrates from the top left side, feeling like a split down my skull. I stumble back, shutting the toilet lid so that I can sit down on it. It's as if a heavy blanket has been set over me, the density weighing down my back and shoulders. Staring at the tile floor, I try to recuperate. I take a few deep breaths in and out, and the feeling lifts as if it was never there.

Before regaining my footing, I sit for a minute more and check social media. As I scroll through the feed, I pass by a black and white video. I continue scrolling with the urge to go back. I once again find it, curious as to what my pull towards the post was. A snippet of a new, fast-paced pop song by Ariana Grande plays as she sings about *the light coming to take back what darkness took away.*

The light is coming? It's as if the song is cheering me on, telling me that I'm onto something with this sending love idea. I feel a sense of strength, a spark igniting in my mind as the song plays on.

I make my way to work down 521 Highway with my arm outstretched to high five the wave of summer heat. The wind fights to drown out the radio but the lyrics of the song playing catch my ear. I've never been one to appreciate or connect to lyrics. Today, however, it seems as if songs are speaking directly to me, now for a second time and correlating with my bizarre idea. I roll up the window and the volume to hone in on the song, "Lovely," by Billie Eilish.

I feel the music, listening to the message of *someday making it out of here.* A violin whines with the singer's angelic sound vocalizing "Welcome home," and it's as if I can catch a glimpse of what the killer's victory would feel like, standing in front of the gateway of light. A radio commercial blares in and snaps me out of my daze. I have no clue what I'm doing or if this is even possible, but it's a hell of a goal to attempt. How wild would it be if I helped this serial killer into Heaven?

I arrive to the fair, my office for the day, and pack mule the equipment to my spot. The sun beats down on my shoulders as I plop the tent onto grass and get set up for the event. The middle-aged DJ brushes off the tip of the microphone with his stained racing t-shirt. "Testing one two, testing one two. Check, check." The DJ gets started with blue grass as the crowd pours in, ready with screaming children and dripping snow cones in hand. Squinting through my aviator sunglasses, I look around at the crowd, wishing I could leave when it's only the start of the day.

I smile as I make conversation with a group and check their spines. "Looking at the screen you can see where your tension lies, and how each color represents a different level of it. The green areas mean that the area is perfectly healthy and good to go. Then, see where these red spots are areas of concern…" I stop talking, overcome with pain coming from the left top side of my head as if my skull just cracked open.

The pain is unreal, and I try to act as if I'm not about to keel over. I take a brief moment to let the feeling pass and rub the top of my head. To the group, I shrug it off as if I was being ditzy. "I'm sorry, I completely forgot what I was going to say!" I laugh. They laugh too, probably out of sympathy.

I've read that psychic mediums can tell how a person passed by experiencing their symptoms. Remembering this, I notice that this same area of the head was where the killer was bludgeoned to death, and it sure as hell felt like I just was. I shut off the thoughts as if they are something inappropriate, not letting them live in my mind for a moment more. What am I thinking?

Each group passing through my tent keeps me occupied and the day flowing along. I check the time with only thirty minutes left and I begin slowly packing up the table. The DJ's grand finale is "Bohemian Rhapsody," and I text a video to Kylie. "This song again lol."

*

I walk in through my garage, the scent of my house welcoming me as I kick off my work flats. I go straight to the medicine cabinet for ibuprofen to rid myself of my lingering head pain. As I look in my reflection, I begin to wonder what another cause of the headache might be. It can't be a head rush from crying because I don't do that anymore, now accustomed to not thinking about what happened a few weeks ago.

It's not only the headaches that concern me lately, but the feelings that accompany them. At night comes the heavy blanket feeling, weighing down my back. I sometimes laugh at the sensation of my knees buckling when it hits me as I walk; it's as if I'm giving someone a piggyback ride. At times it is hard for me to breathe; the pressure in my head and neck area feels like it's restricting my throat. It comes and goes all within 30 seconds, leaving me feeling physically fine but dumbfounded.

I lay outstretched over the comforter. My chameleon, Leaf, sleeps in my hand. As I pet Leaf's cone, I feel something's missing; an empty feeling. On my TV I search for one of the killer's interviews and instantly feel better. "Strange," I think. I set my dinner plate over my lap and allow the bed to envelop me as I unwind from my day. He appears on the TV in his dark green jumpsuit, sitting uncomfortably across from the interviewer. "I try not the think about the victims too deeply because then I get depressed," he says. "Anything I say to the families of the victims will just sound trite and empty. There's no big enough apology, or really anything I can say about what I've done to their sons."

Blink... blink... blink. My gaze breaks with the screen as I look to the strand of Edison bulbs above my TV. Those were brand new for the apartment and yet the third one to the left is flashing. After a few seconds it stops, but I continue to stare. As the interview rolls on the bulb resumes its stillness, shining steadily alongside the rest, and my wheels begin to turn.

*

Dusk falls over the Charlotte skyline as I sit in the stands alongside my family for the baseball game. Popcorn and hard cider in hand, our group is the only one cheering as Syracuse sprints. During an inning, "Bohemian Rhapsody" plays over the field's speakers.

Kylie leans over the row, "Kris, it's the song again."

"I know, what the hell," I laugh.

"What?" Mom chuckles, wanting in on the joke.

I take another handful of popcorn before responding, "We've been noticing this song almost every day for the past, like, week. At the gas station, a restaurant, literally everywhere. I even heard it the other day at work. It's weird."

The announcer's voice echoes through the stadium. Though I'm zoned into the game, I suddenly feel something on my leg. I look down to see that it's my own right hand, tapping my fingers against my skin again. Each finger pats, from my pinky down to my thumb and back up again. I stop my hand, grabbing the hard cider can to occupy it.

At the end of the game, we make our way through the flood of people and to our car. Halfway home, Grandpa switches over the radio station. *"Mama, ooh!"* Kylie and I look at each other wide-eyed. "Told you!" I yell over the backseat. Kylie adds, "I swear, if I hear Bohemian Rhapsody one more time this week…"

Returning home, I kick off my Converse and head to the bathroom. After a long shower, my headache goes away. I tie my hair in a knot, throw on my favorite Def Leppard shirt, and tuck myself under the covers. For the hundredth time today, my mind drifts to *him*. I wonder if my light ever reaches him and if it does, I wonder if he feels better or if he knows where it comes from. The empty feeling returns as I remember him. I search the hashtag of his last name on social media, waiting for his pictures to pop up. The first one I see is of him in an orange jumpsuit being escorted to the defense table, his blonde hair gelled back.

I try to scroll down but find that I can't—the screen is frozen on that image. Frustrated, I slide my thumb up and down the stuck screen. It glitches out, the image pixelating before the app crashes. I bang the phone against my palm as if to threaten it into cooperation. The entire screen stays black and pressing the home button doesn't wake it up. Suddenly, the home screen returns. Without touching it, I watch as the phone switches to airplane mode and opens iTunes. I stare at the screen in fascination as a song plays on its own.

My fingers tap in curiosity. As I let the song play, I open a new browser and type into the search box, "Symptoms of a ghost in your house." The results include "headaches, randomly becoming extremely hot or cold, and the feeling of heaviness. Not being able to get the person out of your head, maybe seeing them in your dreams." The article explains that once a person has turned into a spirit, they are no longer confined to a body and their energy fills the space that it's in. A ghost around might explain the dense, heavy feelings I've been experiencing.

When a ghost "haunts," it's usually an attempt at communication. Spirit can't make signs appear out of thin air; there are boundaries, and they have to work with the physical world. As pure energy, they can telepathically influence a person to notice subtle things for the purpose of giving a message or reminder. It's like being in a store and pointing out something to a friend. When ignored, the signs become more persistent until the spirit gets the attention or message across that they desire.

I keep scrolling, relating to the content so far. The spirit might avert someone's attention to something they know would be a reminder of themselves, such as a number or even someone with a similar face to them. They send these reminders for comfort and acknowledgement that they are always around.

Between the cigarette smoke, the light bulb incident, and now this, it's beginning to make sense that a ghost may be the cause of the strange activity. Maybe the finger tapping comes from the energy of whoever the cigarette ghost is, and I no longer think it is Grandpa T. By opening myself up to meditation, maybe I've opened myself up to spirits. I have little doubts that I'm being haunted, but by who? I set my phone down and stare at the ceiling to cool down my brain.

In a split second, I come up with the wild theory that the spirit may be the ghost of the killer. I think about the insanely real dream that I had about him and the fact that he smoked cigarettes, which I began randomly smelling after taking on an interest in him. I think of the signs that I've been experiencing, like the light bulb flashing while I watched his interview and my phone freezing on a photo of him. I wonder if I called him in by sending him that first prayer. I blink rapidly and shake the idea from my head. He has no clue that I exist, and if he had free roam, I'm sure he would choose to hang around his family or be literally anywhere else but a house in South Carolina. "I need to stop," I say to myself, forcing my eyes to close.

I've tried to let this all go, finding that my mind has become consumed with this ghost theory. With the passing days the signs become more frequent, refusing to allow me to keep my distance. They're so frequent that instead of ignoring the signs, I begin a journal to note every occurrence. Doing this helps me to keep track of the patterns and frequency of activity throughout the day. They're clues to help me find correlations, and to figure out who is around me, since he or she is not going away. *6/7: Light bulb above my TV flickered again when watching his documentary; at night he randomly popped into my mind and my room got really hot; 6/8: TV and phone glitched out at the same time when his face was on the TV. Smelled cigarette smoke when someone on the news said the words "serial killer."*

*

After a restless night, I can't wait to do my daily sending love meditation. I sit crisscrossed in front of my TV stand with flames wavering over the candle wicks, my door shut and locked.

I listen to the man's voice and follow the routine, most excited for the part where I visualize my focus. It's the same version of him as I've imagined every time before, the 1994 prisoner, wearing the army green jumpsuit and aviators. Just from looking at him, I instantly feel love well up in my heart, overflowing and ready for direction. The pink light beams directly to his heart and fills its gap. I can feel the magnetic pull, the latch that the energy holds when it connects. I feel cared for, I feel happy, I feel everything that one feels when experiencing the essence of love. I imagine that if this is working, he feels the same energies. He might not know where the love is coming from, but I'm sure receives it like a drink of water in the desert. As the meditation closes, I open my eyes feeling empowered and lifted.

Sitting with my thoughts as my earbuds go silent, I think, think, and think some more. Unlocking my phone, I commence the internet search and type, "Is it possible to be visited by a famous person's ghost?" I'm nervous as I wait for the page to load. Only two results come up. Both articles share the same answer: yes, and that it is more realistic than we think. One author explains how she draws in certain spirits simply by focusing on and thinking about them. Of course, just as a person can be called over from across a busy room, it is their choice whether or not they will respond. Celebrity status and popularity are boundaries that humans create and are not relevant in the spirit world.

No matter their former notoriety or who they were in life, everyone is a soul. Spirits are often more attached to people than places, and visit those who have compassion for them, just like you would want to pay a visit to a friend.

With these factors in mind, maybe what I've become suspicious of isn't as crazy as I thought.

The first half of my day has passed, and after clocking out I jump into my car and rest my sunglasses over my nose. Winding through the roads of the town, I pick up a call from my friend, Madison.

"Hey! What are you up to?" I answer.

"If you're not busy tonight I want you to meet Ryan, the guy I told you about that I'm talking to," Madison says. "I think going uptown would be fun. Plus, it'll get you out of the house and your mind off of Cameron! Want to go?"

Before answering yes, I hesitate. With the possibility of the spirit being who I think it is, I consider how me going out would make him feel with his lonely mentality: left behind. No way is it time to focus on someone new, and I don't want my interest to stray elsewhere.

Madison interrupts my thoughts. "I was thinking we could come get you at ar…. six… or if you'd rather p… tha… too."

"Hello?" I say. Her voice comes through, popping and crackling like a walkie-talkie. I pull the phone away from my cheek to check for an issue and glance at the duration of the call: exactly two minutes and thirteen seconds, and the time is right at 5:21. 213 was the killer's infamous apartment number where the crimes took place and 5/21 was his birth date. I take a screenshot as Madison continues speaking.

"Yep! Sounds fun, I'll see you guys at six." I hang up.

I laugh to myself, feeling like I'm going crazy. At any given time during the day, a light will flicker or a song will come on and bring me back to him, keeping me from slipping away. Using voice text, I add this new incident to my journal.

I roll down the road, getting closer to my street, when several acapella voices croon through the radio and a piano plays in the key of a B-flat major. The familiar word "landslide" grabs me, and I cannot believe my ears: "Bohemian Rhapsody" again. I turn up the song and anticipate a mention of Heaven or light like all of the other songs I've been hearing. Chills creep over my arms at what I hear instead.

The song serenades my speakers about a young man throwing life away after killing someone. It sings about saying goodbye to everybody, having to go away and face the truth. The singer cries that they don't want to die, wishing that they had never been brought into the world.

The song changes key and the pace of the piano quickens. The message of the last verse felt like it was describing the killer's past; this next verse feels like it's describing his present. The part about seeing the silhouette of a man is just too weird, reminding me of the shadow of the man I see during my meditations. My jaw drops as the singer professes that "nobody loves me" and asks to be spared of his monstrosity. My jaw drops further as the singer declares that the devil will never let him go.

An electric guitar introduces the last verse, the words sounding like the killer's current feelings towards society; being publicly stoned, spat on, and left to die. Then, the part I've been waiting for, *I have to get out of here.* The song lightens; the singer sings *nothing matters to me*, reminding me of the emptiness in the killer, his depression. As the song fades out, I stay silent.

This song holds the most profound message yet. The sign was right there, yet I've remained unaware of its significance for weeks. I can't deny that this song, too, suggests the spirit around me. Is music his way of communicating to me that he really does need my help? Without investing any more thought, I bring myself back to logical thinking. As much as I would love to believe that this is him, my untrusting mind won't let me fully grasp any of this. I let the idea go and switch the radio over.

After I walk in through the garage, I sit at the bar stool in my kitchen with a snack.

Mom joins on a stool across from mine. "Are you doing okay, honey? You seem to keep to yourself lately…I know the sting of the breakup is still fresh, but Cameron didn't deserve you. Do you want to vent about it?"

I want so badly to share with her the real reason I've been "distracted" lately. It's funny, but I truly haven't given Cameron much thought. However, for now, I will use him as an excuse.

"I'm doing fine, and I'll be okay, I'm just still processing and adjusting. I'm actually going out tonight with some friends, so I think that'll be good for me," I reply with a soft smile.

I get lost in conversation with Mom as she shares her day: what this person said and how this person reacted to it. I share drama that I heard about at work. We talk about the clubs uptown, and which places to avoid. We discuss what the temperature might be tonight and what I'm planning to wear.

Suddenly it hits me. Usually, the killer fills my thoughts all day long, no matter where I am. I realize that I've just gone an entire thirty minutes without him occupying my mind. An intense feeling of longing fills my senses. My stomach turns as Mom's words go right over my head. How do I miss someone so badly that I've never even met? Did I hurt his feelings by forgetting about him for that amount of time? Was he trying to reach me, but I was "too busy" for him? I look down as if to check my phone. I navigate to my photo gallery to find a photo of him and feel comforted as I see him, then re-engage in conversation.

With an hour left before I have to leave, I slip under the covers to watch his movie, keeping the volume low so Kylie doesn't hear what I'm watching yet again. I set my phone on the nightstand and roll into a blanket burrito. I pause, feeling eyes on me when no one is in the room. The presence stays by my bedside and my head feels like it's about to explode. Guilt that I'm about to go out for the night and be preoccupied sets in. I'd rather stay here with him. As I continue to lay in my bed, I decide that it might not be so bad, that I *should* get out and make it a memorable night.

I grumble as I get to my feet and raid the liquor cabinet for a concoction that I can make to hype myself up. Mixing two-thirds of cranberry juice with a third of vodka, I take a sip of what tastes like nail polish remover, gagging as I shuffle down the stairs. I really, really don't feel like going.

Through my cloud of hairspray, I glance to the TV to see the killer on the screen, awkwardly making his way to the bar through the crowd of men. The disco ball reflects off of his aviators as he steps side to side with the music, a cigarette in hand. He was awkward just like me, and he did this every weekend. A sense of motivation ignites in me to go out, and I chug the rest of my drink with a puckered face.

Ryan, Madison, and I crowd into a packed club; the smell of liquor and smoke fills the air. Spotlights sweep over the room, shining blue over the heads and shoulders of people surrounding the speakers. I watch my step for spilled drinks and observe the room of people who are half gone, and I feel a sense of freedom.

"That kid's looking at you." Madison smiles at me with excitement. I look over to the one with short blonde hair and ripped pants. "No, no, I'm not even ready for flirting." I sip my cranberry vodka and change the subject. Madison leans on my shoulder to fix her heel. "You don't even wanna go talk to him?" she asks. My mind goes to the killer. "Nah, he looks like a tool," I respond. "The bar sounds fun though."

Three Jägerbombs in and I'm on the mechanical bull, hanging on for a while before flopping off in hysterical laughter. After another drink together I leave Madison and Ryan to themselves and walk loosely to the dance floor. As the bass from the speakers booms in my chest, I notice the entire floor; everyone on it is blurry. Before long, I feel a hand slide down my back, and I hop back over to my friends.

After the night has ended and my friends have pulled up to my house to drop me off, I peak my head through their car window. "Thank you. N'drive home mmsafe. Love you." I hiccup. Still in heels, I stumble over the grass and through my front door, trying to be as quiet as a mouse. My vision blurs as I grab onto the wooden door frame, struggling to take off my mid-thigh boots and ACDC shirt. Happy to see my TV, I power it on and fall to my bed. I turn it to one of his movies, exactly what I had been looking forward to the whole night. When I am sober, I often wonder what my obsession is with this man, and why I am pulled to a character such as him. Tonight, I don't question a thing as I enjoy the opening credits.

A 50's song plays as scenes of a chocolate factory flash across the screen. The candy is poured, molded, and wrapped as it travels through the assembly line. The camera pans to the actor playing the killer; he's dressed in a white coat, hair net, and gloves as he blankly loads at the chocolate Santas onto the machine. I try to keep my eyes open to watch as much as I can before falling asleep.

*

Brightness peaks through my blinds and I open them to the sun just beginning to rise. Feeling surprisingly energized and restored after rest, I decide to meditate before the house becomes filled with noise. Meditating is becoming my retreat, my happy place, and my haven. It's where I escape the materialism of the outside world and drift off to a place where none of that matters, a place with no pressure and no judgment. My own sanctuary where I am in a state of complete peace as my own free being.

After doing my third eye session, I search for a new love meditation technique to break up the monotony of the same one I have been using every day. I often wonder, when doing these meditations, if I'm sending out my energy to complete nothingness. If I'm making myself look stupid while he is unreachable in hell and if this is all for nothing. Though I doubt that he's receiving my energy, I send it anyways for the chance that he is. Scrolling through the thumbnails, one with a bright image catches my eye. I select is as I lay under my sheets. Placing each ear bud in, I press play and shut my eyelids.

I'm greeted with a calming and pleasant female voice. Sounds of a flute and chirping add to the immersion. "Get in a comfortable position and begin breathing deeply in through your nose and out through your mouth," the voice says. A visual of the killer's eyes comes and goes as I inhale and exhale deeply. My mind drifts, and my body sinks deeper into the mattress as I become more and more relaxed.

"In your mind's eye, I want you to envision a bright and magnificent ball of golden light." I watch a golden sphere of energy as it glitters and glistens, hovering softly above my chest. "Feel its warmth, and feel it expand around your heart chakra." In this moment, I swear I feel slight heat emanating from the air above my body. I feel compelled to open my eyes to check if something is actually above me but when I do, I see nothing. I close my eyes and re-center my mind.

The woman's voice advises me to watch as the ball slowly releases from me and expands larger and larger, amplifying in power. To look into it and see the emerald slivers of healing energy that it has absorbed from my own body. "This ball of energy is being intensified by Archangel Raphael, the angel of healing. Whenever you call upon him, he will answer." I see the image of Raphael before me: a fit man with short black hair, tan skin, and magnificent feathered white wings. A perfect specimen. He pours green, healing light out of his palms and into the gold. I want to smile as I feel the energy increasing.

"Now, really feel this as you project as much love and intention as you possibly can into this ball of energy. Can you feel it?" The killer comes to my thoughts, and compassion instantly flows from my heart to the energy ball, filling the entire sphere with a pink glow. The woman instructs me to see the face of the person to whom I'm directing my intentions, and again I imagine the most recent version of him. He lays heavily on the couch, disheveled and completely done in from the weight of his life. I study the contours of his face, viewing every crease and line in his skin. I look at his hair, the way that his blonde bangs rest on the side of his forehead, seeing every strand defined.

The voice breaks my concentration. "I want you to avert your attention back to the ball of golden light, filled with green and pink glints. Watch as it slowly begins to rise." My mind's eye gazes upwards as the orb floats through my roof and to the sky, leaving a glistening trail in its wake. It soars like a comet over the clouds to his childhood home and descends into its roof. It finds the killer, drawing itself to him like a magnet. The energy hovers over his head, beaming like a miniature sun. Its form releases and surrounds him completely in its healing glow.

I stand back as I witness the healing take place. Swirls of gold, pink, and emerald flow over his arms, similar to how waves wash over a shore and soak the sand. "Notice the change on their face. See the serenity and peace, how the contours on their face soften, how radiant and revitalized they now look." The energy gathers, lifting over him, and breaks into a million pieces to rain over his head and shower him in pure light.

"Watch as the speckles of energy soak into them. Their skin sparkles and shines as the energy permeates their body. It will remain there, comforting and healing them for as long as they need…It is now time to let them rest." I don't want to leave, feeling the pull in my energy to stay with him. Despite my protest the music falls silent, and my consciousness returns back to my bedroom as I hear the bubbling of my fish tank. I wipe my eyes after another intense flow of emotion.

After kicking off my work shoes I hop onto my bed with a bag of chips. I turn on the TV, stuff my face, and scroll down the list of documentaries, searching for one of his that I haven't yet seen. At this point I feel as if I'm battling a secretive addiction. I can't quite put my finger on what my fascination with this person is. It's not his crimes—when it comes to that aspect I for some reason zone out. After learning so much about his personal life I sometimes forget that he was known for being a famous murderer. Maybe I empathize with him because I see a lot of him in myself.

After another bite of chips I see the title of a documentary I haven't seen before. I press play and scoot back onto my pillow. The documentary is narrated by the main detective on the case. He explains the crimes, giving details of everything I already know. He shares how he and the killer became acquainted during their daily talks, and what it was like to be around him.

The documentary ends with an interview with the killer's former neighbor talking about the morning of November 28, 1994. While the neighbor was watching TV in public, breaking news came through that the world famous serial killer had been beaten to death in prison. Around her, every person stood up, applauding and cheering, whistling and singing praises. After a life as pathetic as his, even his death was celebrated. The thought of this hurts my feelings and forms a pit in my stomach.

The screen fades to black at the end of the documentary. Eerie humming accompanied by the sound of a synthesizer rings throughout my room. The feelings running through me along with the disturbing song turn my stomach. I look to the screen and see footage of a bulldozer demolishing his apartment building as the music continues to play. People cheer as his apartment is reduced to fallen bricks and ash. All at once I'm consumed with grief. I lose myself, wailing into the pillow until at least five minutes after the credits have finished.

Lightheaded and exhausted, I try calming down. I stare at my ceiling as I breathe in and out when suddenly, the door chimes from upstairs. Remembering Kylie and I are supposed to go out to eat together, I wipe the tears from my cheeks and rush to the mirror. Black streaks of mascara have streamed down to my chin and my eyelids are swollen. Perfect. I compose myself with a dash of makeup, and head to the stairs.

I flip up the light switch but the stairs stay dark. Stumped, I flip the switch up and down; it still doesn't work. I find a new bulb and screw it into the fixture. Even after replacing the bulb, there is no light. My wheels start to turn. "Kylie! Come here and watch how weird this is."

Kylie hesitates to turn the corner and see. Delighted to share, I demonstrate. "Okay, watch." I flip up the switch and it doesn't work. My grin gets bigger as I do it over and over and nothing happens. "Maybe the switch down at the end of the stairs is the problem," she says, trying the one at the top. We stare at the light together, anticipating illumination, but we're met instead with no result. I can sense the alarm rising in Kylie with every failed attempt, while I feel a thrill. I put the old bulb back in and try it again. Nothing. She tries once more and the light finally turns on, beaming from the ceiling as if nothing out of the ordinary had happened. Kylie pauses. "That's so weird," she says. We exchange uneasy smiles from across the staircase.

I'm glad when my family witnesses these occurrences. It's reassuring to know that this isn't my imagination, and it serves as proof to back up my story if I ever decide to share my theory with them. I want to believe that Kylie would be accepting of my suspicion, but I'm worried she'll judge me for it. Today, this light bulb incident feels like a sign that I should share my thoughts with her, in the hopes that she might now hear me out.

*

Sitting across from Kylie at the high top table of the restaurant, I take this one-on-one time as an opportunity to bring up my theory, using the light bulb incident as an icebreaker. I expand on it by bringing up other strange occurrences, and she shares a few of her own. I take that as my green light. My heart pounds as I muster up the courage to hit her with what I'm about to say.

I grab the straw wrapper as I hesitate, the paper crumbling in my fingers as I roll it back and forth. "So, I know this most likely isn't the case, and I know how crazy this is, but I'm starting to wonder if the ghost in our house is... uh, someone..." Cutting myself off, I reach for a sip of my water.

"Wait, what?" Kylie laughs.

I stutter, "Well, you know how we've been smelling a lot of random cigarette smoke?"

She waits. "...Yes?"

"I just have to point out that the timing of our *hauntings* started when I became interested in, you know who."

She widens her eyes and shakes her head, not following.

"The serial killer, Kylie"

Kylie rolls her eyes and smirks. "Oh god, Kris."

"No I know, but listen... You know how depressing his life was and how he didn't know love..." I draw back, embarrassed by her reaction.

I continue, "It occurred to me that he's probably still suffering and it just...I feel for him. I don't know why. Well, I found out that you can send the energy of love to people through meditation. So I started doing it, sending love to *him*. I didn't expect it to actually work, but now we're getting all of this weird shit in our house and every time I watch something about him, something weird happens. Also, I can't stop watching things about him or get him out of my head. It's like something just has such a hold on me. I don't know though, it's all pretty farfetched."

She stops chewing and flashes a "that's ridiculous" smile towards her plate.

"He smoked a lot of cigarettes, and now we keep smelling them. I'm just saying." Studying her face, I can tell she's half considering what I'm saying and half not. The conversation tapers off, leaving me in a state of embarrassment.

On our way home from dinner I figure I'll offer one last shred of evidence. "Do you wanna hear something crazy? You know how 'Bohemian Rhapsody' has been following us around? Well, listen to the words. It literally describes him, right down to killing someone. It's bizarre."

Quickly, I begin searching for the song on my phone when Kylie snaps, "I already know that song, I don't want to listen to it."

I hesitate. "Well, want to just listen to the beginning? It's just so interesting and I haven't been able to share this with anyone."

Quickly she responds, "I really don't want to hear it, Kristen!"

Sheepishly I put on the radio, hunch in my seat and look out the window. The night ends unsettled, and I head to my room the moment we get home.

The next day I feel tense, trying not to think about the awkward exchange between Kylie and I. I hate that I let my excitement get the best of me, but in the moment, I really felt that she might share my enthusiasm. I feel discouraged and consider if I should abandon this whole idea.

I lower my tight shoulders and allow social media to engulf me on my lunch break. I scroll post after post and catch a makeup video with a "light" song. *There's a moment meant for us, like it or not. Despite the laws I get around, I'm over here but I have to get across. The sky above me is on fire, the lake is a golden sun.*

Mesmerized by the correlation, I allow the video to loop once more. The song cuts short as a call comes in from Mom. She answers brightly, "Hey Kris! Real quick, the weirdest thing just happened to me. I was just sorting through bills downstairs and kept hearing footsteps upstairs? I thought one of you girls came home early but saw that both of your cars were gone. I went upstairs to check the living room and the lights were turned on. It really is like we have a ghost in our house!" She laughs.

I beam. "That's what I've been telling you guys!"

I hold back, considering if I want to take the opportunity to tell her. After a deep breath, I confidently begin my explanation in hopes for more understanding than Kylie offered me. As I share my theory, I feel a release and eagerly await her response as she stays silent on the other line.

Mom responds in an elevated tone, "I don't care how bad you feel for him, he was a serial killer! He is a bad person and he is not welcome here. He better get the hell out of my house!"

I don't say a word as I press my hands to my forehead.

"If you want to help, tell him to move on, that's how you can help."

I explain, "That's exactly what I'm trying to do." I feel crazy. "Well, I don't know. That's probably not the case anyways but I just wanted to share it with you. I told Kylie last night and she didn't believe me."

The silence on the line makes my skin crawl, so I break it. "Anyways, don't even give it a second thought. I'll be home around five, I can pick up dinner on the way!"

Mom coldly replies, "Okay. See you then." I want to kick myself for bringing it up again.

*

I'm really beginning to enjoy my time alone, when I can feel this presence the most. I find comfort in hanging out in my room, embracing and connecting with his energy. Oftentimes I'll be distracted while watching TV, and he will pop into my head moments before the screen glitches. Other times, static cuts through the sound as if he's telling me that he is here.

Today feels different. I sit in my room waiting for something to happen, finding that I'm waiting for nothing. My room feels desolate. Even while watching his documentary, I feel nothing. I think back to Mom's reaction yesterday. "He better get the hell out of my house" plays over in my head. She either got upset because she was worried about my state of mind, or because she truly believes the killer is here with us.

His absence suddenly took place the day after mom heard about him. When something bothers Mom, she takes action. Mom prays, most of the time for Kylie and me. Even spirits have to abide by laws and boundaries, and I wonder if she prayed to banish "this ghost" from our house. Given how insecure he was with rejection, I'm sure that if he didn't feel welcome anymore, he would leave. I try not to stress about it. He'll probably come back by tonight.

Three days pass with not one sign. All three days I have sent love, but it doesn't feel like it's been going through. Once again, I am truly alone. My worry turns to anger as the day passes and I knock on the frame of Mom's door. She smiles at me to come in.

I walk to the edge of her bed and anxiously grip the wooden frame. "I haven't been able to feel the ghost since we talked. I noticed that he disappeared after

I told you about everything the other day and I have to ask. Did you pray him away or something? This is the first time I've felt alone since it all started, and I know you pray a lot."

She looks shocked that her prayer was effective and replies timidly, "No..."

Like catching a toddler with chocolate on their face, I flash her a look to let her know that I can tell she's being dishonest. Mom remains quiet, unsure of what to say. "I know this is bizarre. Like, *really* out there. I don't know what to think of it myself, but I really feel like I might have a rare opportunity here. The signs are undeniable, and I feel like I'm being called to something." The light shining through the window fades from a dim yellow to deep navy as I explain my reasoning. Her demeanor changes from defensive and confused to sympathetic as she hears me explain his story.

In the midst of listening, Mom challenges, "It's been over a month since your breakup, I just want to see you going out and having fun." I fumble with a pillow to help steady myself. "I still am, but this situation isn't something to ignore. Going back and forth about whether this spirit is the serial killer is exhausting and lately I do get burnt out, but something always brings me back and that's what tells me to not let go. It's been hard not being able to talk about this. 'What's new with you' has even become a hard question to answer, but I want to do this. If I actually end up crossing him over, everything will go back as it was before. Until then, I want to enjoy this journey."

Mom looks at me, still unsure. Her expression seems supportive and I feel a bit of solace. We hug with both discomfort and understanding. As I walk down to my room, I realize that the support from Mom might not be relevant anymore if the ghost never returns. I click off the lights and hope for resolve in the morning.

*

It's 7:00 A.M, bright and early. My room still feels empty, but I rise from bed and make up the covers, setting up the pillows just how I like them. I turn on my chameleon's lights and prepare my space for meditation. I lay rose quartz in my right palm for the vibration of unconditional love and use it for the session. I remain tranquil as the beam of light flows to the killer. After a moment, I feel that latch that I had been hoping for. The familiar happy and light feeling hits, and I feel relieved that my energy has reached him. As the meditation ends, I feel density behind my head as if someone is right behind me. I smile at the return of his presence.

Chapter Four:
Putting the Pieces
Together

I struggle with this more than I feel confident about it, often asking, "Why me?" My mind is beginning to lean more and more towards the idea that the ghost in my house might really be who I think it is, but the theory leaves me feeling ridiculous half of the time. If this was happening with the ghost of an everyday person, I wouldn't question anything.

In meditation, the way to distinguish if a message is from spirit and not just the subconscious is to pay attention when getting an image or word outside of your thought pattern. Thinking hard enough about a butterfly will most likely make one appear in your mind's eye. If a tiger pops up unexpectedly, that's a symbol from spirit. I've been starting to notice that happening to me more often than not.

I sit motionless on my bedroom floor. My expectations, thoughts, and memories fall away as my blank consciousness stares into black. I get out of my own head, beginning to forget my identity as I fade into a form of subconscious energy. In the midst of my empty state, my own voice calls out from the back of my mind and reminds me of what I want answered. "I call upon Archangel

Michael, and only Michael into my space. Michael, can you bring clarity and show me who this spirit is around me?" My eyes lock ahead of me, watching grey particles swirl in the abyss. Something is fading in. Within a second, the image appears in crystal clear form. It's the most vivid image I've ever seen in meditation, and it's the serial killer's face.

Frustrated, I come back to myself. Clearing my mind of what I've just witnessed, I take three deep breaths to go back in. "Archangel Michael, I need you to guide me to see who is truly leaving me signs. This next image I see, I will take as my answer." Faster than the first time, the killer's face appears directly before mine. I stare past the aviators and into his blue eyes wanting to believe, but I can't.

Like a ball gaining momentum I find that the more signs I notice, the more frequent they become. That third light bulb over my TV still flickers almost every time I put on a documentary about him. I still find my fingers tapping in that one-by-one pattern when I zone out. The killer does have a common first name, but I'm now hearing it up to five times a day. In the moments that I doubt myself, "coincidences" occur and correspond directly with him, persuading me to rethink my doubts. As I think, "How could this possibly be him?" spirit shows me exactly how, as I see his first name on a billboard or sign, right at 2:13, the number of his infamous apartment. I can't escape the synchronicities as they chase me, and I log each and every one.

*

The sky is midnight blue as I lounge in my room with a chocolate bar in one hand and a book about *him* in the other. The pastor who helped the killer study Christianity shares the moment he received the request of his services for an inmate at the prison. Starting off fully alert, I become drowsy by page seven.

I flip the page as my eyes droop. "He walked into the room himself with no guard and no chaplain. Just how he looked on the news, he stood 6 feet tall with blonde hair and- 'purdishin.'" I pick up my head and look to the right. Sitting in dead silence, I'm certain that I just heard someone say that out loud. Purdishin? After glancing around for a minute more I adjust the blanket and ignore the word that my imagination made up.

I continue reading but can't let "purdishin" go. The fact that I've never heard that word before says something to me. Before I forget it, I set the thin black book in my lap and reach for my phone. I scrunch up in a ball and type, "Purdishin," into Google, but no results appear. Tapping my finger, I think of another spelling. "Perdishon," no results. "Did you mean: Perdition?" Google asks me. I select the correct spelling, perdition. "Perdition is a state of eternal punishment and damnation into which a sinful and impenitent person passes after death." Holy shit.

My mind races as I grip my phone. Was that a sign that he really is eternally damned and past the point of saving? This could mean that everything I've learned is wrong and that he is stuck forever.

My heart beats fast as I squeeze my eyes shut and pray for mercy on his behalf. Feeling a lift, I unclench my fists and ease my eyelids. As astonishing as hearing a word from the spirit realm was, the grimness of the message clouds my excitement.

I'm pretty convinced that this is in fact the killer. If it is, he's able to roam around my house, not trapped in Hell. But how is this possible in a state of "perdition?" What I know of the afterlife is that Heaven is a euphoric place where loved ones can visit Earth, and I know Heaven is not where he is. Souls are trapped in Hell for eternity, and ghosts stay wherever they died until finding "the light."

I'm having a hard time figuring out where his soul may reside if he is a ghost but also in hell. The light from the phone screen hurts my eyes in the dark room. I look up more about the definition of "perdition." The word is explained as purgatory, or a state of limbo. I read up on how a soul becomes trapped. They are not trapped in physical places on Earth, but they can be stuck in dimensions or planes. According to psychic medium Ed Carlton, one's belief system and mindset will manifest where their soul ends up. If a spirit feels they were bad in life, they're most likely convinced they're going to Hell. As a result they avoid the light and end up caught in the dimension of the living. Once a person passes, the plane that they go to will match either their high or low vibration, a vibration being the overall energy or presence of someone.

"Better" people go higher, "bad" people go lower, which is where we get the ideas of Heaven or Hell.

The lowest planes are where dark beings and lost souls reside. The atmosphere is despairing, similar to the feeling in a nightmare. The highest planes are where angels and light beings are. The energy is full of unconditional love, joy, and peace, and there are multiple planes in between the two. Once the soul is spit out into the plane that they gravitate to, they are taken through a review of their life.

Life review shows the spirit every moment in which they impacted another's life. They will experience their actions through every witness's point of view, including passersby's, to learn from their mistakes. After life review is complete and they've learned what they need to learn, they move up to a higher dimension with a greater understanding and better mindset. Learning about the physics of dimensions help me better understand why I feel the killer's spirit might be in so many places at once. After bookmarking a page, I retire the book on my nightstand. I lay my head on the cool pillow, heavy with disquiet. I try to shut off my incessant thinking and drift off to sleep.

Originally, I didn't want to accept the fact that I wanted to help somebody who did the things that he did. I still randomly ask, why am I doing this for someone who doesn't deserve it? Diving into deeper understandings of him, I find myself truly caring about him. I wonder about the dimension he is in, what he might see or feel. I imagine it's one of darkness and misery. Assuming that he actually is with me, I think of what might bring him hints of comfort in the darkness, small beams of hope.

When I feel he's present, I put on his favorite music in hopes that he hears it. He liked Iron Maiden, Black Sabbath, and Def Leppard. I'm not sure how this all works, so in case he can't hear the songs through the speakers, I sometimes sing them to him. When I'm hanging out in my room, I play humpback whale sounds for background noise, what he listened to in solitary to remain calm.

I feel a density behind my back as I walk up the stairs. The smell of toast and tea greets me as I heave up the last step and give an enthusiastic "Good morning" to Mom and Kylie. Kylie's shoulders tense as she sits across from me.

As I speak Kylie fidgets, antsy, as if she wants to say something. After another sip of her coffee, Kylie pipes up. "I didn't want to say anything, but I am getting kind of freaked out. The same thing has been happening to me for almost a week now, and it happened again last night." I lean in, showing her my interest. "You guys know what a heavy sleeper I am. Lately I've been waking up almost every hour throughout the night. It creeps me out, like someone's in my room."

I grin. "Interesting, isn't it? I'm just going to feel so stupid if this isn't really him."

Kylie sets her coffee cup on the granite and looks at me with consolation. "Even though it might not be who you think it is, you're not crazy. There is somebody in our house. At night I have to shut my door when I'm in my room because I feel something staring at me from the doorway," she reassures me. I notice her wall of skepticism slowly breaking down with her experiences.

I've always been a light sleeper, waking up at least four times during the night. I've read that spirits often try to visit during the early hours of the morning, and now I wonder if that's the reason I never sleep well. Since all of this has begun, I wake up even more frequently and automatically think of the killer when I do, like a power switch that flips on as soon as I become conscious. Hearing of Mom and Kylie's individual experiences help me feel more secure in my thoughts. It's outside proof that this isn't only in my head.

After breakfast, I skip back downstairs into the comfort of my room. Plopping onto my bed, I search a true crime community blog for new content on the killer. I scroll through the feeds of users with clever names, reading their comments under the meme posts. I feel like the awkward kid, laughing at everyone's jokes from across the room. I decide to join in, making an anonymous account. My thumbs twiddle over the screen as I try to think of something stupid for the username.

I observe what people in this community share about him, finding it less judgmental than I would expect. There are a handful of people I stay away from, the ones praising how he killed. The rest don't condone his actions, relating to him by way of loneliness and family issues; they've come to this community as a way to feel less alone in their own struggles. It's beautiful that something positive can still come from him despite the bad, that people can use him as a tool for understanding and learning.

The true crime community is all about well-known killers and crimes, but I'm surprised to come across users claiming they have connections with this killer specifically. I raise my eyebrows as I see some say that they feel his soul resides in theirs, and at least five swear that they are the reincarnation of him. Aside from those, there's a few that say they feel his spirit around them. I can't tell if they're being truthful, but I click the blue icon at the bottom of the screen to reach out to them about their experiences.

Maybe talking to others who are possibly going through the same thing will give me some clarity. These are people who will understand and want to help him, too. I can tell them about sending positive energy to him if they're not doing it already. Maybe all of our energies combined can help him through to the light. Within minutes I get one rude message back; the person is pissed that I may also share a connection. From their response and the responses two others, I'm shocked to realize I'm the only one trying to help his restless ghost.

Spirits go to those who have compassion for them. I'm sure he is happily drawn to these people, given how lonely he was in life. The small handful of people who feel for him are all on this app, which may explain why they're also having these encounters. I don't know if this is a normal thing, if they're lying, or if they're delusional. Is everybody who feels sympathy for this killer visited by him? Am I just another one out of the many?

My excitement has shifted to doubt and sadness that once again, I'm not so special. Once again, I'm in a position to be easily forgotten if I'm not needed. Millions know his name, and he is bound to visit more than just me. I should be happy for him that he's finally finding the friends he never had but for some reason it stings. I lock my phone in discouragement and set it down.

My socks shuffle over the hard wood floor as I walk to the fridge. I wrap my hand around its silver handle when suddenly a streak of white smoke passes in front of my face. I take pause, soaking in that I have just seen my first spirit in thirteen years. I'm astonished, noticing that my abilities are manifesting into multiple gifts. Physical touch, smell, sound, and now sight. I want to be more excited, but it's just not the same with him now. As I reach for the juice a push of energy makes me lose my footing. I chuckle in amazement at the efforts of the ghost.

Back in my room, I'm ready to release all of this mind clutter. Meditating feels different this time around. What was once our time alone feels invaded, as though it's no longer just me and him. I shut my eyes and once again see that streak of white in front of me. It's as if he's shouting, "I'm right here!" over the wall I'm holding up.

Dismissing him from my thoughts, instrumental third eye opening music soothes my mind. My thoughts, ideas, and memories disappear, and I look into the distance at a grey, glowing outline of a tree before it dissolves. A horizontal black rectangle awaits in the distance, staying fixed until I shift my focus to an outline of an eye. The grey moves and sways around the visual field, forming a blurry image of the back of the killer's head. He's wearing his glasses and what looks like the orange jumpsuit, washed of color. The music malfunctions, skipping about five beats before he goes away.

With gratitude for his reassurance, I let the appreciation bundle up in my heart chakra. In my mind's eye, I push forward its energy with my astral hands. The ball expands in a glowing pod, enveloping him in its warmth. I smile as he does, feeling the goodness that my energy is projecting onto him. As I close out my visuals and open my eyes, I have a new-found confidence and a stronger sense of our bond.

I think of him with every song, feeling our connection strongest during my long drives to work. In my car with music is the space where it's just me and him. I'm alone with my thoughts as I drive, windows down with the wind blowing through my black hair. My logical mind questions if this is all too good to be true. This might be that demon tricking me into thinking that it's the killer. My heart tenses as I come to that realization. But what would it want from me?

As I gaze at the road, static pops through the car speakers and I stare at the dashboard. For some reason the static makes me feel safe, as if he's communicating that it's really him. I notice the time on the clock, 3:11, an angelic number and a good omen. The color red beams from the stop light. I look to my phone for something new to listen to and select shuffle on an EDM pop playlist.

The light turns green as the song buffers, giving me no choice but to listen. *On the way descending down I've been waiting for you. I've been calling out for you, putting my writings on the wall. All you did was run from me. You take your time and I'm on fire as I wait. Keep moving.*

The sound muffles behind me, like someone is taking up the space behind the right side of my seat. I suppress the urge to turn around knowing that every time I do, the presence goes away. But I can't help it and turn around anyway. I look at the empty back seat and turn back to face my steering wheel. Just like I knew would happen, I don't feel him over my shoulder anymore. The music returns to its original volume, and I continue listening to the song as he stays in my head.

Returning home, I flip through the stack of mail and see one white envelope addressed to *Kristen Lauren Halder.* For me!? I rip open the top to reveal a reimbursement check from an appointment one year ago for $7.77. How odd. Seven, a number I've always seen as a Godly one. Lately these heavenly numbers have reached me through a milk carton, a total at the gas pump, or even on my receipts. I feel my angels are communicating to me that this ghost is an okay energy. I want to trust what they are saying, but what if it's another manipulation?

The only light in my room is the soft amber glow emitting from my lamp shade. I'm hugging the killer and look to see a warm smile on his face. He makes me laugh, sharing memories of his past. It feels so good to be with him in the physical form, to be able to see his real face. He starts chuckling. I giggle, "What's so funny?" His chuckling turns into laughing, getting heavier and more intense. Louder and deeper, it breaks off into multiple bellowing voices. With one blink I'm no longer holding him. I look in my arms to see a girl wearing a tattered white dress with long black hair covering her entire front. She reveals her disfigured teeth as she flashes a sinister grin. I move back with a chill down my spine.

My room turns pitch black, and I wander with outstretched hands to feel my surroundings. My hand runs along the cold wall and brushes up against the light switch. I can make her disappear with the light. As I flip the switch, nothing happens—just like the switch in the hallway the other week. Nerves heightened, I walk to my fish tank light, finding that it won't work, either; it's like the power is cut. I peer out of my door and into the hallway to run out. The lights work everywhere but my room, and as I attempt to step out, I'm unable to leave the boundaries of the doorway.

The plane I'm on is exactly how I imagine the killer's: dark, frightening, and constricting. I calm my breathing while staying low to the carpet to hide from the demonic girl. The ghost's presence latches beside me as I hide. He's on a different level, invisible and unable to do anything but spectate. She's coming.

I wake up on my bed in a sweat. Coming to my senses I realize that it was only a dream. Taking a deep breath, I reach for my lamp. I click it twice, and it won't turn on. I'm still in it. Like Groundhog Day, I experience the dream loop two more times, desperate to get out.

As I crouch by my bed and next to the ghost, I anticipate the girl around the corner of the bed when suddenly, my consciousness returns to my bed top. I struggle to open my eyes. I'm able to reach for my phone to check the time. My thumb clicks the lock button and the bright screen makes my eyes ache. I squint to see the time is 3 a.m. Hesitantly, I reach for the lamp switch. With one click, my room brightens. I do a reality check, looking at my hands to see if they're warped, only to find them normal. I sigh, relieved to be out of the nightmare. The gravity of the realm I experienced motivates me to want to help him out of his faster. I make a trip to the bathroom, waking myself up so I don't fall back into the loop.

*

The morning sun rises. As I lay in my bed, I ponder the significance of last night's dream. Has the presence always been the demon, or was the dream made from my own worries of that? Did I possibly encounter what influenced him down the dark path? I put my hands together over my chest and recite the Lord's Prayer. I follow with my own personal request for clarity and protection, to rid any evil that may be latched to my space. "In God's precious name we pray, amen."

The kitchen floor creaks as I pull out the barstool across from mom. "Good morning, Kris!" Mom greets me through a bite of toast. With bags under my eyes, I explain why I didn't sleep well. Mom offers, "What if we try saging the house? If the presence is something bad, you'll know because the ghost will go away." I look down at my feet, hesitant to agree. "That's probably a good idea. I'm just nervous to have an absence afterwards, proving that I've been wrong this whole time." Mom looks at me, almost relieved that I may discover the ghost isn't *him*. I chime in, "I don't know what to buy or how to do it. I'll have to look it up." My nerves are jumbled as I begin the online search, bringing me closer to a possible reality.

After my last bite of oatmeal, I run to the mall's goth shop that I know will have white sage. With apprehension I bring a pack of three white smudge sticks to the register. The long-haired man behind the counter mindlessly scans it and announces, "Your total is $11.11." I smile as I reach for the receipt. On the car ride there and back I feel the spirit clinging to me, either trying to encourage or discourage this house cleansing. Pulling into my garage I take one last glance at the dashboard, 3:33 p.m., another angel number. I shut off the ignition and really hope these numbers are my sign.

Mom and I stand in the TV room. I hand her the stick of sage and instruct, "The article says to sage from the farthest corner of the house all the way to the opposite point. I think this room is a good place to start, also because this is where the demon was in 2014." With all windows open, a cool breeze crosses the halls. I pull up the saging prayer and light the first bundle. The flame from the edge of the sage lights and turns to a cloud of smoke. I blurt, "It smells like weed."

"Kristen, we have to be serious." Mom giggles. "Ready?" She waves the smoke as I say the words, "Okay, um. *I call upon my...* wait what was it? Oh. *I call upon my angels and guides along with the energy*—I feel stupid." We look at each other and can't help but laugh. I try again. "*I call upon my angels and spirit guides along with the energy of this sage to assist me in ridding all evil, negativity, and density, to transmute it into positivity, love, and light. Any dark or evil entities that are present in our home are to be banished, you are not welcome here.*" With the demon in mind, I repeat the phrase in each corner of the room, getting louder and more confident each time.

Over and over I repeat the prayer until suddenly a sense of peace fills the air, like the relief of taking off tight jeans. The density that once felt so normal to me subsides, and I feel safe and relaxed. Mom looks at me emotionally. "Did you feel that, too?" she asks. I nod my head in acknowledgment, teary-eyed myself. She wipes her cheek. "Why are we crying?"

I laugh. "No clue, I guess it just feels *that* peaceful." With all of the goodness in the air I can still feel him, but this was only the first room. We smudge every nook and cranny of the basement, saging even the staircase.

I become nervous as we step into my room. With a click of the lighter, I re-burn the dried leaves and head for my closet. I say the prayer by my rack of shoes on the far end. Walking back out, I find Mom holding the killer's book, uneasily waving the smoke around each side. I can't help but find it funny. She notices me standing there. "Sorry, Kris," she says, "just in case." I close my eyes as I repeat the prayer, feeling the transmutation of energy. Just as in the TV room, the lift in density moves us. We finish the last room of the basement, and now the entire downstairs is cleared of negativity. The ghost doesn't match the energy we're banishing, and follows us upstairs. I feel free and light with the presence that apparently *isn't* negative still by my side. I blow out the burning embers of the sage after clearing the last room of the house.

The ghost stays shyly behind me as I check my phone. As I scroll through my text messages, I get the feeling of a heavy blanket on my back with a sharp and heavy sensation pounding the top of my head. Happiness rushes in from the feeling of him here. The feeling is interrupted by the messages in the group chat aimed for me. "Kris, I met this guy the other week and he's such a cutie! He's single too, wink wink." Another message: "Girl go for it. He's your type." Back and forth my friends message amongst themselves, sharing what cute babies this guy and I would make. I put down the phone and lean back.

I'm not going to be yet another person that makes *you know who* feel like there will always be something or someone more important than him. Whether this is really him or not, I'm playing it safe. I hastily type, "I am honestly done with men for about a year lol. Thanks for thinking of me though!" I put down the phone with a sigh of relief and get ready for my shower.

I flip on the light as I turn the corner of my bathroom. As I turn the hot water handle I gaze to the top of the shower. I observe the shower curtain rod, seeing that one side is pushed halfway down the wall. I inspect it closer in amazement, knowing Kylie or I would've put it back in place if we had knocked it loose. Excitedly, I hurry to Kylie and Mom in the next room.

I peer through the TV room doorway. "Did one of you guys happen to mess with the shower?" I ask.

"No," they reply indifferently. Taking a second look, they see the smile on my face and know I'm about to have them follow me. I proudly march them to the bathroom and point to the shower. "Look at this shit, I found it like that. Isn't that wild?" Balancing on the edge of the tub, I put it back in place and begin to test the rod, yanking on the curtain. With force, I pull it in different directions to find that it won't even budge. They watch, intrigued at my discovery.

"That is pretty crazy, I'll admit." Kylie says softly. I grab onto her shoulder and jump back down.

The three of us return to the TV room and huddle under our blankets. I reach for the remote and begin a movie search. I joke nervously, "We could always watch a family-friendly serial killer documentary." A rush of embarrassment floods through me as I hear crickets. Then, quick like lightning, the lights in the room flash and I count three times. Like something out of a horror movie, the lights blink rapidly. Wide-eyed and excited, I glance at my sister, who isn't saying a word. Nobody is.

It takes a lot of energy for a spirit to move and manipulate objects or electricity, just as it would tire out a person to move something heavy. "Good job," I say proudly in my head. I stare at the TV screen, imagining a white light flowing to him to replenish his energy. Although we don't pick his documentary to watch, throughout the night I notice that my mom and Kylie hold a new respect for my theory.

*

A new day begins. Gathering everything that I need to work from home, I reach down to grab my planner and notice something out of the corner of my eye. I look to it, seeing a puff of white smoke about six feet in the air by my nightstand. My head pounds as I watch the mist slowly rise to the ceiling before vanishing. That makes four times this week. They're not the same full-body apparitions of what I saw when I was little, but I'm sure that with time I'll develop that back. However, I wonder what it means when a ghost takes on the form of a puff of smoke, being that I have also been seeing others as a flash of light. I don't have to start work for about five more minutes, leaving time for a quick investigation.

Through online articles I read that there are several types of ghosts. Their vibrational energy influences how they manifest into their form. "Ectomist" describes a cloud of white smoke about five to seven feet in the air that causes density throughout the room. Because he pops into my mind whenever I see this phenomenon, I believe the ectomist is the killer's energy. I keep that in mind and set aside my ghostly research. I reach for my planner, open my call list, and begin with the stale work script.

A few hours have passed as I pencil in another spinal screening for next week and shut my laptop for lunch. Taking a bite of salad, I pull up the true crime community app. I stop scrolling as I come across pictures of the killer's childhood home. The post shares that the house was on the market back in 2015 but is now occupied by a professional guitarist. I notice a picture of a room dedicated to display his guitars, and my mind goes back to what Martha mentioned in the reading about "J" and the guitar room.

I look over the original pictures of the retro decorated rooms and vintage furnishings in awe. Scrolling down the post, I come to photos of the interior, taken just two years ago. Holding the screen closer to my eyes I examine how the house has evolved with the times. I stop on a picture of the dining room to take a longer look, noticing something out of the ordinary. Above the table and across the ceiling is a streak of white in midair. It's not a glare and looks like motion caught on film. I realize that the white streak in the picture looks strikingly similar to the ectomist I've been seeing in my own home.

*

A few days have passed since I found that picture of his old dining room. As I settle into bed, I put on his movie for background noise. Looking up to the screen I see the part where the killer and his two friends are standing outside of his house. As the killer talks, two small puffs of white smoke come out of his blonde hair. I stop in my tracks, find the remote, and rewind the scene three times to confirm what I saw, baffled by my discovery. With the scene paused, I pull up the dining room image to compare the entities and find that they are a match.

The exploration in this unspeakable journey is maddening. A true test of intuition. The worst part is not knowing if I'm on the right track or spending time on an energy that is non-existent. At this point, I know it is time to be brave and seek out the truth. With hesitant hands, I go to Martha's website and see what days are available for a medium reading. The worst case-scenarios run through my mind as I gaze at her booking page. If she says it isn't actually him, who is this ghost? If he's not getting my help, where is he and how can I help him? Can he even be helped? I already regret it as I click "book appointment" for next week, July 12th. With the appointment now locked in all I can do is wait and try not to think too hard about the outcome.

I distract my mind from all things *him*, attempting not to stress over what I might find out tomorrow. My nerves have kept me distracted from work, friends, family, and even myself, consuming me as if it's life or death. I can't understand why I feel so strongly about the outcome. I assume it would be hard, letting go of something that I believe in so faithfully and something that I've invested so heavily in. Knowing that what's brought me to the world of spirituality is all based on a lie would be crushing. What would hurt most of all is living with the knowledge that I can't help this person that I now care for, knowing he is to suffer indefinitely. Since booking the appointment last week the ghost has offered me signs of reassurance, but the consolation fails to reach my over-driven mind.

Nervous for tomorrow, I channel surf through multiple titles, none of which appeal to me. I scroll past a comedic show, one where celebrities narrate historical events while intoxicated. The episode is about Joan of Arc. Joan received visions and guidance from Archangel Michael who picked her for a divine mission in leading the French army to victory. At just 19 years old, she was burned at the stake for witchcraft. I continue watching, intrigued that this episode out of the many that could have been on was what found me. I relate to her; the guidance of Archangel Michael, being seen as "crazy" from her prophecies, and the backlash she received when she spoke her truth. Receiving this sign perks me up for tomorrow. That night, in bed, I rest my head a little lighter as I turn out the light and await the morning alarm.

*

The next morning, I awake to the alarm blaring from my phone. I press the button to silence it. I remember what I set the alarm for and the thoughts flood in. After scrounging an outfit together, I make my way up to the kitchen with no appetite, feeling like I could puke at any given moment. It's surreal to think that after all of this time, I'll finally get my answer. I prepare myself for disappointment, knowing that the odds this notorious person even knows who I am are slim to none. With low expectations, I can either walk out feeling the exact way that I did walking in, or better.

I get in my car, looking forward to connecting to him for what might be the last time. I roll down the window, put on my sunglasses, and hit shuffle on my music library. The song that begins is one that I heard in the very beginning of my journey, and yet it manages to inspire me today as much as it did then. *You feed my dying light, your eyes give me something to believe in. The darkness will lead us into the light as you call me home. A touch from you and I ignite.*

The car feels empty as the EDM song plays. Hoping that our music will call him in, I desperately try to connect. No presence feels like a bad sign. What if he ghosted me for our reading, literally? What if I show up just for Martha to say, "Sorry, there's nobody there," and then I'm stuck right where I began?

I arrive at the entrance to the building and tightly grip onto its metal door handle as I inhale deeply. My heart pounds out of my chest as I walk down the hall with clammy hands. Coming to meet me is a familiar woman with curly, white hair and bright colored clothing—it's Martha. The hallway is quiet, filled only with the sound of our echoing voices as we catch up. I smell the familiar scent of essential oils radiating from her door as we approach closer.

She leads me to the dimly lit room, and I sink deeply into the plush seat opposite her chair, which mimics the feeling of my sinking chest. Martha reminds me that she never remembers previous readings because of the dream-like state that she goes in to communicate, similar to how we often can't remember dreams upon waking.

"So, with that being said, what is it that you want to focus on today?" She smiles, reaching for her notepad and colored pencils.

I pause. "Well, I might save my questions for the end to see what comes up for you. This might be an interesting one."

"Holding in questions can block the flow of the reading, because the energy I'm going to be getting will be worry and confusion," Martha explains. "Ask away." With a deep breath, I explain my experience and then hesitantly offer, "The reason I'm so confused is because I think this is somebody famous."

She stops sketching and her face takes on a look of concern. "Everyone that I've read who believed they had a celebrity attached to them ended up being attached to a demonic presence. I've gotten my ass kicked a time or two with stuff like this, so I try not to mess with dark entities anymore... I will look into it, I just have to put on my spiritual condom. More psychic protection."

As she closes her eyes, my hope dims. Even though I've already prepared for a hard no, it's not making the hurt any less. My train of thought breaks as Martha asks, "Your last name is spelled H-A-L-D-E-R, correct?" A loud sound effect comes through the speaker of her phone, interrupting my answer. "What the *hell* was that? My phone never makes that sound," Martha announces. I smile knowing he's here.

I hear the excitement in my own voice. "Exhibit A, things like that happen to me daily. The other week I was listening to my music app and a song that I've never downloaded before just started playing."

She stares at her phone on the table, contemplating what I've said. "Like I said, I don't usually read for things like this, but…that's interesting."

I perk up. "I don't want to quiz you. I can tell you who the person is, if that helps."

"Well, I don't want you to, I want to find out."

"I wouldn't want to put you in a dangerous situation either, if it is demonic," I say with a sense of guilt.

Martha looks curious as she rests her chin on her hand. "Well, with my phone doing that weird sound, that's interesting. Of all coincidences that sound had to happen right now, and exactly in your reading time period. That's definitely his doing."

I hold my hands together. "Do what you're comfortable with for sure. I don't wanna push anything."

"No, that's alright. I'm getting a strong man presence," she begins, surprising me.

"I feel like I'm supposed to acknowledge the yellow flower, like he is referring to *you* as 'the bright flower,' a daisy. He said he's getting the flowers you're sending." The killer is the only person that I'm sending love to, which I assume the flowers are a symbol for. This is him.

All of the tension in me releases. "Really?" I ask.

"Mhmm. He's coming across to me as artistic and creative. A depressive vibe, like a Kurt Cobain. He looks a little like him too, are they alike?"

"It's not a musician, it's far from a musician," I answer. "He wasn't particularly liked?"

Stumped, she sets her notepad in her lap and leans forward. "Alright, he is not unmasking himself so do tell me what's going on. Who is this?" I think of the right way to say his name, but there's no nice way to say it.

"Okay, don't judge," I tell her.

"Not to judge," she reassures, and I laugh.

I shyly announce the killer's name. "I know it's weird."

I can see her disconnect from the reading as I say it. "No, it's not weird… but you know you're playing with fire, right? I have to know your intentions. I know that you want to help heal his soul, but have you considered that maybe he didn't have a soul to begin with? That it was possibly a demonic presence occupying a cellular body?"

I explain my view, although she's not persuaded.

"Well, I've been looking at your aura field as you've been talking, and I see you as a healer of broken souls, a warrior angel. What I see in you is an angel in a human body. You get the craving to help these lost people, because helping them is your soul's purpose." She closes her eyes again. "I feel like this child broke at two years old, and you're doing this for the young boy. I believe his soul was already taken to heaven at that young age when he was inhabited by a demonic presence. You may think that you're connecting with him, but if you're connecting with what possessed him, you will end up being possessed, too. I guarantee it." The pit in my stomach doubles in size. I should have known better, that my worst fear was the truth. I find myself itching to leave early for the comfort of my home.

"I will continue reading but I have to cut us both off from that presence. It is making the room so heavy. I'm going to just talk directly to your angels and guides."

She shouts "OUT" every time she feels him come back. With every "out," I feel more and more naive, more stupid; stupid for bringing this not only upon myself, but upon others.

"Archangel Michael and Joan of Arc are here. Are you aware of your connection with them? Like her, you are a soldier angel. Joan says that you have been called, just like she was. But she says, I was burned at the stake. You may not be burned, but might have your reputation destroyed, so she says, 'Quiet!'" Martha says with a laugh.

Martha continues, "They're here to assist you in guiding these lost souls. A show they say you saw last night was there to give you validation of their presence for today, otherwise you might have questioned it."

The timer dings, indicating that the time is up. I'm temporarily elated from the information about Michael and Joan, but I leave the reading unsure of my exact feelings. I hug Martha goodbye as my eyes adjust to the bright hall. As soon as the door shuts behind me, he floods my thoughts. Afflicted, I shoo him away.

I open the car door, letting out the stale air. The killer's soul is in Heaven, which was the whole point of this in the first place. I don't have to worry about his state of being. In fact, it's a relief to know he was never suffering. I call Mom as soon as I start the car. "In a nutshell, he was always possessed and what took over his body was what I drew in. It's gone now, though, Martha cut him off from me. I feel good about it, that he was never truly suffering throughout his life because it was never really him." Mom seems relieved that this will all be behind me. I feel like I'm lying as I convince her and myself that this is all great news.

"Well, I'm glad you got an answer, honey. I think this is a good thing. Now you can focus on your acting, and maybe look into some agencies!"

"Yeah, that would be cool. Well, I'll see you in about 30 minutes. Love you." I hang up and turn on my music, pausing as I see the screen full of our songs that I can't listen to anymore. One by one I delete each song before driving home to the sound of the radio.

Just like the last time I found out this was a demon, we have an upcoming cruise for next week. Even after yesterday's session the dense energy remains around, following behind my every step. The smell of cigarettes fills my senses and I angrily banish it out of my space, repeating the Lord's prayer with intensity although it doesn't seem effective.

If it weren't for this "demon," I would've never opened up to spirituality the way that I have. Despite the change, I want to continue reaching for my full psychic potential in spite of the entity. At home in my bedroom, I light the candles and sit cross-legged in front of my angel altar. With a guided meditation, I focus attention on my third eye.

The woman's voice in the mediation leads my thoughts, but I find that they continue to stray elsewhere. "Deep breath in... and long breath out. In...

and breathe out. Good. Now, I want you to imagine breathing in indigo mist, representing psychic energy. Inhale deeply, breathing it into the point between your brows, energizing your third ey- ch...a bei...g li..." Static pops over the last words.

"OUT! You're not welcome here!" I shout. Sadness washes over me as I feel the spirit leave. On the carpet I sit heartsick and empty. I already miss sending love; feeling him grasp that beam of light that I send out to him. I turn off the meditation before it even gets started. Wiping my cheek, I stand up and blow out the candles.

*

Morning comes and we leave for our trip. A "Welcome to Charleston!" sign greets us as we cross the state line. As my eyes focus on the road, my mind drifts towards the reading. I dissect the situation, evaluating and re-living each conversation in Martha's session and each moment in my journey that led me to my conclusions.

I grip the wheel, tensing as my thoughts battle each word Martha shared, comparing it to what I've learned about the ghost on my own. Some things just don't add up. She didn't sense a demon in the room at the time that the phone went off and was communicating with a male presence in the beginning up until I mentioned who it was. Martha cut off contact before tapping into the presence's energy and didn't give herself a chance to feel what the energy was besides something that was dense. The fear she felt from her past experiences may have created in her a bias towards my own situation. If I never said the dreaded name, she may have kept reading that man who referred to me as a daisy.

"This child broke at two years old and from then on a demonic entity took over his body." He didn't start withdrawing until he was *four* after a traumatic surgery, and was a good child, although shy. He was also baptized after turning to God during incarceration; can a possessed person even touch the holy water?

Everything I'm doing with this spirit relates to my relationship with divine energy and bringing it to somebody else. I don't see how a demon could handle all of the light, although I can't be stupid and naïve, either. My gut is telling me not to write him off completely. I can't tell if I'm listening to my intuition or my heart; I'm still learning to distinguish between the two. Just when I thought I would have my answer, I find myself more confused than before.

We pull into the gravel parking lot of a seafood shack to meet with dad's side of the family before the cruise. For the time, I'm able to forget about it all. Being around my family helps me to feel better. Excusing myself from the table, I head for the bathroom. As always, the minute that I disconnect from other people, the killer fills my mind so loudly that I can't think of anything else.

Reminded of his absence, I shut the stall door behind me. "I miss you. I wish that was all real." The bathroom goes dark. I stay calm, ignoring the demon's attempt at my attention. Instead of excitement, I feel scared until the lights come back on. After a brief moment, they do. Water and suds over my hands as I repeat the Lord's prayer three times in my mind. I collect myself in the golden framed mirror and exit to rejoin the group.

Tonight during dinner, I catch myself not thinking about him. My stomach turns; the homesick returns. I guess that's something that hasn't gone away. Now that I know that the entity I felt was never him, I have to simply push through my feelings and move on.

I let loose on my first cruise as a 21-year-old. On the first day, I attend a kickoff party by the pool and down an entire margarita pitcher and a half. I make friends, but don't remember any of them. By 6:00 p.m., I'm passed out on a deck lounge chair. At 8:00 p.m., a guy from the pool deck knocks on the door to ask me to dinner, but I'm dead asleep on the top bunk. After several attempts to wake me up, Kylie and Mom go to formal night. In the middle of the quiet dining room I stumble in right in time for dessert, drunk and in a misbuttoned dress.

With a headache in the morning, I vow to myself to be coherent for the rest of the time, and not over-do the beer towers. For the first time since my breakup, I meet somebody I feel a little connection with. We stick by each other, sharing social media information and phone numbers for when the cruise is finished.

Our families sit at a round, white-clothed table, complete with candles and fancy folded napkins. As the person I'm interested in talks to me, I feel myself tapping my fingers pinky to thumb, thumb to pinky, and stop myself. "I don't want you here," I say in my mind. I feel the entity leave and pour myself another glass of wine.

The ship horn blows as we dock in Puerto Rico. Stunning scenery and warm, breezy weather greet us as the crew helps us off of the metal bridge. White sand lines the sidewalks, which runs parallel the perfectly turquoise water. I enjoy the culture and Hispanic music, strolling around in my maxi-dress under the hot sun. As we pass the market, locals compete for our attention, trying to sell their handmade baskets and clothes. Coming up on the shops, our ears are pulled in different directions as music playing through each doorway mixes with the sounds of street vendors.

Among the sounds, my ears tune in to a familiar beat. "The light is coming" plays from across the dirt road; another metaphysical tap on my shoulder, reminding me of the unfinished journey. Out of all the cultural music we've heard on the trip, this is the one American song I've heard the whole time. I keep walking with that realization in mind, and suddenly begin feeling him again.

Our week of paradise comes to an end and once again, I'm back to reality. Feeling giddy about the guy I met, I text him as we load into the car. The three of us talk about him, excited to see where things might lead. Kylie turns up the radio and the words interrupt my thoughts. "I'm struggling to deal with the withdrawal from you. This has all got me feeling so helpless."

"Can you turn this song up?" I ask. From the speakers come the lyrics, "I see you've found someone, you're moving on and don't get me wrong, I'm glad for you but sad for me." Am I going crazy, or is this the song that's on right now? I look up the lyrics online to confirm what I'm hearing with my own ears. It's "Happy Sad Song" by the group ChampionsLeak.

Noticing these songs feels similar to hearing my name called in class while daydreaming. It draws my attention when I'm not paying any, and at the exact part that I'm supposed to hear. I see him in my mind as the song plays and anchors me back to him. My gut tells me something wasn't right about the reading. I can't believe the killer is automatically in Heaven. It doesn't feel right. Maybe he's not the ghost around me, but something in me still wants to do what I can to bring him peace, wherever he may be. I can't accept leaving him behind that easily. In this moment, I decide that I will take my own leap of faith and continue with my original plan of healing this killer. Music; always our bridge back to each other.

CHAPTER FIVE:
BELIEVING IN YOU

Allison and I sit across a brightly painted table at our usual Mexican restaurant. I order the jumbo margarita, figuring it will give me the courage to fill her in on "what's new." I trust that out of all people, Allison will believe me. It's funny how little I thought the hauntings would amount to a few months ago. Because those same hauntings gained so much momentum and turned into something bigger than I could've ever imagined, I decide it's time I can share it with her, just as I have everything else in my life. A heavenly choir sings in my head as the giant green glass is set in front of us.

As Allison makes small talk, I find that hanging out with her feels different now. The friendship that once felt so humble and familiar now feels ingenuine and forced. We've grown into different lifestyles. I don't want to admit to myself that Allison, Beverly, and I have outgrown each other, but it's beginning to feel like the truth. She looks at me while I count to 10 and suck in the icy tequila, breathe, then sip for another 10 seconds. The taste of lime dances on my tongue as my body starts to relax.

With a looser tongue I ease into the conversation. Allison stares in shallow fascination as she sips on her drink, listening to my most recent ghost stories. I remind her of the movie we watched together and who it was about, studying her reaction as I emphasize the timing of it all. I can't read her any further and struggle to sense if she's *acting* like she believes me as not to make the situation uncomfortable.

Allison adds, "Another weird coincidence, I think my mom's side of the family is from Milwaukee, like him. Let me text her." If anything, at least she's pretending to be interested. I feel relief that she's on my side and relax more into the booth.

Allison exclaims, "She responded! 'Your aunt lived a block from where apartment 213 was. She could see the crime scene tape from her driveway.' Creepy!'"

"That's wild. How weird," I reply with a bite of a queso covered chip. I've noticed before that Allison's mom resembles the killer's mother quite a bit; I wonder if they have a distant relation. What a small world that would be.

I slurp the last drop of my margarita and am reminded of how I came to this conclusion in the first place, how everything lines up with him. I still don't know what to believe, but I think I'll have to figure this out on my own.

*

A new day brings in a refreshed mind. Today, I tell myself, I am going to get an answer. With a bundle of white sage and the house to myself I bless every room, reciting the saging prayer in each one. The powerful intentions bring so much light and so much God into each room that evil can't possibly survive here. There is a lift, a quietness to the entire atmosphere. I extinguish the burning edge and close the door behind me, laying down for a meditation titled *with assistance from Archangel Michael*. I follow the guidance, cleansing myself to rid negative entities from my aura.

I feel pure and peaceful, adrenaline rushing through me from the good energy. With only pure spirits and angels around, there will be no deceit. Now is my time to connect with them. I look through the black veil, calling to Michael and Joan. I call in God himself to give me a clear answer as to who this is. "I need to see this sign today, so I know when to expect it. No grey area, the sign has to be black or white. Please, give me a sign that will wash away all of my doubt, one as clear as day."

I squeeze my eyelids tighter to see through the swirling grey, looking for a symbol or a name. "Come on…" I encourage. The color black circles around my visual field but nothing is happening. I open my eyes. No epiphanies have hit me, and I don't feel any different. I blow out the candles, put back my crystals, and put on workout clothes. I just have to be patient; it's only the afternoon. To run outside or on the treadmill today? I decide on the treadmill.

I flip on the TV room lights and turn on the TV with the volume already loud. The channel has been left on National Geographic. Odd, because none of us ever watch that. As I tie my sneaker laces I listen to the narration in the background. "Models are super thin, and athletes are very tall. It's the fact that they're rare that makes them appealing." I reach for the remote and draw to a halt when I hear a familiar voice say, "Thanks, thanks for your help."

I gaze up to the screen and watch a brief, three-second clip of the serial killer thanking his lawyer as he leaves court. I stand with my hands over my mouth as my eyes lock on the TV. Is this really happening? I look at my hands for a reality check; to confirm that I'm not in a dream. I could have gone running outside, but I chose to stay in. That exact channel was on, with the exact part that he was in, at the exact time I turned on the TV. I've only seen the killer on streamable TV, shows that I select myself. I've never caught him on cable before, until now.

I rewind the show to see how far back it goes, realizing that if I went into the bonus room thirty seconds later, I would've missed it. Pressing the "info," button on the remote, I find that the name of the show is "The '90's: The Last Great Decade." The show is not even about true crime. This is one of the many episodes in the series, and I happened to catch the one that he was in for less than a minute.

Here it is, my clear as day sign that I asked for less than an hour ago. I rewind the clip over and watch him stand in the orange jumpsuit. He lip swallows, nervous from the crowd looking at him, just as I do when I feel uncomfortable. Mom's footsteps click through the house. She must have just gotten home.

I go upstairs and greet her with puffy eyes. "Hi Kris! …Oh no, what happened?

I smile as I share the experience. "I really think it's him, Mom."

She approaches me with a hug. "Oh, honey, I'm sorry you got scared. We'll figure this out."

I correct her. "No, I'm crying because I'm happy. That was amazing."

She pauses, saying a quiet, "Oh..."

"Do you wanna see?" I eagerly ask.

I lead her to the bonus room. I press play, walking her through what I was doing at the exact moment. "Okay, and then I heard someone talking and I'm like, wait a minute. I looked up and that's what I saw." Together, we watch the blonde man stand to his feet from the defendant table.

"Is that him?" Mom asks.

I smile, "Yeah, that's him."

A crime writer narrates, "The truth is these people aren't monsters, they're human beings. There are factors that go into turning them into this perfect storm of a person." Mom responds to that statement as if she never thought of it like that before.

His one-minute part ends and Mom raises her eyebrows. "Wow, that *is* pretty interesting," she says, looking both surprised and uncertain. A rush of joy fills me as I thank God for the clarity. I tell myself this is it. He gave me my answer, and I now need to trust it.

We head back up the stairs, discussing what to cook for dinner. A new grocery store down the street has its grand opening today, so we get in the car to make our way there. We walk through the balloon archway and I notice a colorful display of flower bouquets, a sea of pink, red, and purple petals. Of all of the colors, one single bundle of yellow roses is right in front of me. Martha's words flash through my mind: "He's referring to you as a bright yellow flower." I buy the flowers and bring them home for him as something to brighten his space.

Returning home, I set the bags on the counter and search the cabinets for something to put the flowers in. I clink through each glass and find the perfect vase to house them in. The word "Love" across the middle of the vase feels symbolic of the meditations I've been doing, while the flowers represent the energy I'm sending him, just as he communicated in the reading.

Walking into my room, I feel heaviness behind my back. I smile as I set the yellow roses on the stand under my TV, completing my angel altar. I throw on my oversized AC/DC shirt, put on humpback whale sounds for him, and fall back on my bed to chill. My stomach flutters as the presence settles in my room. This right here is what I look forward to every day, my new favorite feeling.

On days when I doubt his presence, I don't get many signs. When I let myself believe that the presence I feel is him, I receive signs in abundance. The signs stop only when I tell myself none of this is real. It's like the spirits hint if I'm getting "colder" or "warmer." Some days I believe it, some I don't. Despite my uncertainty, I send love every single day.

*

It's my day off, and I decide to relax with a horror movie. I stuff my face with quinoa chips and scroll through a true crime message board. I scroll past Ramirez, Columbine, and Gacy. Next is a picture of the killer as a teen next to a six-foot bong that he made out of snow. I chuckle as I slide up my thumb to keep scrolling, but the screen freezes on that picture. The app crashes, turning the screen black for one second before returning to the home screen. The slightest breeze caresses my right cheek, yet there is no window open. I find the timing of these malfunctions fascinating, like a finger pointing directly at my answer when my logical mind tries to throw me off.

Everyone is gone for work, and finally, it's quiet time. The cold rose quartz weighs heavily in my right palm, and I close my eyes to drift away as the meditation video begins. A shimmering sound comes through the speakers along with the words, "Welcome to a guided love meditation. With this meditation, you can direct your love towards another person, a situation, or even towards yourself." I scuffle around to get comfortable before the meditation begins.

I inhale and exhale as instructed, falling deeper and deeper into myself. The last awareness I have of my body is the weight of the crystals in both palms. That falls away, and I am completely emerged in the scene. I listen to chimes ringing in different tones as the voice instructs.

"In front of you is the focus of your love meditation. Imagine them either in their house or a nature setting, whatever comes to you." Standing on a cliff next to a barren tree is the killer. He looks like his most recent self; a green prison uniform and grown out hair. His back faces me as he looks over the remote valley. "As you find your person, see them as peaceful, calm, joyous and content."

I walk closer, stepping barefoot over rocks and pebbles and around to his right side. His eyes are closed behind the aviator glasses as a gentle wind moves through his golden hair, complementing his slightest smile of tranquility. "Using your intention, see them completely surrounded with an intense loving light. This light is pure, unconditional love and acceptance." He turns to face me, enveloped in angelic white.

"Allow it to grow stronger and more effective until it not only radiates around them but penetrates every cell in their body." The white cocoon of light gleams around his aura and cleanses away the sorrow, replacing it with the highest of vibrations. His heart chakra glows pink as the energy transmutes from hate into love.

I witness what feels like the eye of a storm, a place of calm in the middle of chaos. Ten minutes of no worries, no guilt, and no hate, a moment of pure peace unraveling a life of distress. Smooth pebbles support my feet and the birds chirp in time with the chimes as I observe.

I grab onto him tightly and press my face on his chest. "Look into their eyes and tell them, *I see you with only unconditional love and acceptance. I see you with only unconditional love and acceptance. I see you with only unconditional love and acceptance.*" I struggle to look into his eyes clearly, as if I'm not lucid enough. My eyes hurt from trying to see past the haziness; it's like trying to force my eyes open in a dream.

I look into the blurry image of his blue eyes, feeling compassion pour out of me as I repeat the phrase. "I see you with only unconditional love and acceptance."

"Feel the words deeply as you radiate this energy to them. Let go of all judgment, of all resentment. Share this moment with them in their divine form as well as yours and stay for as long as you need."

The woman repeats the phrase as the chimes, and then her voice, fade out. In the stillness at the top of the mountain I hold onto him, not wanting to let him go. Without words we stand in the embrace and I can feel his energy purifying me. It is unlike anything I've ever felt before. Our minds are still in the present moment. I repeat the phrase from the meditation again and again, as if to make up for all the times he was never told he was loved. A few minutes pass and I decide it's time to go back to my day.

I feel a sense of peace and leave him with the white light, strength, and motivation. I feel the presence is gone as I open my eyes. I notice that lately, after I send him love, he disappears for a while. I assume that after his boost of love-energy he does his work on the other side, so I patiently await his return. As I ponder if the meditation *truly* reached him or not I realize that the energy has to go somewhere, so why wouldn't it go directly to where I intend? Besides ten minutes, I don't have anything to lose by continuing to try this.

*

I tighten my scrunchie, wipe the sweat from my brow, and begin a workout video. The timer sounds for a 60 second break before the next circuit. Thankful for the rest, I toss back half of a bottle of water and return to the carpet. The timer lets out three beeps, warning me of the seconds that remain before I start again.

On my stomach for frog kicks I lift my alternating legs, wondering when the torture will end. The song tones waver, sounding like an instrument from another time period. "I'll make it through the gates someday. I lose hope and you tell me to keep holding on. I hear the call, I see it all. We can soar higher if we keep faith. At times I'm merely just a whisper but grow stronger if you keep believing in me." These songs never fail to amaze me; they seem to reach me through any available source. The synchronicities in these words are so uncanny that I don't believe I'm listening to a real song until I look it up online. I notice how the messages in each song reflect the changing situation and give me clues of his status.

I can't understand why this would happen to me out of all people. Regardless of my experiences, I don't want to go on believing something if it's not real. I wanted to try this on my own, but I think I need a second opinion from a different medium. This time I won't say a word in the session. I will see what the medium says for themselves. I want an honest, unbiased answer. Gripping my phone tightly, I begin another search for a five-star professional.

I scroll down the list of locals and notice the same three names that appear in every top list, one of them being Martha. The other two are "Psychic Medium Ed" and Denise. My thumb swivels to select Denise's website. I'm intrigued as I read testimonials describing her as friendly, humble, and incredibly authentic. I dig deeper, searching the internet for dirt and finding nothing but happy clients. I study the photo of her on her website, in which she gives off a gentle look. Do I give this another shot? Checking her calendar I see that she's pretty in demand: the soonest reading she has available is the 21st of September. After stalling, I click "Book Now" and toss my phone aside.

In the evening I share Denise's page with Mom. I can sense her hidden enthusiasm at the chance of hearing from Brad again. "It's a two-hour drive, we can make a weekend trip out of it if you want to go with me?" Her response makes me smile, and I book her an appointment right after mine. As it is, the anticipation has been slowly eating away at my sanity. Can I even wait a month for a reading? This is another trial of my patience, another test of my will.

Back in my room, I fill my suitcase for a chiropractic conference trip in the morning. The entire office is going, and we will be in the city for a quick day and a half. I'm more excited than I should be, being that of all places, the destination is Chicago, Illinois; a second home to *him*, as he would spend weekends there when not in Milwaukee. I neatly tuck in a shirt and wonder if he will follow me to Chicago, or if he won't want to revisit the place where he caused such destruction.

*

The plane touches down on the runway, skidding on the asphalt as I look out of the oval window. I arrive to the hotel room and set my Converse next to the mini fridge. With two hours to myself, I draw the curtains and slip under the white down comforter. I take this time to heal the killer for the weekend. I feel him lift as I send him the ball of light, then nap for the remainder of my down time.

The alarm beeps and I squint my eyes open. Suddenly I remember that I'm in a hotel room in Chicago. The TV greets me with the music from a local commercial; the feather comforter and pillows lay clumped to my side. I stretch and yawn, throwing my feet to the floor in an attempt to sit up. I walk over to the window and part its heavy curtains. The brightness blinds me and I narrow my eyes to observe the sunset kissing the skyscrapers. The city looks a lot like the scenery from one of the killer's movies, resembling almost its exact setting.

I head downstairs to meet with the staff and load the L train to head for the city. I pick my seat next to the window with Kelci, the receptionist, beside me. Sitting on the blue carpeted chair, I observe the surrounding metal rails and wonder if he ever rode this same train.

"Kristen, get in our picture!" one of my colleagues exclaims, interrupting my train of thought. I make conversation with the girls behind my seat and Kelci turns to me. "I brought wine, but I don't know how the doctors will feel about it. Do you…" The rest of her words become a mumble as I look away from her and directly out of the window. My eyes take their own control and lock directly onto a sign for Milwaukee and then I return Kelci's attention. There it is again, my hourly something that reminds me of him.

As we walk the streets I feel someone over my shoulder, only to turn around to a vacant sidewalk. Heaviness and a headache follow along, although these symptoms have now become so constant that I barely even notice them anymore. A giant Ferris wheel makes its way around and around, with purple light illuminating the white metal. Drums echo in the distance, drawing us in before we head back for the night. We walk closer to the sound of percussion to find a crowd watching a live band perform in the biergarten.

The crowd rallies as the drummer thrashes the cymbals. "Thank you, thank you, lovely people! Now, this next song we're doing is by a little band named *Queen*." The drunk crowd loves that. If this is Bohemian Rhapsody, I'm going to lose my shit. The singer makes the crowd wait with anticipation, slowly setting down his water to grab the microphone. I hold my breath, hoping that my group won't lose interest and walk away.

A piano in the key of B-flat major begins, and I stand in disbelief. Even miles away from home, this song manages to find me. I feel him standing behind me and refrain from turning around. Chills run down my arms as I hear the crowd singing along, and I hold on to this moment.

Midnight approaches as we stand on the sidewalk with sore feet, figuring out how to get back to the hotel. A short man approaches our crowd and speaks broken English. "Excuse me, you looking for way back to hotel? I have party bus, for you. Uh… $10 a person, and a beer for everyone?" The tinted bus windows behind him flash with colored lights as loud music bumps over its speakers. Sketched out yet intrigued, we take him up on the offer.

Exhausted, we load onto the bus one by one. As we slump in the seats, the driver comes up the stairs with an arm full of Miller Lites and a few Coors. He passes one out to everyone but me. "Oh, we need one more?" he asks.

"No, it's okay, don't worry about it!" I say but he steps off. A couple of moments later, the bus bounces as the driver hikes back up the stairs. He hands me the only beer he could find, Pabst Blue Ribbon, the killer's favorite. "Really?" I laugh to myself.

*

Our return flight leaves at 5 a.m. The staff and I drag ourselves through the airport and sit at the gate. Resting my head on my hand, I look to the McDonalds line. The guy waiting turns around and I notice the way his eyes are set, the color of his hair, the curve of his nose. It is a funny "coincidence" to see someone who resembles the actor so closely in a place that reminds me of that very movie. Realizing that the spirit wants me to know he's with me at the moment I'm thinking of him feels surreal. The ghost's validations throughout this short trip have offered me more faith about my upcoming reading, and I leave Chicago with more confidence than when I arrived.

The sun is up as I return home, and I'm greeted by Jack's meowing. I scoop him up like a baby. In search of breakfast, I open the empty fridge. Hungry, I make a trip to the store and drive with the windows down to enjoy the crisp fall air. After gathering a basket full, I load the items on the belt one by one. "Have a good one!" I smile, putting coins back into my wallet.

With my eyes focused on my purse, I turn to leave, barely noticing that I'm about to run into somebody. I bring my hands up in front of my chest, scrunching my face to brace for impact. "Sorry!" I apologize. No one responds and I open my eyes to an empty aisle. I look to my right, then my left, to see one other person over by produce and the cashier staring at me. I fix my purse strap and walk out awkwardly.

My mind wanders on the drive home, and I think of how Cameron might be doing. I think back to the first time I told him "I love you" and to our first trip to Charleston together. I'm shocked, finding myself missing him for the first time as I reminisce on the faded imprint of my past.

"The call disappears inside you. I'll lift you up, always here beside you. I'm here to comfort you. Whatever you need, I'm here to comfort you." My eyes draw to the car diagonal to me and see that its license plate has a 213 on it. I slap the steering wheel in disbelief. "My God, are you serious!" I turn up the song, my mood brightening.

Because of the constant activity, my spiritual life is overpowering my normal one. When I try to focus on other things besides the killer and spirituality, I find that the break is short lived. When I take a break with a movie or show, I discover a subtle hint in the storyline that reflects my situation. I always find a sign of the paranormal, if not a specific reference to him.

In conversations where I talk about everything *but* the supernatural, it almost never fails that the person I'm talking to will change the topic to something otherworldly, regardless of what we were discussing before. I'm always snapped back into my reality, as if my guides are urging me not to steer too far away from my focus. There's just no getting away from it, but I must say I love it.

But at times I feel burnt out, exhausted, and moody. I'm falling asleep during meditations, and the energy that I'm sending to the killer feels forced. Instead of a graceful flow from my heart to his, it's become a heavy brick, ripped from my core and weakly shoved over to him. Pushing out any bit of positivity that

I have left, I know that he needs it more than I do. Still, I wouldn't trade this for the world.

*

Moonlight streams through the shades and beams off of my gray wall. Amber light flickers from my candles, adding to the serene glow. I put on the movie and tuck myself under the covers.

I'm comforted just being in my own space, undisturbed by both my internal and external worlds. My relaxation is interrupted when I hear a buzz come from beside me. I look at my phone to a text from Madison. "Hai, do you wanna come uptown with us tonight?" I sit in contemplation, huffing and puffing at the thought of removing myself from my cocoon. Why must people make plans with me? I rise to my feet to get ready and meet them out.

Walking the streets of Charlotte, I gaze up at the skyline. My heels click over the sidewalk as I look for a club called "Roxbury". I stumble upon the exterior and see the sign lit up in blue bulbs, with ROXBURY in horizontal letters. Among the line of people waiting to get in, I hear someone yell my name. I search the crowds for the source and see my group behind the rope. I yell as I run up to my friends to attack them in a hug.

As the bouncer checks my ID I hear the bumping of 80's pop music. "No way, is this an 80's themed club?" I ask, peaking in the entrance to see a disco ball hanging above an illuminated paneled dance floor. Next to it is a lounging area with three neon, light-up couches. 80's movie posters and memorabilia fill the walls and create a nostalgic atmosphere.

I hold my purse to my hip as I make my way to the bar. My eyes search the room, first noticing a tiny retro sign advertising Pabst Blue Ribbon among a sea of posters. I order a whisky and coke, gagging as soon as I realize how strong it was made. I am in love with the space because it reminds me of the killer. Being surrounded by reminders of him comforts me while I'm away from home. Just like Chicago, I've been led to another place that feels like *him*. I become disoriented and giggly, and the hours fly by as I start remembering less and less.

The following morning I get through my hangover by working from home.

I hear a knock at my door moments before Kylie steps through to talk to me. "Hey Kris, did you need something?"

"No, I've just been in mi room, why?"

Kylie looks with a blank stare. "So you never knocked on the bathroom door? Great."

I smirk as I ask what happened.

"Well, I was in the shower and I heard three like, slow knocks on the door, and I thought it seemed weird. I kept yelling for you to come in, and the door never opened," she responds.

"Hmm, strange! I wonder who that could be!" I tease as she shuts the door.

I forget that most people aren't as comfortable with paranormal things as I am. I figure that Kylie usually avoids the topic either because she's skeptical or annoyed by it.

*

He is always my first thought upon regaining consciousness each morning. I feel him already present in my room. I expect to wake up one morning to find that none of this ever happened, that it was all just a dream. To my surprise, I awake every day immersed in the same reality. This morning, I stretch and step my feet onto the plush carpet. I make my bed, pulling up the comforter to the top with no wrinkles, and display my pillows with the biggest in the back and the smallest in front. I'm greeted by the hissing of my chameleon as I turn on his light and humidifier. I attempt to pet him lovingly, but he lunges at me. I hear Kylie say something as she passes my room.

I call out, "What'd you say?"

She replies louder, "Tell your ghost to let me get some sleep."

I laugh. "Did something happen to you again?"

Kylie comes through my door and sits on the bed to begin her story. It was 3 a.m. when she woke up to the sound of tapping.

"How strange," she thought to herself as she tried to find the source of the sound. Gathering her awareness, she noticed that the middle blinds had been repeatedly knocking against the window. They had never done that before. It was specifically odd that only the one set of blinds were moving and not all three. All of the windows were shut, and the only wind was coming from the fan swirling above.

In the darkness of her room, Kylie stumbled out of bed for the switch on the wall, seeing if the breeze from the fan was the cause. After a few minutes of the fan being still, that single panel continued to tap, louder and louder. Annoyed, she exclaimed, "Fucking stop!" The tapping stopped at that very moment. A dreadful feeling crept up her spine.

"What the fuck, what the fuck, what the fuck." Her hands searched for the remote in her sheets. Relieved to feel her hand hit the plastic object, she flipped on the TV for light and background noise. She sat in the darkness, wide-eyed and silent. An hour passed, and her eyes became too heavy to hold open. She turned off the TV, tucked herself back under the covers, and closed her eyes. One last tap from the blinds was a spiteful "goodnight" that kept her mind awake for ten more minutes.

I notice the timid look on her face as she finishes her story. "I'm sorry it scared you, Kye. Don't be afraid to set boundaries, tell him to not bother you anymore. You can kick him out when you think he's there."

I yell out, "Love you!" as she walks back to the bathroom. It dawns on me that she's not distant from this situation because it annoys her, but because it freaks her out. I wonder if the things happening directly to her are because she doesn't believe. If she didn't before, that's starting to change. I unlock my phone and log the activity. -8/27: Cole's blinds were tapping in the middle of the night.

Hours later, I'm lugging my equipment through gym doors. I set a spine model on the table right next to my sign advertising, "Free Spinal Screening Today!" Standing awkwardly at the table I wait to be approached, observing the room of bodybuilders. "Rainbow in the Dark" comes over the speakers and catches my attention. Just as he called me a daisy, I feel he's referring to me once again through the words of this song. I turn to the laptop, seeing that a lousy thirty minutes have passed. I return to my stance, and my section of the gym goes dark as the lights cut off. No one was by the switch, and the rest of the gym stayed illuminated. A confused muscle head takes out his ear bud as he looks at the ceiling. I watch as he walks to the wall and simply flips the switch back on. *-8/28: The killer popped into my head just as "Rainbow in the Dark" came on and the gym lights shut off.*

I come home drained and watch something unrelated to the killer to give my mind a break. Flipping through the channels I see *Supernatural* and select it for nostalgia—I haven't watched it in years. In this episode, brothers Sam and Dean, who are paranormal hunters, wake up in an alternate reality with no memory of who they are. They aren't hunters; they work 9-5 in an office cubicle and have no recollection of knowing each other.

Placed in this alternate life they don't even believe in ghosts but could swear they're experiencing hauntings at their work. Feeling they're the only two going crazy, they work together to get to the bottom of this mystery, acting off of their gut feelings. By the end they find that there is in fact a ghost haunting the building—the ghost of a man who killed 17 people and is now stuck on the earthly plane.

Once Sam and Dean figure it out, an angel zaps them back into their own reality. The angel explains that they were put through that test to realize their true purpose. The angel slyly says to Sam and Dean, "So are you with me? Are you ready to stand up and be who you really are?" As I watch the scene, I feel as though the angel is speaking directly to me.

The ghost in the episode was a killer of 17 people, the exact number of the killer's victims. When the angel explained the lesson was to prove their calling for that life, it resonated with my own situation. There have been times where I've wanted to give up on all of this, when I've become so mentally and physically drained that I no longer thought I could do it. I still question it all, but seeing Sam and Dean in that test re-engages my motivation.

At a tavern with Allison the evening after, I see a man at the bar who looks exactly like Dean, and later that night bump into a guy at a different place who looks like Sam. The universe always finds a way to get a message to us, but oftentimes we don't realize that it's there, instead writing it off as a *coincidence*. Spirit language is all about timing, and I have to train my mind to understand that.

CHAPTER SIX:
A STRANGE COMFORT

I relax to the scent of fresh linen and sounds of humpback whales. The days tick by at an irritatingly slow rate; I'm still three weeks away from my reading. I look at his yellow roses, noticing the petals browning around their edges, doomed to fall off with the single touch of a finger. Taking any excuse to be in my car for a while, I blow out the candles and head out to get a new bunch for the week. I enjoy my uninterrupted time of losing myself in my music, feeling his presence at its strongest as it plays.

I look out at golden hour, a time when the sun is just about to set, and put my visor down to shield my eyes from the orange glow. The view reminds me of one of our light songs, *Sun in Our Eyes*. A lot of the songs I've been listening to lately mention the sun, this being one of my favorites. I hold my hand out of the window, feeling the wind on my sun kissed skin. "You're miles and miles away, Heaven knows i. ..ade.. heav… fade." I beam at the static popping, "AH!" I exclaim, outstretching my right hand for his.

I log the malfunction as soon as I pull into the garage. As I change out the bouquet, I put on his interview. The dull headache comes back. I sense him with me as I watch. Something about having him on in the background comforts me, filling the void of his physical absence. I can never figure out why I get emotional as I watch him. Watching as he carries himself and even the sound of his voice makes me tear up almost every time. I can't tell if I'm connecting to my own emotions or his.

I throw three more shirts and a pair of high waisted shorts into my old duffle bag, ready for our road trip to visit family tomorrow. My room goes dark as I turn everything off except for the interview. The interviewer looks firmly at the killer. "Why did you do it? Is there any one thing that drove you?"

The killer shifts in his seat, "To this day I don't know what started it. For years, I resisted the urges and stayed away from temptations but then one day I… gave in." My sight goes dark as the killer nods with a sigh.

*

My mind is clouded as I wake up to movement. Without opening my eyes, I can tell that the room is pitch black, the TV turned off after hours of inactivity. Laying on my left side, I bunch up the pillow beneath my head and feel like someone's...spooning me? It's the same feeling as when Cameron would pull me closer in the middle of the night.

I wasn't physically moved, but I can feel the energetic presence surrounding my entire backside. I reach the length of my right arm behind me and feel the other side is warm, like someone was just lying there. I feel comfortable with it, instantly nodding back off after the few moments of being half awake.

The sun is up as Kylie and I load our bags into the trunk. I reach for nana and grandpa's, fitting their luggage on top. Talking to mom with my eyes half open, I rest my head on the passenger seat. After some time, I wake up to the sound of our tire hitting a pothole in the road and check the time to see how long I've been sleeping. After making sure Mom is still good with driving, I put on my music and gaze out at the autumn trees as we pass the highway. A couple hours into the drive, ten more to go. My ear buds sing to me and help me through the tedious ride.

I observe the colors of the changing leaves when suddenly, piercing pain spreads over the top left side of my head, radiating to the top of my brow. It's as if someone stuck a dull steak knife through my brain; there was no warning and no build up. It hits me all at once and it's excruciating. Discreetly, I stare at the floor mat and clench the side of my head until the feeling passes. In a moment, I pick my head back up and look out of the window, staring at the sign as we pass it. "EXIT 213." Quickly, I grab my phone to snap a picture, ending up with a green blob.

All of a sudden, I remember the encounter last night. I was so out of it that I almost forgot it happened. I know that after a few days, I'll overthink it and convince myself that it wasn't real. As of right now, there isn't a doubt in my mind that what I experienced actually happened. But the killer was gay, so why would he do that? Maybe he misses companionship and I was just there. Maybe he was just bored.

My headache subsides shortly after we pass the exit. I scroll down my growing list of signs. *-8/30 on road trip looked up at exit 213 at the same time I had the bludgeoned headache.* Over the song coming through my ear buds, I hear a muffled voice. "Kris? We're going to stop to eat." Mom smiles through the rear-view mirror.

Opening the car door feels like lifting the seal of a container. The fresh northern air hits me as I step stiffly out of the car. Walking around to the walkway, I glance at the license plate on the hatchback next to us and notice the three letters that make up the killer's initials. The plate on the car next to that contains the numbers 213. My jaw drops and quickly I take a picture of the two plates together before holding the door open for everyone.

Last night, I packed myself a protein bar in an attempt to save my bad eating for the trip and not on the road. As everyone looks over the menu, I slip off to the bathroom. I walk into the dingey, white tiled room and notice that the music in the bathroom is a lot louder than out in the restaurant.

Clear as day, a song begins as soon as I sit down. "It's three in the morning and I just want to be with you, let me in. Last night we fell asleep and woke up in a euphoria, though, no one needs to know. I'm not leaving you alone." From the stall I listen in awe of the significance relating to last night. The lyrics repeat, "Oh, I'm not leaving you alone." As the song ends the volume seems to quiet back to normal as the next one begins. Lazily, I swing my foot up to the toilet handle to flush. Before I leave the bathroom, I log *-8/30: Presence song* *reached me in gas station bathroom.* I rejoin my family with their brown bags of food in hand, and we hit the road.

We drive until we're too tired to continue, pulling into a hotel for the night. The desk clerk smiles as she hands me a key to room 312; 213 backwards. Of course. The red light turns green as I slide the card over the sensor. I open the heavy wooden door and am confronted with the smell of must and tobacco swirling from years of guests. I fall back on the mattress, thankful for a place to stretch out. The game show channel occupies my ears as I wait for the shower. I still can't get over what happened last night, let alone over the last three months. I know that I should give my mind a break from all of this, but how can I? The bathroom opens up; it's my turn to shower next.

I shut the door behind me and wipe the fog off of the mirror to look at my rough appearance. I run the water, waiting for it to get hot. As I hold my hand under the stream, the brightness in the bathroom dims and brightens. I look up at the light fixture, figuring that the bulbs are old. As I shower, the lights subtly waver from bright to dim, blinking calmly.

Feeling better, I turn the shower knobs to the left and wrap myself in a white towel. I walk over to Mom, who is blow drying her hair by the vanity.

"Just out of curiosity, did the lights in the bathroom flicker when you were showering?"

"No, I didn't notice it," Mom answers as she brushes.

"Hmm, interesting." I walk back to the bathroom as Nana puts on her face cream to see that the light seems just fine. I'm noticing more than ever how my believing sets a momentum, strengthening his signs and my ability to notice them.

As we all turn into bed, Mom shuts off the TV. The room falls dark and silent, the only light being a small red dot on the fire alarm. Since the demon experience, I've never let myself sleep in complete darkness. In 2014 I would go to bed every night feeling its presence watching me. The only comfort would be my fish tank light and TV; without them, I'd panic. Normally, I would be extremely paranoid in this situation. Tonight, I notice I'm not so afraid of the dark anymore, because I know who is in it.

Loud beeping startles me awake. I pick up my head to read the digital clock: 7:00 a.m. I shove my face back into the pillow and mumble, "I don't wanna get up."

Mom yawns through her words. "Me either. I couldn't fall asleep for almost an hour last night, and then I got a text at 2:13, like who texts at that hour?"

I pick up my head. "That's a specific time, let me see." Mom flashes me her screen, and I read the text, delivered exactly at 2:13.

"Rude." I remark. Going to the bathroom to brush my teeth I flip on the light and eye it intently. It doesn't flicker once.

*

The tires roll over the gravel driveway of my aunt's house as we pull up to the small country home. I get out, stretching my legs and inhaling the fresh upstate New York air while taking in the landscape. The wide-open land and rolling green hills are so tranquil compared to the crowded buildings and construction in the South Carolina town that I live in. I glance to the bend in the road that leads to our family farm down the street but within walking distance.

We haul our suitcases, pulling them over the three wooden steps inside the dusty garage. After doing my share of packmuling, I begin walking alongside the country road towards the farm, happy for a few minutes of my own to bring the ghost to this beautiful scenery. The golden sun hangs over the cornfield, covering the entire area to the right of the road. The farm was started by my great grandfather—who came to America with only a nickel in his pocket—in 1930, on 450 acres of land. For generations it's been a dairy farm run by our family but was recently abandoned as a business and now sits empty.

I look at the giant pine trees that line the road across from the field. Coming up to the farmhouse, I approach the window and take a peek inside. I climb three flat, concrete steps to the entrance. I rest my forehead on my hand as I look through the dusty glass. It's as if the house is frozen in time. Floral wallpaper, the same brown leather couch and tan recliner with a pea-green blanket draped over its back sit ready to welcome family. The kitchen looks timeless, still furnished with the original countertops, flooring, and fixtures.

It's painful to see, knowing what the land once was, but I find its desolate state beautiful. The wooden barn that was once fresh with red paint now sits slumped, the color flaking off its surface. The tractors sit idle, covered with spiderwebs. The aisles that once housed Holsteins are now bare concrete floors with vacant pens. Behind that, the grown-in pasture is alive with the creek running through the middle, reaching all the way to Niagara Falls.

This creek is often one of my go-to spots in my meditation headspace. To see it in person after imagining it for so long feels like I've stepped right inside my mind. The meadow is overgrown with wildflowers colored pink, yellow, and purple, the crab apple tree standing in the middle of it all. The land is so peaceful; I feel as if I'm the only person in a still world.

As I stand embracing its beauty, I feel the presence behind me. Turning to an empty dirt ground, I'm pleasantly surprised to realize that he's here admiring these surroundings with me. I close my eyes, feeling the pull of energy as I channel the beautiful and happy vibration of what this all once was. The energy rises from the flowers, the home, and the memories, sharing its positivity with us as it flows into his frequency. I open my eyes with serenity.

After reconnecting with family, we spend most of the time in the garage, sanding and repainting furniture for my little cousin's room makeover. My uncle brings out a black and red bag of tools and ironically hands me the power drill, a tool that the killer was famous for using. It is Milwaukee Brand. I didn't even know *Milwaukee* was a brand. Dusk begins to settle. The construction lamp that has been shining all day becomes our main source of light. Our hours of work are beginning to come to a close as we stand around in a circle discussing what to do next.

I notice that my phone has been stuck at 34% for almost twenty minutes now. 34 is the age that the killer was when he died, and I've been noticing the number more and more often. As I respond to a text, my attention falters from the screen to a light flashing in the corner of my eye. I look up and see the construction lamp blink three times. Mom and I look at each other, and I flash a smirk to Kylie, who isn't amused.

We make our way into the room to set up all of the pieces of furniture. Five of us in that one room plus all of the furniture makes me feel claustrophobic.

"We could put the bed facing the wall, but then it would be blocking that window," my aunt offers.

Mom chimes in, "Well, the dresser is going next to the closet so that wouldn't work." A song screeches from the radio, interrupting our conversation.

"What the hell? That radio was off," my aunt says as she looks at us in disbelief. "That's bizarre."

Mom and I give each other the look. "Well, I guess we'll just keep it on," my aunt laughs. We continue talking and the song gets noticeably louder.

"What is happening with that freaking thing?" My aunt walks over and unplugs it.

As I tuck myself into bed, I begin to feel the sickening sensation of missing him. I pull out my phone and find a picture of him. He is sitting in a chair, one foot on the floor and his ankle crossed over his knee. He's wearing his khaki jacket, smiling with the aviators on. I study the picture like taking a hit of an addictive substance, and I instantly feel much better.

I log every sign for the day before nodding off. *11/2: Anxiety in car, then Bohemian Rhapsody started playing and made me feel better/Noticed exit 213/ Battery percentage stuck on 34% twice/34 on milk can/Noticed minute :34 almost every hour/My order number was 34 at McDonald's and the girl who served it to me was wearing a Queen hoodie/daisy next to number 34 on a license plate/The lights flickered in two separate stores as soon as we walked in.* I find that when I am away from home, signs happen in front of the people I am with as if he is proving his existence to them.

Being in the remote country with family grounds me back to Earth and refreshes my mind. Although preoccupied, I still receive ectomist sightings, his name, and his numbers throughout the weekend. I'm flattered to find that he's following me everywhere, attached at my metaphysical hip. After three days, the trip is over, and we head back home.

*

Walking beside Mom, I push the squeaky cart down the aisle of the home store. We've always shared everything and anything that we have going on in our lives. Recently, however, the one thing I want to talk about most is the very subject that I constantly have to bite my tongue on when I'm with her.

I can tell she worries; worries that I'm too sucked into the spiritual world and not the physical one. It's also likely she worries about my sympathy for a person such as him. I can't blame her; if the tables were turned, I'd feel the same way.

"What do you think about this geode painting for the TV room, Kris? I like the bling on it." A puff of ectomist rises over the shelf above me and distracts me from answering. I avert my eyes, snapping back into conversation, "Oh yas, I love it! The gold would look good in there." As I grab the painting to load in the cart, I look back up to see that the smoke is gone.

Walking towards checkout line, we stumble to the left in unison. I look at my Mom and start laughing.

"What was that?" Mom chuckles, "That was weird."

I get dizzy and weighted down as if someone sat on my shoulders.

"Oh. All of a sudden I don't feel good," Mom says with a heavy breath.

"I just got the same feeling right before you said that," I reply. Even she finds it bizarre, giving me an amused look.

Another window of opportunity opens to talk about spirits. I reserve my words, careful as I articulate them to explain the phenomenon of feeling ghostly energy. She appears concerned, unwilling to believe the possibility of who's around. "I really want you to see the movie, Mom. I think it'd make you see him differently," I nervously suggest.

"Okay well, maybe when we get home." That little agreement brightens my entire day, meaning more to me than she realizes.

At home, I feel like I made a mistake by putting on the movie and it hits me as soon as the music begins. I wonder if showing her this will have the opposite effect of what I intended and instead disturb her even more. From the bus scene until now, I've been on the edge of my seat waiting for her reaction. Surprisingly, her sympathy grows as the scenes play on. She shows interest in his story by commenting and asking questions. I smile as I answer them.

The scene with the teen faking seizures in school is coming up and I begin sweating, ready to be embarrassed on his behalf. This is going to ruin everything. He throws his arms up, letting out the first yell, and I cover half of my face with the blanket. "Bleh. BLEH!" He rolls around on the tile floor as his peers stand around, watching and laughing. Over the sound of them, I hear Mom laughing, too. Was this kind of humor a 70's kid thing? I laugh in relief with her and relax a little more for the rest of the movie.

The ending credits roll. As we discuss her thoughts on the movie, I notice the shift in her demeanor from afraid and put-off to supportive and understanding. Without warning, my phone dings. It's Madison. "Hey, come up town with me and Sydney!" I look to Mom with a puckered lip. "I don't want to cut into our time together."

Mom smiles. "Go! Have fun with them!" I contemplate as I always do, and within a few minutes decide to get up.

"Thank you for watching that with me," I say before leaving.

"I'm actually glad I saw it; I do feel better about him." Mom smiles.

Following my routine, I mix together vodka and juice to pump myself up for going out. Walking into my bathroom to get ready, I notice an emptiness. Normally, as soon as I separate myself from people, his energy bombards me. This time I can feel he's not with me. Maybe he's with Mom as she's more open to accepting him now. Since I'm going for a night out, maybe he left to visit somebody else. I try not to worry about it and focus on my look.

At our usual rooftop spot, we walk past the ivy-covered walls to the bar in the middle of the patio, invisible inside the sea of people. The swamped bartenders pour without looking, giving out drinks that are two thirds liquor. I look over the surrounding glass railing; the skyline is in perfect view. I'm ready to feel free for the evening, surrounded by a crowd of strangers when I'm so used to being alone.

I don't know what it is about Spanish music, but I've been having a recurring daydream of the killer trying to make me laugh by dancing to Mexican music, pulling me in for a tango. I have no clue why, but that scenario crosses my mind every time I hear Spanish music play. We're sipping on vodka cranberries and taking videos and pictures when a bald man slides across the floor to us. We all prepare our, "I have a boyfriend," in case he tries to make any moves.

The man yells something in my ear that I can't understand over the techno beat. He grabs my waist and hand and shows me how to salsa. I laugh; I don't know else what to do. This is random, especially for a club setting, with club music. This ends up happening to me the next two times I go uptown in the span of three weeks, all with different people. I have never tangoed before, but the dances are just like the ones in my recurring daydream.

Spirits influence people through thoughts. Sometimes they get someone to notice a sign, sometimes they borrow them to *be* the sign. Could the killer be doing this through these people to validate something for me? Maybe he's showing me that he is the one present and proving our connection, or maybe he's showing me that he's here and paying attention to my thoughts. Maybe this all has no meaning, but the timing of the situation is strange and worth considering.

Three days have passed since the night Mom and I watched the movie and he is still absent. The extensive passing of time is concerning me. I never know what he's off doing, and I pray he's not in trouble or trapped somewhere. What if he just left me? There's a world full of people way more special than me that he can choose. Why would I be any more important to him?

I sit in my room alone again. The sickening sensation of missing someone that is gone forever punches me in the stomach. I need someone to talk to about it but I know I must keep it to myself. I lay on my bed playing "I Am The Walrus" through my speaker, hoping to call him in, but I only enhance my worry.

I walk into mom's room, managing to steer the conversation towards the topic of the ghost after a few minutes of small talk. She finds sincerity and pain in my words, realizing just how much all of this means to me. She stumbles on her words. "Well… you don't know…Maybe he has things to fix on the other side or something. I mean, he has *a lot* he needs to work through. Just be patient, he'll come back." Despite my anxieties, I'm humbled that she offered kind words towards him.

*

The next sun rises, and I open my eyes, feeling the now familiar vacancy. It is going on day number four. My music plays with no static, my phone works without malfunctions. What the hell? The density that once hung habitually over my shoulder is now just empty space. It feels like weeks have passed, and I'm beginning to question if any of what happened was even real.

I try a meditation and press play on the third eye music. After closing my eyes with a few deep breaths, I'm in. My physical senses fall away and almost instantly, I snap into the black of my subconscious. With closed eyes I plunge into my neutral space within. For the first few minutes I sit, emptying my mind to black nothingness. Focusing on the chimes and humming keeps my mind from wandering. Fifteen minutes go by as the black begins forming patterns of grey and white. In the grey, a still view of the killer forms right in front of me. It is a faded black and grey vision not put there by me, but by a visitation. His back is facing me. I can see from his shoulders up. His head is turned slightly to the left, just enough so that I can see a bit of his profile and the side of his glasses. I lean to see the front, but the picture doesn't change. A static pop comes through my right earbud. The vision fades away and my attention reverts back to black. Heaviness releases from my heart with gratification at his returned presence.

Minutes pass as I sit with a vacant mind. A horizontal rectangle appears in the distance, white glowing behind it. Is that a door? Before I figure it out, it too disappears. I'm fidgety and anxious to get out after some time and open my eyes. I feel the carpet beneath me, the bed pressing against my back, and the rose quartz in my palm. My body is energized, my mind sharp. The presence around me feels good. Finally, it feels there. I take the day to relax before leaving for a work event tonight.

*

Ready for the teachers to charge in, I stand politely at my screening table. Thirty minutes in and the room is packed, with my line having at least six people at a time. Among the crowd, I look up and lock onto a man standing awkwardly by himself. I do a double take at the uncanny resemblance as I stare at the tall, blond-haired person wearing glasses. He seems to be the killer's same height of 6'1, with the same broad shoulders, even holding the same posture as him. With a can in his hand, he looks like the socially awkward guy at the party, walking around with a beer. But there are 200 people in the building, and he's all the way across the venue; he'll probably never make it over, but at least I got to see him.

My concentration breaks as a woman hands me her finished survey. Fifteen more receive their assessment, and I'm on autopilot as I go through the line, unaware of what time it is. With a smile, I hand the next person their survey. I look up to see that it's fake him. Up close, he looks even more like him. I try to keep my composure, but I'm a little nervous talking to him. As he shares his neck pains and aches, I play it cool and hold the scanners on his back to read his results. Of all of the people that I screened, he spoke to me the longest. Of all the people in the crowd, I spotted him directly. Of all of the vendors, I was one of the few he waited in line for. It's times like these that I feel the most connected. In this moment, there isn't a doubt in my mind that the killer is coming through this man. As he walks away, I feel a great sense of validation. At the end of the night I log the sign in my notes and notice the list's rapidly growing length.

*

Normally my room reaches close to 80 degrees as soon as the door shuts, but tonight my room is freezing. I always figure the fluctuation in temperature has to do with different spirits entering my space. I put on my oversized sweater and cozy into my room when Allison texts me to tell me she's here for wine night. Running up the stairs, I greet her with a high-pitched screech hello and bear hug.

I keep my own life quiet, encouraging Allison to share hers instead. Sipping red wine, she continues on about her boyfriend drama and I listen intently. My phone buzzes from the other side of the room and I jump up to go check it. It's a message from Kylie. "My blinds are tapping again. I'm going to punch someone."

I laugh. "I'll be right back, Allerson." I prance across the hall, creaking open Kylie's door with a dopey smile.

"I'm so annoyed," Kylie laughs. "Come sit next to me and listen." We lay side by side in the darkness, staring up at the ceiling. As I wait, Kylie breaks the silence. "I swear they were just doing it for like, two straight minutes." We wait longer, talking at a whisper so as not to miss anything.

Silence falls between us as we hear the blinds lightly patter against the window. "See!" She points. There is a pause between each tap, as if the blinds are catching wind behind them and gently floating back to the frame. I lay listening to the ever so lightly tap... tap... tap. She chuckles. "When it was just me in here they were almost banging and now it's so polite since you're around." After about a minute, it stops. I beam as I get up, happy that she's as enthusiastic about blinds tapping as I am. Walking back to my room, I'm blinded by my lamps after sitting in pitch black. I tell Allison what just happened, glad to have the opportunity to share a little extra proof in case she doesn't believe me. "That's crazy, Kylie is experiencing this too?" Allison asks. I nod and toss back another sip of wine.

When I received the sign of the killer on TV, I told myself I would never doubt his presence again. After that wore off, my certainty continued bouncing back and forth. Just as I was beginning to doubt again, he reached me in front of other people for external validation. This happening for a second time can't be just a coincidence.

Kylie's blinds never creak on their own again. I don't believe in "coincidences" anymore; I'm beginning to see how spirit talks to us daily. Everything we see or experience is for a reason, and within every moment holds a meaning. Throughout the days I find that these signs have a ripple effect, leading me to believe again as I await the upcoming reading.

CHAPTER SEVEN:
THE 21ST NIGHT OF
SEPTEMBER

R ain patters on the glass of my window and gently wakes me up. It is mid-September, and right in the heart of hurricane season. Our entire state is preparing for hurricane Florence to hit South Carolina tonight. With all of the hype, it has been impossible to find bread or a pack of water bottles in any store; the shelves are wiped clean from the little bit of excitement in our hum-drum town. Around 6 p.m. tonight, a friend will be having a gathering at their house in the spirit of hurricane season, and I've been debating on whether to go out before the storm hits.

I keep my eyes closed as I reach for my phone on the nightstand. My finger merely brushes the screen as I go to grab it. Just from the mere contact, the sound of a bass guitar begins strumming through the speaker, playing an alternative rock song that I've never heard before. I don't pick up the phone, and instead listen.

"Tonight the world is going to be spinning fast. I'm so happy you're past is behind you. You've been out in the wild, out in the night. You've been feeling out of your mind, do you live in reality or is this all a dream?" I unlock it to see what is happening, finding that "Volcano" by U2 started playing from iTunes.

"You're like a volcano, and you don't want to know. Something in you is going to soon blow." I jump up and out of bed to show someone. It's too early for Kylie to be awake, so I run up the stairs. "Mom, look!" I yell. She comes out of her room with a confused smile. "So, I just woke up, and before I could even touch my phone this song just started playing. I've never even heard it before, it just started on its own," I say with excitement.

I click up the volume and hold the phone between us. "That's crazy. It's a good song," she comments, making me smile.

"I've never even heard this song before," I repeat. We listen as static pops through the next phrase. "You we..re ....alone and... now you're not alo...ne..." We look at each other at a loss for words. As if the song playing on its own isn't enough, there's static to further prove this is not just a coincidence.

A long strum of electric guitar cues the end of the song. "What do the words mean? Could you hear what they were?" Mom asks.

"No, I wasn't even paying attention. I'm going to replay it in a second to listen." We each make a cup of tea, sit in her room, and listen. "Tonight the world is going to be spinning fast. I'm so happy your past is behind you. You've been out in the wild, out in the night. You've been feeling out of your mind, do you live in reality or is this all a dream?"

"Tonight the world is going to be spinning fast, like the hurricane! Wow," she comments. Her enthusiasm opens the door for me to elaborate on my interpretation of the lyrics. Amidst my rambling, I notice her retreat. "Well Kristen, I think that you're getting too wrapped up in this. You need to focus on other things," she snaps.

"What? I thought we were just talking about the song together?"

"Yeah, but you can't let this all hold you back from actual life."

"What? Where is all this coming from, I thought you thought this was cool?"

Her response inspires me to show myself out of her room. I get up and leave in an entirely different mood. Shutting my bedroom door behind me, I plop back onto my unmade sheets and dwell on her words. Some people won't understand this, and I have to embrace that. I know what I'm doing with this, and I know my truth.

I lay back and press resume on the song, closing my eyes to listen to its words. "You used to see as clear as the color of your blue eyes, now your vision is hazy. Your future is going to land on you. You used to be alone, now you're not anymore." That's wild. That was the part where the speaker crackled. The strum of the electric guitar rings through the speaker. *-9/15: Woke up and Volcano started playing itself off of iTunes.*

The day comes and goes, and the sky falls dark just as I'm about to leave for the night. Lacing up my combat boots in the kitchen, I look over my arm to observe my cat growling at the corner wall leading to the basement. "Jack, whatcha lookin at?" I ask. He emits a low meow as his black fur twitches and his eyes lock onto the blank wall. The sound of Mom's footsteps come from behind. "Hey, Kris. Are you still going tonight? I worry with how the weather's going to be."

"Yeah, I figured since it hasn't started raining yet I should be fine. I'm not going to stay long," I respond.

Mom pauses. "I'm sorry about earlier," she says.

I tie one last knot. "It's okay, I just don't know why you got mad at me for that."

"I wasn't mad at you. I reacted that way because I don't want you to start feeling towards him…how I feel towards Brad. I still miss him every day and…" Her voice pitches higher as she fights tears. I rush up to hug her, holding on for as long as she needs to collect herself. "I think of Brad every day, and I just feel so stuck. It's taking me a long time to accept that he's not here, and I can't stay stuck on him like this."

I was not expecting that response, and stutter as I find my words. "Oh, no. My feelings for him aren't romantic, it was never like that. He's even *gay* if that makes you feel better." I laugh. "I look at it like… if this actually is him, I have a big duty to fulfill. If I can actually do it, this would be something really special. Trust me, once I get him to where he needs to be, my life will go back to normal. I'll get a boyfriend and all that. But this is going to be a part of my life for a little, and I want to embrace the time I have with him while it lasts."

Mom relaxes her tensed shoulders.

I hug her again and say into her shoulder, "Everything is going to be fine, just please trust me." I grab my black-studded purse and smile. "I'll text you as soon as I get there." As I walk to my car, I feel a sense of relief from our talk.

I arrive at my friend's house, finding that the group started drinking before I even began my drive over. Liquor from the mini bottles burns my throat as I toss them back one by one to catch up with the group. The wind starts to pick up, whistling and hooting through the cracks of the windows as the rain beats down on the roof.

Madison and I sit under the multicolored lights. She sips out of her cup and asks, "So, what's new with you?" Instead of confessing a love for someone or ratting out a dirty secret like most would as they are drinking, I find that now when I'm intoxicated, I want to expose the suppressed, unspeakable topic of my paranormal experiences.

Sober, I don't dare tell about the killer until I know it's him for sure. Will I manage to stick by that while inebriated? I begin, "Well, you wanna hear something crazy?" With an eager ear, the poor girl listens to my tales as I tell her everything, leaving out only the name. "And even today, my phone it started playing a song by itself."

"Dude, that's crazy! What song was it?"

I tell her, and Madison automatically pulls out her phone to type "Volcano by U2."

"Madison, Kristen, get ova here!" our friends call from the pool table, ready for a game. I pour another vodka soda and listen over the break in music to the sound of the storm growing stronger. Over the beating of the rain, I hear a song begin to play with acapella voices and a piano in the key of B flat major.

Tingles of excitement spread from my head down to my spine. "Oh my god, this fucking song." I say, holding back emotion. Madison says, frozen, "Did 'Bohemian Rhapsody' really just start playing after we were just talking about that… That's insane, dude."

"See what I mean about the timing?" I say with a chuckle. *MAMA, OOO,* everyone sings in unison. I laugh, noticing that people can never resist the urge to sing that part. I join in, singing my heart out with the red solo cup in my hand. Even away from home and out with people, he's still here by my side. I continue the night happy as ever, knowing that both aspects of my life can exist in harmony with one another.

*

I wake up on September 20th with my stomach in a complete knot. Even after holding out for all of this time, the thought of having to go another day without my answer is agonizing. I can already see how this reading is going to go. I'm going to sit in front of Denise with my hopes up. She's going to close her eyes, open them and say, "I'm sorry, this isn't him." I study her picture online. Even though she looks so humble, all I see is the lady who is going to crush me tomorrow.

Lightheaded from the stress, I ease into my car to go get my paycheck from work. I stick my key in the ignition and notice the radio was left on from when I was last in the car. I imagine the ghost gripping my shoulders and looking into my eyes as if he's the one singing me the song that is playing on the radio, the message in the lyrics being, "It's all going to be alright, it's all going to be okay."

I'm amazed at the coincidence of catching the song at that exact part with those words of consolation. I'm calmer than I was before, though I can still feel my own rapid heartbeat. The radio announcer's voice blares out, and I switch the setting to my phone for new songs.

Three dots bounce on the screen as the recommended song loads. My mind races with each possibility, each reason this ghost may not be the killer. I begin to get overwhelmed, and a melody begins. For the second song in a row, the lyrics offer the message that everything is going to be fine. "Don't stress your mind, dry those eyes. We'll be home together with the keys to the universe if you just stay with me."

Tears well up as I reach my right hand to the passenger seat for his. I just need to know if this is him, just one hint before tomorrow is all I need. I continue down the road deep in thought. After a few minutes I pull up to the gas station to deposit my check. A white delivery truck is blocking the ATM that I was planning on using, so I pull in closer to show that I need to get in.

Rolling up next to the truck's side, I see the blue circular logo: *Pabst Blue Ribbon Beer, Established in Milwaukee 1844.* Every Friday around 1:30 p.m. I come to this gas station for the ATM, and never have I seen this truck parked here before. If this isn't a sign, I don't know what is. As my check processes, I stare at the truck in desperate hope that it means something. I want to believe it so badly, but my mind still taunts me. Back at home I kick off my shoes and head to my room. I can't believe that in less than twenty-four hours I'll have my answer. I attempt not to anticipate the session and brace myself for tomorrow.

The morning comes and I turn on the TV for background noise while gathering my things before leaving. With a weak hand I zip up the duffle bag and tuck my phone charger in its side pocket. The TV is dead silent as the killer walks into the meeting room filled with the news crew. His arms hang low to his sides as he walks swiftly to meet his dad and stepmother. Quickly, he says with a slight smile, "Hey Dad, Shari. Good to see ya." His father says the same as they embrace in a hug. "What a way to start a week, huh?" he says, hugging Shari before the three of them stand around. Watching the screen, I realize that this is probably the last time I'm going to watch this video. I gaze at the prisoner's face as I reach for my packed bag, holding my stare as I press the off button on the bulky, grey remote.

My thoughts race at the speed of our car going down the highway. "Again, I'm just going to feel so stupid if this isn't really him."

Mom's voice quiets me. "Well... you don't know. I think you're psyching yourself out. Either way it'll be okay. You know you have a lot of support, a wonderful future with acting and everything. And I'm here for you." Anxiety eats at my stomach; nothing seems to ease my mind.

"Don't stress about it, let's talk about things we're going to ask her." Mom glances at the map on her phone. "I want to see if she hears Brad say, 'Aww snap' like he always did. You know, in his low voice, the 'Awwww...owwww.' I don't know, I can't do it." She laughs.

My thoughts drown out her words; everything goes silent but my mind. Her phone rings until I silence the call. "Can you see who that is?" she asks, keeping her eyes on the road. I sit up to see an unknown number calling from Milwaukee, WI, smiling as I tell her where it's from. Feeling better, I concentrate on the mountainous scenery.

Arriving at noon, we step into the quaint hotel, styled in 1800's fashion. Red floral wallpaper and woven baskets occupy every nook and cranny. The woman at the front desk smiles as she hands us a key to room 211, close to 213 but not exactly. Our first day in the town is the most fun we've had in a long time. After walking off dinner we shop and return back to the room for movies and ice cream.

My eyes grow heavy as the time gets later and later. I step off to the bathroom for a shower. My finger taps the bathroom counter as I ponder what song to play. "Volcano" by U2 might make me feel better, being that it was such a recent validation. Under the bright bathroom light, I bounce my head to the rhythm as I tie my hair up in a knot. "Tonight the world is going to be spinning fast. You've been feeling out of your mind—" My eyes shift from my reflection to the flashing light above. Three times. My mood brightens, knowing he's here. After my shower, I confidently lay my head on the cold white pillow and close my eyes for tomorrow to come.

*

Waking up on the morning of September 21st brings a mixture of emotions. I'm excited but anxious, ready but not ready.

I announce, "Geudmerning, Mom!"

"Merning!" She chuckles. As I get out of the plush, white sheets, a rush of butterflies shivers through my body.

"Oh my God, it's today. I don't know if I can make it until 6 tonight."

Mom stretches. "It will be fine. Deep breaths."

With the day to explore the town, we head out with a destination wish list. After an hour of deciding which cafe to visit for lunch, we walk to the one surrounded in flowerpots on the corner of the street. Walking in, I notice vases with two yellow flowers on each table, a comforting reminder of the yellow flowers in my room for the ghost.

Taking small bites of my French dip, I wince at my non-existent appetite. Mom leaves the table and without her, I think about what's to come in the next few hours. I feel my face flushing, my hands clamming up, my pulse racing. I really can't do this. Suddenly, there's a touch on my right upper arm that pulls me out of my nervous spiral. I'm comforted as the energy lightly grips me, a subtle message telling me to calm down. The feeling sends tingles across my skin, giving me goosebumps. My automatic thought is that this is the killer's spirit, but I can't be sure. It lingers for less than a minute before dissipating.

Mom comes back with a smile and continues our conversation. Ever so quietly, I recognize the lesser known alternative song playing as one of mine and the ghost's songs. I attempt to record it, but the song is too low for my phone's speaker to catch. Hearing the song stills my nerves.

After lunch we walk back out to the brick sidewalk, enthusiasm and worry stirring my gut. We shop the boutiques and crystal shops to kill time as 6 p.m. taunts me, being so close yet so out of reach. I glance in my bag full of new crystals and oils, then look up to see a group of people huddled under a tree. They're crowding around a man holding something delicately in his hands. Mom and I approach closer and see a small green animal sitting motionless on the man's palm.

Mom's eyes light up. "Oh wow it's a hummingbird, they're my favorite!" The man squints from the sun as he holds up his palm.

"Yeah, I work in the restaurant right there and came out for a smoke break and almost stepped on him. I'm glad I saw; he was just lying on the sidewalk. I don't know what happened to him." He stands with his hands cupped, looking at the hummingbird as if he's scared to break him. The man looks up at me. "I have to go back to work in a minute, will you take him?"

Without hesitation, I happily scoop the small bundle into my hands. He feels like a warm, soft stone, barely weighing anything. We stare in awe, studying the bird's small, green feathers and tiny beak. My bottom lip puckers. "We need to help him, he's so precious!"

Mom's eyes scan the street. "They have to drink nectar every fifteen minutes.

We need to find a flower bush, or he'll go hungry since he can't fly."

"I feel like Snow White," I joke as I hold the small bird to my chest and stroll past people. He lets out a small chirp, perking up as we walk up to a red flowered plant. His sword-like beak brushes up against the petals and I glance up to the door behind the potted flowers. I'm fascinated to see that on the door is a "23" in golden metal letters, similar to the killer's apartment number font, "213," just short of the 1 in the middle.

After minutes of anticipating his cooperation, we soon find that the bird is not going for it. Continuing our quest, we stumble on a small public garden surrounded by a white picket fence and multicolored clay pots. With high hopes we walk up to each plant but the bird still shows no interest. With the time drawing closer to 6, we have to think of something fast. We find a burger joint to ask for simple syrup, a mixture of water and sugar.

The sun beats down on the picnic table outside of the restaurant as we sit, trying to get the bird to eat. I hold him ever so gently, dipping the tip of his beak into the syrup, and watch as he begins to lap it up. We watch in childlike wonder as he continues drinking. We stay quiet, careful not to scare him. As quick as lightning, the hummingbird perks up, ruffling his feathers and chirping.

His fluttering wings hum as his small body lifts off of my hand, zooming away like he was never hurt at all. "That was so beautiful!" I say as Mom panics, wondering if he is okay to fly so soon. I search the trees for where he may have gone, but he's nowhere in sight. This happening right before our reading might mean something. It's possible that the wounded bird is yet another sign from the killer. A symbol that he will one day be able to fly free out of my hands, which nurtured him.

My heart pounds out of my chest as we pull into the wooded area at 6 o'clock. "Mom, can you do your reading first? I feel like I'm going to puke." As we put the car in park, Denise steps through her front door. My mouth is dry and my head is light as we step out to meet her. I attempt to act as natural as I can in my shaky state, going in for a hug instead of a handshake as I introduce myself.

She is everything I imagined she'd be. Quiet, sweet, and welcoming, yet reserved as she holds her hands together in front of her. I notice her tendency to giggle at everything, easing the tension. Upon meeting her, I'm more at ease. "I know you're both having a reading today, so who would like to go first?" Denise smiles, searching our expressions for an answer. I point my finger at Mom, volunteering her to go before me. With a smile and a "good luck" from me, Mom and Denise head inside, and I make my way back to the car.

My eyes grow teary as I rest my forehead on my fingertips. "This better be you. Please let it be you." I resort to what I always do when I need comfort and pull out my phone. I rest it on the steering wheel with his interview playing. The words usually calm me like a lullaby, but I don't find it helpful this time around. I study his face, desperate to feel an authentic connection. I think of the hummingbird, trying to see it as a sign from him as I watch him speak with the interviewer. I'm impatient and uncomfortable as I focus on the man in the jumpsuit. I shut off the video to be in silence and look at the trees for consolation. "I can't figure out anything else on my own, I need a clear answer through this reading. Please God."

The silence is making me antsy. I try putting on the movie, but it only makes me feel worse. What's supposed to be an hour feels like two. I wait as I bounce my leg and stare at the branches, hoping that nature's beauty will have a calming effect. A few minutes after seven, I see the door crack open and I perk up. Looking for the expression on Mom's face, I see a smile and notice that she's in high spirits. Mom and Denise make their way down the steps and Mom turns around, laughing at something Denise just said.

For some reason this worries me more, knowing how legit this medium is. I don't even have the chance of her faking it to make me feel better. She's going to tell me the flat-out truth, that I've been wrong. I meet them on the gravel walkway. "She's the real deal, Kris. That was incredible," Mom says as Denise giggles. Rambling like a child who's just come home from a field trip, Mom stops herself to say that she will fill me in later.

She sees the worry in my eyes and gives me a hug of support before I go in. I follow Denise to what feels like the guillotine. I swallow a lump in my throat as I step through the threshold. The familiar humming of meditation music and smell of essential oils help me feel at home. I observe the crystals and spiritual tools displayed around the room, admiring how many she has as I find my place on the couch. She hands me a pad of pink paper since we're not allowed to record sessions, and I clench the edges of it. In case she can't tell already, I tell her how nervous I am. She chuckles, "You'll be fine! Just take a few deep breaths and have fun."

Denise finds her spot on the couch while explaining her reading style to me. "I don't want you to give me any details; doing that will ruin the validation of what I receive for both of us. Okay, so, are you ready to start?"

Flashing her a timid smile, I say quietly, "I think so."

Closing her eyes, she announces that she's setting the intention to only allow beings of light and a high vibration to communicate with us. Nervously I ask, "Have you ever read anybody with a dark entity attached to them?"

"Oh, yeah, a few. I will not read the energy if it's too dark, I am not doing that." She chuckles.

"Well, this reading's fucked," I think.

"So, what is it that you would like to focus on?" she asks.

Careful with my words, I begin, "Well, there has been a spirit leaving me signs since the summer. The only problem is, I don't know if this is who I think it is because he was somebody famous? The signs started when I became interested in him and there's been some pretty wild coincidences. I'm here to see if it's actually him or not." I refrain from saying any more, sitting up as straight as a pin.

She nods understandingly. "Okay, well, let's just see who comes through." With a deep inhale, Denise begins tapping in.

I close my eyes, making myself more aware of my fast pulse and heavy breathing. I have to calm down. I put myself in my room as if this is just another daily love meditation by myself. Denise whispers, "Okay, so now just give me a second."

She's not going to pick up on anything, I can just feel it. I sit on the edge of the couch, trying to calm my shaking leg. Concentration falls across her face as her eyes stay closed. "There is a dominant male presence that has been around you. He's presenting himself in a civil war uniform."

I slouch in disappointment, "No, he wasn't from the civil war."

"Well, you may not know him as that, but I'm getting the impression that this was him from a past life and that's how you have this connection now."

I draw back as my mind opens to that possibility. "Are you serious?"

"Mhmm." Denise hums as she concentrates. "Yeah, I'm pretty sure that's civil war, it's the grey uniform with the flat hat."

After a pause she continues, "Did you take a tour of somewhere that he lived, or visit somewhere he would visit a lot?"

I contemplate her question, but nothing comes to mind since I haven't been to Milwaukee or Ohio. "No, I don't think so…" I reply.

She hums questionably and my brain clicks. I chime in, "Oh wait, yes! I went to Chicago just a few weeks ago, he used to visit there. Maybe that's it?"

Denise responds, "That feels right. I just heard him say, *she walked exactly where I walked,* and he's showing me a visual of you walking past a quirky coffee shop, bookstore type hangout he says he visited often." I sit up a little taller as things start to connect, remembering how I felt him during that entire trip.

Denise stays concentrated as she pulls for information. I thought that by now his presence would hit her like a load of bricks and she would blurt out his name. I clear my dry throat. "I could give you a hint to help you along?"

Denise's eyes remain closed in meditation. "No, I want him to tell me. He's just being a little shy," she responds with a laugh.

Although we haven't yet received a jump out answer, the good news is that she's communicating with a spirit, not a dark entity. With eagerness I ask, "Can you hear what his voice sounds like, or an accent?"

"I feel like he had a sort of nerdy or nasally voice?"

I agree with a smirk of confidence, piping in, "I really can give you a hint if you need one, I trust that you're honest."

"No, really, it's fine, I'm actually kind of determined to find out through *him.* But, if you want to tell me just a first name, I might be able to connect more directly."

I offer the first name. Denise perks up with confidence. "Okay, now I can distinguish his energy line much better and he feels stronger. I'm hearing him say, *I crossed a line that I couldn't go back from, a point of no return.*"

I scoot closer on my seat, knowing that was something the killer has actually said in an interview before.

Denise continues, "He's saying that he's made a lot of mistakes in his life, talking about having to make a lot of amends…He's really down on himself about it. I'm trying to tell him that we all have to make mistakes to grow, don't be so hard on yourself." Denise chuckles innocently, unaware of the volume of these *mistakes*. "He feels like he didn't do enough for the people in his life. And again is just dwelling on making amends. He was trying to *walk the straight and narrow*, but something always distracted him from the life he truly wanted. He was very creative and had a lot of passions that he never got to grow on. Was he involved with drugs?"

I try to find my words. "Well, he wasn't a user. He actually, um, drugged other people. I'm sorry that this is so weird." I laugh awkwardly.

Denise sits gracefully with her hands daintily at each side and adds, "At this point, this is my mission to find out who this is. It's so interesting."

In saying that, I watch as her smiling face drops to a look of confusion.

"Oh…" Denise says, shifting in her chair, "He's showing me some, um… very graphic visuals. Like a crime scene." I cover my mouth, waiting for what she will say next. "I'm watching it from his point of view, as if they're things that he did? I'm not going to go into detail." This could actually be him. I watch her tilt her head in confusion.

Fidgeting with the paper, I ask what else she sees. She opens her eyes to look into mine, afraid to upset me. "I don't want to tell you who I think this actually is, Kristen."

My heart beats faster and my face lights up, "Just say it. I think I already know!"

Denise laughs, not knowing what to say.

"Trust me, you can say it."

"Well… was this guy around in the, say, 70s or 80s?"

I hold a giddy smile as adrenaline soars through me. "Yes!"

"Holy shit," she replies, taking in the realization that she is correct. Denise asks, "Is this Jeffrey Dahmer?"

My heart and the world around me seize as I bury my face into my hands. My emotions release all at once, overwhelmed by the answer.

Tears stream down my cheeks as I look up. "Really? Is it really him? Not something tricking me?"

"Nope, that's him alright." Denise laughs, passing me the box of tissues.

"But is it actually Jeffrey Dahmer who's been around me?"

"Oh yeah," she reassures me, "this is definitely him." I exhale through my mouth as I dab the tears from my cheeks and fan my face. "I'm sorry if you're freaked out about this."

"Oh no, I'm just in shock. I love true crime!" she laughs. I have so many questions that I don't even know where to even begin.

I crumble the tissue with my shaking fingers and compose myself for a question, "So, how long has he actually been with me? I think the signs started in May, but I'm not sure."

Returning to her meditative state, she responds for him, "*Longer than you've been aware of, and I've come through to you in many forms.*" Denise opens her eyes and shares, "And he said that he showed me a crib... your crib." Unaware of the magnitude of our connection, I'm at a loss for words. Up until this moment, it never even crossed my mind that "my ghost" as a child could have possibly been him, because, how? I sit in pure shock and process that the ghost I've grown up with is the same one that I have now, Jeffrey fucking Dahmer.

"He's showing himself watching over you as if he was responsible for you. Believe it or not, he seems a little over-protective."

I listen in awe, but ask the question, "Why me?"

"He knew you were going to be the one to help him, and I feel it's one of your main purposes in this lifetime. Also because of your connection through past lives, his soul recognized yours. When you saw him you recognized him back, your energies are drawn to each other."

Denise snickers, "I just heard him say that he couldn't find a way to stop himself from what he was doing, so he told himself, *I'm going to be the worst motherfucker that I can be.*" My eyes pop open as I ask if he really said that. "Word for word," Denise answers. Diving into my theory about a demon latching onto Jeff, I explain the séance at his house right before the first murder.

Denise turns her head as if to listen to a whisper. "*I saw the Devil and the Devil saw me.* Hmm, that's kind of terrifying." Denise laughs. "I feel like he's using that as a crutch, kind of blaming his actions on a darker force, not having to deal with it mentally. Those were still *his* crimes." I thought he was remorseful, owning up to what he did. I'll look at him a little differently, knowing he so cockily brushed off his crimes. If what Denise just said is truly how he looks at what he did, I have to say I'm disappointed.

Denise continues, "This is going to sound weird, bear with me. The world has to have villains to bring out the light in others. I'm getting that he was what the world needed at the time, to bring society together. He had to be the "bad guy" to raise awareness, in a sense, changing how we look after each other. Even though he was this horrible person, he served that destiny for the greater good."

As Denise concludes that thought, I relate that to my own ideas. Even as a child, I've always wondered if we write out our lifetime before coming to Earth. Jeffrey always said how his life seemed out of his hands in some way; psychologists could never put their finger on the cause of his actions. Predestination may be the missing puzzle piece to that mystery.

Denise interrupts my thoughts as she asks, "Was he abused? There's cuts on his arms, and signs of molestation as a child… Not from a parent, someone outside of the family. Either an uncle or an uncle figure, do you know who that would be?" He always denied abuse, not wanting to shift the blame onto anything or anyone else but himself. I can't think of who the uncle figure would be. My heart sinks and takes away the beauty of the moment, saddening and infuriating me at the same time. As opposed to my fond memories of being little, I'm lucky I was protected from what he had to endure. It was said that Jeff was pure evil because "nothing ever happened to him." If only he had shared this publicly, it could have been a key sign to understanding him more. I feel honored that he shared that with me; he didn't with anyone else while he was alive.

"He's clingy to you because you give off this healing energy." I smile, knowing that I didn't yet mention anything to her about helping him. Denise shares, "He has a very child-like energy; he's curious about things, but still timid and a little afraid. He clings to you the way a child would hide behind their mother."

My hand cramps around the pen as I scurry to write everything down. The sheet of pink paper is ruined with sloppy letters and circled words scattered around the page. "He's sharing that there are these obsessive 'fans' worshipping him for what he did to these people. He shows that you're different, your feelings towards him are genuine. He struggles with this 'tug-of-war,' going back and forth between the bad energy and the good. He accepts this as a consequence for what he's done, however. His 'fans'" encouraging energy tempts him towards the darkness as you try to bring him light. "

I notice the time. "Oh my gosh, my thirty minutes ended a while ago! We can stop, I'm so sorry."

Denise smiles, "Actually, this is really cool for me, too. We can add another thirty minutes to it, on me!" I resist, uncomfortable taking the gift. Insistently, Denise continues reading, and I smile as I reach for the pad of paper.

"Do you know what life review is? It shows us the scenes of our life choices and how they affected others so we can learn from our mistakes."

I share my knowledge of it and Denise continues, "His review is too troubling for him to face so he remains stuck in his own Hell. This takes a spirit anywhere from a few weeks to a few months to finish. You said Jeffrey passed in 1994, and still has yet to complete his life review as of now in 2018. That's twenty-four years..."

Denise takes a breath and wipes her brow, then resumes conversation with the other side. She looks stumped. "Huh. Out of all of the things that he has done, one thing he can't get past was from childhood. He had a friend or a neighbor... Alice? To this day, he's guilty over something he did to indirectly hurt her; not physically, but her feelings. Maybe he harmed her dog or something and seeing how it broke her heart always stayed with him." Alice has never been mentioned in any of the documentaries or interviews. Quickly, I scribble the name down.

My voice breaks the silence. "Is there anything else that I can do to help him?"

Denise sits with her hands in her lap. "He's trying to act fine and keeps saying *I got this*, but I really don't think he does." She laughs. "Just keep sending love, that's perfect for him."

I look outside of the window behind her and notice the pitch-black sky. Denise's messages become less frequent as the spirit tires out. Denise concludes, "Do you have any more questions for him?"

I have my answer, I have plenty of proof, but for my own sanity I need something more. "Is he showing you any signs that he's left me?"

Denise inhales and closes her eyes, "Do you ever smell cigarette smoke?" Amazed, I explain my breakup and how it happened on his birthday. "Oh, well, happy birthday to him. He's like your breakup buddy." Denise laughs.

The room grows quiet as she focuses to hear more. "Do you ever sing… like to him? He likes when you do." She smiles.

She asks about the daisies and I reach for the tissues again.

"Jeff said I was like a bright yellow daisy in our first medium session."

"Aw, that's actually really sweet." She giggles. "Daisies represent friendship and yellow is the color for joy, which you've brought him. I also feel like he might've liked daisies, and was into the flower power thing in the 70's." Denise nods as she delivers the channeled message.

"Thank you. Thank you, thank you, thank you. Thank you for seeing parts in me that I didn't see in myself." I blink back tears in hearing the words that I will hold onto forever.

I dab my eye, not expecting these kinds of tears by the end of the session. I sit for a moment in disbelief of the hour I just had. With a deep breath I get off the couch and embrace Denise with a hug of gratitude. I thank her over and over. As we let go I ask of her one more favor. "Can you, like…tell my mom?"

"Oh yeah, I was planning on it." We walk outside into the chilly atmosphere of the fall evening. I'm surprised as I walk down the steps with the same enthusiasm my mom had an hour ago.

Mom notices us and meets us on the walkway with anticipation. Denise breaks the silence. "Let me just tell you, your daughter is not crazy."

Mom gasps in disbelief, amusement playing on her expression. "It's Jeffrey?" Denise nods in confirmation. "You're kidding!" Mom says, impressed, locking her eyes onto me in amazement. She asks, "So it's not a demon or anything evil?"

"No, I would have refused to connect if I felt it was something bad." Denise fills her in as I listen, still in astonishment. I feel a sense of unity as they converse about our connection. My situation is now a part of their lives, too, and I'm no longer alone in this. I'm proud as I listen. We share more hugs and thank Denise for the peace she has given us both with her gift. Walking back to the car, I can't help but smile.

Mom and I decide we want to celebrate the successful readings. As we buckle our seatbelts, I look online for a place where we can talk about our sessions with a tall glass of cider. At the local pub, I feel as if I don't have a care in the world. Mom seems to not only accept my situation, but to accept him, too, knowing we share such a connection. Now, she really listens. My phone begins to ring, and we put our deep conversation on hold. I see the caller ID and look at Mom as if I'm in trouble. "It's Kylie. She still has no clue." I laugh.

Timidly, I answer. "Hey Kris, how did it go?" Mom and I exchange humorous looks before I begin the spiel. Kylie's reaction is what I expected it to be: surprised but still reserved. I tease her about the blind tapping that Denise brought up and continue sharing, careful not to overwhelm her with the information.

"Wow, this is a lot to take in. I can't believe it," Kylie chuckles. I conclude the call. "Okay I'll leave you alone now. See you tomorrow! Love you!" I can't believe I feel so free in being able to address him. I take another swig of hard cider and bring up the civil war past life connection to Mom. The idea of that is unfathomable to me, so incredible that I can't wrap my brain around it. Somehow, a tie from another life makes everything click. Time rolls on, drawing us closer to midnight and the end of our trip. After a great night, we turn in and set our alarms for the morning drive home. As the morning sun rises, our magical weekend comes to a close and I take one last look at the town in the rear-view mirror. Exhilaration and gratitude are all I can feel, knowing my experiences are as real as I wished them to be.

Upon coming home, I set my purse next to the vase of withered yellow daisies and sweep their fallen petals into my palm. On the TV I select his documentary as I unzip my luggage and reach for the bundle of dirty clothes. It feels so good to be back in my element.

"Your honor, it is over now," Jeffrey says, standing at the podium. That's him, my ghost. It feels so surreal to be able to say that. "I know society will never be able to forgive me. I know the families of the victims will never be able to forgive me for what I have done." The screen goes black, displaying the message, "AMERICA'S MOST NOTORIOUS SERIAL KILLER WAS BROUGHT TO JUSTICE."

I hear a quick scuffle behind me. Turning around I see that the bag of chips sitting on my nightstand has flown off, landing two feet away. "I wonder who could have done that," I say to myself, amused. I embrace that he is here with me at this exact moment. I don't have to repress this idea anymore out of fear of being wrong. I never have to doubt myself again.

CHAPTER EIGHT:
HIS STORY

J effrey Lionel Dahmer was an American serial killer, known for killing 17 men from 1978 to 1991. Born May 21st, 1960, he grew up living in Ohio with his mother, Joyce, and father, Lionel. For seven years, it was just the three of them. The first few months of baby Jeffrey's arrival were one of the happiest times in Joyce and Lionel's lives.

After a short while, Joyce grew distant from the baby. While pregnant with Jeffrey, Joyce took a mix of over twenty antidepressants and other substances, and it was at this time that her habits started again. She became frustrated with basic motherly tasks and would eventually hold him only for photos or diaper changes. Joyce didn't want anyone else touching or holding baby Jeffrey, so he was left in his crib daily without the experience of human bonding during this crucial time of development.

Being complete opposites, his parents constantly argued. Lionel was mild mannered and introverted, while Joyce was confrontational and difficult to get along with. To escape the chaos of the frequent yelling matches, Lionel spent almost all of his time at work as a chemist in his lab, leaving Jeffrey with Joyce for the day, which continued for years.

However, Jeffrey was still a very loving and playful child, often acting goofy in front of the camera in home videos. His favorite activity was spending time with his dad outdoors and observing wildlife. It is a common misconception that Jeffrey tortured animals as a small child—he never did. He had a love for animals and would often save baby birds that would fall from a nest on their road.

Up until the age of four, Jeffrey was often in and out of the hospital for infections and illnesses. At four years old, he developed a double hernia in his groin area. The process of the surgery was a scary and traumatizing experience for the young child. He would repeatedly ask what was happening to him and never received a response. The pain from the surgery was so traumatizing that he thought the surgery amputated his genitals, and that his life would be forever altered. During the nights at the hospital, he would offer to Joyce, "You can go home now, Mommy, I'll sleep." Before the procedure, he was a funny and outgoing child. After the surgery he became very reserved.

As Jeffrey grew older, he began to show little interest in anything. One day as Jeffrey and Lionel were out in the yard, Lionel went to dispose of a dead animal under the house. As he was dropping the remains in a bucket, Jeffrey seemed interested in the bones as they would fall in. Lionel was happy that he was finally intrigued by something, and something biology related that he could bond with him over.

In April of 1967, the family moved to a home in Bath, Ohio. That same year, Joyce gave birth to Jeffrey's younger brother. Joyce and Lionel wanted Jeffrey to feel more involved in the family and decided to let him name the baby. He chose the name David. As David grew older, Jeffrey began feeling left out as the interest in him from his parents dissipated. No longer was he tucked in at night, read stories, or asked how his day at school was. The focus was solely on David. Around the time David was eight and Jeffrey was fifteen, their parents' arguing got progressively worse, causing an environment of constant tension in the home.

All day, every day, they would hold a yelling match over the littlest things, whether David and Jeffrey were there or not. At this time, Joyce continued her habit of pill-popping. More frequently, Joyce was in and out of mental institutions for attempted suicides. The fact that his family didn't get along really bothered Jeffrey. He would often keep to himself, venting his anger by whacking the trees in his backyard with branches.

High school was where he began to lose himself as he uncovered who he was becoming, and he discovered he was homosexual. Aside from the intimidation he experienced from women, he found that he never felt attracted to them. He disliked his homosexuality and had a tough time accepting it, knowing his religious parents would have a hard time as well. Feeling shameful, he kept his preference to himself.

During his sexual development, he started experiencing feelings of violence and necrophiliac desires. He had no clue where the feelings were coming from, and that terrified him. He began to have dark fantasies about lying with an unconscious body, somebody that he could be with for hours, somebody that would never leave him. The thoughts would invade his mind like a freight train. They weren't the kind of thoughts that could be banished with a shake of his head; they were stuck to his mind like a powerful adhesive.

The first fantasy he experienced was about a jogger that ran by his house every day. He planned on hitting him over the head to knock him unconscious so that he could act out his desire. One day he mustered up the courage to do it, but by a miracle, the jogger didn't pass by that day and Jeffrey didn't attempt it again. He didn't know how to tell anyone about the disturbing feelings that he had, so he suppressed them in his mind and tried to drown them out with alcohol.

More and more, he began to emotionally withdraw as the tension in his house grew. His time alone in a shed behind their home became his getaway. This space was where he could escape the arguing and devote time to his interest in biology. He would find dead animals on the side of the road and take them back to the shed to dissect and study.

He was fascinated by figuring out how everything in the body worked, eventually building a collection of jars containing the bones that he had found. Lionel noticed how this hobby occupied him and began to think that the fascination was becoming too much. Shortly after his discovery, Lionel had the shed torn down, leaving Jeffrey with nothing to distract him from his inner conflicts.

Lionel and Joyce divorced his senior year, leaving Jeffrey devastated. The weight of his unhappiness along with his growing desires drove teenage Jeffrey to become an alcoholic by his senior year. In school, Jeffrey would act out in bizarre ways for laughs, just like the film portrayed. He would fake epileptic seizures, as if to mimic the episodes his mother had from often drug overuse, to turn the pain of what he experienced at home into something to laugh about. His humor seemed to be geared towards getting a reaction out of people. It included bleating out sheep noises during class, and running down the halls yelling, "Hurricane drill! Hurricane drill! Hide!" The student body referred to his acts as "Doing a Dahmer," and he gained reputation as the class clown.

Although school was his escape from the fighting at home, he was bullied there both physically and verbally. From being shoved into lockers, thumped on the back of the head, or called belittling names, he seemed to have no getaway from conflict. With broad shoulders and a height of 6'1, he was built like a linebacker and could easily intimidate. He could have fought back but never did, and never said anything to defend himself. He instead internalized the bullying, carrying it alongside his other troubles.

Drinking liquor from a styrofoam cup, he would often be drunk by the time he arrived at class and referred to the alcohol as his "medicine." Teachers alongside his peers turned a cheek when it came to his alcoholism and bullying. He participated in little to no school activities but took part in marching band and tennis. His group of friends remained small, and they kept little to no contact after graduation. John Backderf described him as "the loneliest kid I had ever met," and "a tragic figure."

Bridget Geiger, a classmate of Jeffrey's, shared a story about her experience with him at prom, which he had shyly asked her to attend. She shared that he was very polite, and very nervous. Before taking pictures, Jeffrey was told to pin the corsage on her light pink dress. Anxious that he would stick her with the pin, he fumbled around with it for a while before Bridget's mom offered to take over.

As Jeffrey approached graduation day, Lionel moved into a motel after the divorce, leaving Jeffrey in the family home with his mom and brother. Come graduation day, Joyce had packed up, taking David to move in with her family, leaving Jeffrey to the surprise of an empty home. It was at that time where Jeffrey developed severe abandonment issues. For the next few weeks, he had parties at his house to fill the silence. After the parties stopped happening, he began to feel extremely depressed. He was alone with his unwanted, intrusive thoughts, the isolation making them grow worse.

He hated sleeping at the house alone, and the idea of somebody never leaving him became more comforting than ever. His fantasies became an obsession that he couldn't shake. Jeffrey continued having that specific fantasy of picking up a good looking hitchhiker and rendering him unconscious in order to make sexual use of his body. No matter how much booze he drank, he could not rid himself of these thoughts completely.

One fateful day, Jeffrey went driving to the mall when he saw a shirtless and very attractive man with his thumb up on the side of the road. "Don't look, just keep driving," he told himself. But he couldn't help but contemplate whether or not he should pick him up. It was the exact scenario that he had been waiting for, the opportunity being laid out perfectly. With his heart racing with excitement and uncertainty, he turned the wheel around and picked up Steven Hicks, who was looking for a ride to a concert that day.

Pulling to the side of the road, Jeffrey offered him the ride and asked if he wanted to hang out at his place for a while before the concert. With time to spare, Steven agreed, and the two went to the house for a few beers and weed. They quickly became buddies and hung out until the early evening. Hours passed, and Steven suggested that he better get going. Jeffrey became anxious and tried to talk him into staying, but Steven insisted that it was getting late.

In a panic, not wanting him to leave, Jeffrey attacked Steven and the two got into a physical fight. Jeffrey then hit him over the head with a barbell, and Steven fell to the floor. He laid there motionless. Jeffrey felt for a pulse, and he found that he had killed him. In the quietness of the empty house, Jeffrey stood over Steven's body. Fear, shock, and adrenaline overwhelmed him when he realized what he had done. Hours went by as Jeffrey tried to compose himself, thinking of what to do. He resorted to what he knew helped ease his mind: alcohol. The following day he chugged down a bottle of liquor and began disposing of the body. At around midnight, Jeffrey placed the remains into garbage bags, set them in the back seat of his car, and headed to the dump.

Being intoxicated, he drifted to and from the center line. As he swerved down the road, something perked his alertness. Red and blue lights flashed directly behind him, blinking through his back windshield. Thoughts of how this was going to end up raced through Jeffrey's mind. Afraid, he pulled over, the cop car following closely behind. Jeffrey took deep breaths as the officer stepped up to the vehicle. As the officer informed him that he was being stopped for drifting over the center line, he noticed several suspicious trash bags in the backseat.

Examining them with a flashlight, the officer questioned what was in the bags along with why he might be out driving so late. A strange wave of calm washed over Jeffrey for his answer. He explained with ease that he couldn't sleep from his parents' recent divorce, so he decided to take a load of trash to the dump to take his mind off of everything. The officer was persuaded, letting him off with a traffic ticket. Jeffrey had just gotten away with murder and couldn't believe it.

Shortly after the Steven Hicks incident, Lionel and his new wife, Sheri, decided to visit David and Jeffrey in the Bath, Ohio home. They walked through the front door to find counters covered in empty beer bottles, a cleared out kitchen and living room, and Jeffrey alone. Clueless that Joyce and David had moved out after graduation, Sheri and Lionel moved in immediately to be with Jeffrey. He was relieved that they would be there with him, and they noticed an upbeat change in his personality upon hearing the news that they would stay.

Sheri and Lionel noticed a sense of loss in Jeffrey. They wanted to guide his life in a good direction, enrolling him into college for that fall as a business major. When the time came, Jeffrey seemed enthusiastic and proud to be in college. He kept his dorm extremely neat with the bed always made, clothes always put away, and everything in order. When it came to his grades, the motivation was short lived.

He spent the time in college haunted by what he had done. The guilt was unbearable, making him unable to concentrate on anything else. Barely putting effort into his classes, his GPA dropped to 0.45. Jeffrey was never one to make friends, and his roommates frequently took weekend trips or night outings without him. He spent the experience in college as he always has, alone. More and more frequently, he was found absent from class for the greater portion of the week, skipping to get plastered in his dorm. As class went on he lounged drunkenly on his top bunk, listening to the same Beetles record on a loop. His roommates would hear him daily, singing along to *I am the Walrus* as they stopped by to get their books for the next class. Jeffrey flunked out after one semester, ashamed as his dad came to help pack his things.

Back at home his alcoholism worsened, and Lionel and Sheri began seeing just how serious his problem was, but little did they know why he drank so heavily. Lionel tried to lead his son the best that he could, but it was hard for Lionel to give him direction in his state of mind. Almost daily, he would find that Jeffrey was completely intoxicated, slurring his words and stumbling around the house. There were a few occasions where Jeffrey drove somewhere and forget where he left the car, sending Lionel and Sheri on a hunt for it.

In January of 1979, Lionel urged Jeffrey to enlist under the strict environment of the army. He trained as a medical specialist in Fort Sam Houston in San Antonio, Texas. By July 13th, he was serving as a combat medic in 2nd battalion, 68th Armored Regiment, 8th infantry division, stationed in Baumholder, West Germany. He loved the structure of the army, the feeling that he was a part of something so great. Doing exceptionally well his first year, he was ranked as an above average soldier, according to records.

Jeffrey's new bunker mates were astonished as they learned he never kissed a woman and took it as a challenge to help him lose his virginity. Grinning ear to ear, they brought Jeffrey to a brothel in Vogelway. He kept to himself as he walked in, avoiding the sea of women. Right away, the boys introduced Jeffrey to a woman that worked there, leaving the two to a one-on-one conversation.

Minutes later, they found Jeffrey nowhere in sight, assuming that he was too shy and left. The next morning they asked where he went, and he responded, "I don't need any girl."

By 1981 he fell back into his drinking habits, resulting in punishment for the entire barrack when he was caught intoxicated. After the second time, a fed-up group of men from his bunker cornered, jumped, and beat him, busting his eardrum, which affected him for years to come. Owing to excessive drinking, his military performance deteriorated, and his reputation of above average soldier plummeted.

By March, Jeffrey was released with honorable discharge and sent to Fort Jackson in South Carolina. From there, he was given a one-way ticket to a destination of his choice. Ashamed to return home early, he decided to spend a few months somewhere new and chose Miami Beach, Florida. Although he found a job at Sunshine Subs, his expensive drinking habit became a financial black hole. No longer could he afford his nightly motel, leaving him to find refuge at the local salvation army. Other nights he spent sleeping on the beach. To Lionel and Sheri's surprise, a trunk full of Jeffrey's belongings appeared at their doorstep. After seeing that he was no longer enlisted, they bought Jeffrey a one way ticket back to Ohio.

Two weeks into his return, another failure ensued. Jeffrey had been asked to leave a hotel lounge because he was drinking straight out of a vodka bottle in the lobby. In a drunken stupor, he refused and was escorted out. As Jeffrey continued to drink from the bottle, the police were called, and he began to get testy. With a flip of the middle finger, he was arrested for the first time for drunk and disorderly conduct.

Desperately, Lionel tried to get his son help with ultimately no success. In hopes that her positive influence might inspire him to live responsibly, his grandmother, Catherine Hughes Dahmer, welcomed Jeffrey with open arms to her home in West Allis, Wisconsin. His grandmother was the only family member towards whom Jeffrey displayed affection, and Lionel and Shari were hopeful that he would want to change in her presence.

They got along famously, enjoying each other's company. She mothered him lovingly, and he reciprocated by doing her yard work, shopping, and cleaning. Attending church with Catherine every Sunday, he aimed to drive out his darkness and homosexuality. He found himself handing money to the homeless men he passed, tipping generously at bars and restaurants, and helping people in need when given the opportunity. Before long he landed a position as a phlebotomist, proud that he was finally in a good place.

He began reading at the library in his free time to quiet his loud mind. On a quiet afternoon, Jeffrey sat reading at a table as a man walked by him, dropping a note on his lap. Curiously, Jeffrey opened the paper, reading, "Meet me in the bathroom if you want a blow job." Avoiding the offer, he left. Days went by as his mind raced with those words written to him. That simple gesture re-awoke his homosexual urges; his mind once again stirred with desires to be with a man. This at first frustrated him after he had worked so hard to push his sexuality away, but from that point on, he decided to embrace it. According to an agent that he would later meet with, he referenced his homosexuality by saying, "That's the way I am, so fuck it."

The dark desires continued to snowball as he formed an obsession with having complete control over a person, and staying with them as long as he wanted. He tried to fight the violent urges, thinking of ways that he could satisfy these strange feelings without hurting anyone. Walking past a department store one evening, an idea came to him. He stared at the male mannequin through the display window, noticing the perfectly submissive "partner." After hours, he stole the mannequin to bring home. It fulfilled his urges, and he was relieved to have found some kind of solution. He continued going to church, his desires under control, his secret, closeted. But after a couple of weeks, Catherine stumbled across the store mannequin in his closet and insisted he throw it away.

With nothing to satisfy his lust, his longing for a submissive body resurfaced. He fell into a new routine of frequenting gay bathhouses. Night after night, he kept the company of men to whom he was attracted, but the void in him lingered. Twisted and gory desires stirred in his mind, growing persistent with the passing weeks. He studied men's bodies with morbid curiosity. After being

133

with them and satisfying their needs, they would leave, as expected. Hurt, empty, and once again alone, Jeffrey sat with his thoughts.

In January of 1985, Jeffrey was hired as a chocolate mixer at the Ambrosia Chocolate Factory after being laid off from the plasma center. Because of his graveyard shift six days a week, he was prescribed sleeping pills. It wasn't long before he began using the pills to his advantage, drugging the men he met. They would be all his for the night and until morning. Although he knew that this was wrong, it was what he resorted to in order to keep from killing.

One evening soon after, Jeffrey offered a drink laced with sleeping pills to the best looking guy on the dance floor. He then invited the man to the back room of the club. On another evening, Jeffrey was carrying on with his ritual, crushing and spilling pills into whisky and coke before offering the drink to his partner for that night. He spent all night with this man, holding him as they lay, uninterrupted.

Noticing the time was almost up, he prepared to leave before the pills wore off. More hours had passed than usual, and Jeffrey grew concerned. He placed his two fingers to the man's neck, noticing that his pulse was extremely slow. In a cold sweat he called for an ambulance, leaving the bathhouse before he could be caught. Eventually, numerous complaints of being drugged by the same man added up. The managers grew suspicious of the accusations and banned Jeffrey from their club.

Alone, dreadful thoughts filled his mind day in and day out, thoughts of morbid sexual fantasies as his violent desires intertwined with lust. He didn't want to believe he was capable of such thoughts; they shook him to the core. His loneliness and longing for companionship began to cripple him. The nightlife was his only conduit for finding strangers, but he couldn't bring men back to the house at such a late hour.

Under the flashing lights, he began observing the crowd in the gay clubs on the strip of Milwaukee, Wisconsin. Keeping to himself as he drank by the bar, he looked for someone who caught his eye to bring back to the Ambassador Hotel. The routine stayed the same: he would search the dance floor, drug someone he found attractive, and invite the man back to the hotel so that he could have his way with him.

One night, he met Steven Tuomi, who happily accepted his offer to join him. Jeffrey slipped him the sleeping pills and watched as Steven chugged his drink down to the last sip. Jeffrey got blackout drunk himself, eventually falling asleep next to Steven. As Jeffrey opened his eyes in the morning, he looked down at his arms to see sleeves of bruises and dried blood. His heart sank to his stomach as he looked down to Steven Tuomi's lifeless body lying underneath him. His chest had been beaten in, and a stream of dried blood ran from the corner of his mouth as he lay cold.

Jeffrey was stunned with no recollection of what happened. The nightmare from nine years ago came back to haunt him; his victim even had the same first name. In complete disbelief, he spent the day overwhelmed with anxiety.

It was from this point on that he spiraled out of control. He had given up on trying to control himself, feeling that there was no point in fighting something he would end up losing to. His thoughts were too strong, overpowering his resistance. In later years, Jeffrey said in an interview, "The killing was just a means to an end, I didn't enjoy the act of that, but it was the only way to get them to stay."

He began actively seeking victims that were his type, muscular men with dark features. He drank alone at all-you-can-drink beer busts, downing bottle after bottle. He sat at the bar and waited until closing time to approach the men. Posing as a new photographer, he offered them $50 in exchange for modeling pictures.

Back at his grandmother's house, he would take provocative photos of their muscular physiques on his Polaroid camera. Afterwards, they would sometimes engage in sexual activity, and that's when he would give them the drink laced with sleeping pills. He waited until they were unconscious and engaged in sexual activity with them for hours. While they were still unconscious, he fatally strangled them. He never killed them while they were coherent for the purpose of making it less painful.

Although the scenarios didn't always end in murder, he committed three murders in his grandmother's basement before moving out. One of his victims was a very handsome young man and aspiring model, Anthony Sears, born January 28, 1965. On the evening of March 25, 1989, the two met outside of club *La Cage*. Anthony approached the tall man in glasses standing outside of the doors and asked him for a smoke. He walked up to Jeffrey with caution. Jeffrey heard Anthony ask, "Got any coke?"

"No, this is just whisky actually," Jeffrey answered, swirling the ice in his glass.

Anthony laughed as he explained what he meant.

After an evening together, Jeffrey felt like this one might actually work out. "If he would only stay, I wouldn't have to kill him," he thought. As the morning hours drew closer, Anthony suggested that he should get going. Jeffrey slumped in disappointment as he offered him "one last drink" and carried on with his routine. During Jeffrey's confession, he described Anthony as being "extra special," and someone he wished he could have had more time with.

A smell emitted from the basement of Jeffrey's grandmother's house, one that Catherine couldn't put her finger on. Puzzled, she questioned her grandson, but he offered only excuses. She was growing tired of the same routine, the late night company, the excuses, and his drinking. In speaking with Catherine frequently, Lionel noticed the burden that Jeffrey was becoming on her and suggested that he should give his grandmother a break and move out. He had money saved up from the Ambrosia Chocolate Factory and was able to afford his own place.

In September of 1990, Jeffrey moved into apartment 213 at the Oxford Apartments in Milwaukee, Wisconsin. The beige building stood tall in the middle of a rough part of the city. Inside of 213 was a quaint space adorned with tan carpeting, racy paintings, lava lamps, and cigarette smoke. His across-the-hall neighbors befriended him, becoming possibly the closest friends he ever had. They described him as a kind-hearted and generous person who always shared what he had with others, explaining that if you asked him for a cigarette he would also give you an extra one for later.

The apartment was spotless, complete with a fully populated fish tank which he took much pride in. He found serenity in watching the fish swim. He read up on fish care books to be sure to keep up with the environment properly. In his own space, he didn't have to limit himself. Jeffrey began dabbling in the occult, reading books on the practice as he considered pursuing it. Placing two griffin statues and a devil face wall plaque in his living room, he began to feel more in touch with a dark power, stronger, and as if he belonged to something bigger than himself. He placed a black table in front of his shiny blue curtains, intending to build an altar from it. On it he'd display the skulls of his victims so that he could draw energy from them. In a later interview even Jeffrey admitted how "bizarre and strange" the idea was.

Jeffrey developed a fascination with *Star Wars: Return of the Jedi*, and *The Exorcist III*. He watched the movies numerous times a week. It wasn't so much the plot that caught his interest as it was the villains. He was attracted to the power that the "Emperor" and "The Gemini Killer" had over others; their ability to control people drew him in. These films became part of his routine and would serve as his inspiration in a sense, putting him in the mood for murder.

Jeffrey worked the graveyard shift six nights a week at the factory. The clubs were his scene every Saturday night. On some weekends he would venture out to Chicago. While he was there, he visited the bookstores and taverns by day, clubs and bars by night, taking the bus to and from as he didn't have a car. He spent the nightlife alone in a crowd, tossing back Budweiser and Pabst Blue Ribbon to the sounds of 80's funk. As the night progressed and his cares dissipated, he would seek just the right man for his twisted fantasy.

Months went on as he acted on his gruesome desires, unraveling more and more madness. In the dismemberment of the bodies, he got a sense of the tragic waste. Sometimes apologizing as he looked upon them, he would have moments of reflection, thinking, "What have I done?" The tremendous potential of these bright young people was gone by his own, blood-drenched hands. But something in him pushed away his remorse and revulsion. Just like the flip of a switch, he would put on a stone cold face and clean up. "It became an incessant and never-ending desire to be with someone at whatever cost. It just filled my thoughts all day long," said Jeffrey.

As time went on, his actions became more twisted. He had a bizarre idea of experimentation so that he wouldn't "have to kill anymore." With extended knowledge in biology, he pondered ways to create a "living zombie," someone who would never leave him, following his orders as their own will would be non-existent. His thought was to use a power drill to make a small hole in someone's head and then pour a diluted acid solution into the brain to try to create this effect. In the three times he tried it with his unconscious victims, it never worked.

He began saving and preserving the skulls and body parts of his victims in order to feel closer to them. He went so far as to see what it would be like if his victims *became* a part of him. Disgusted but also curious, he wondered what it would be like if he consumed the parts that he kept. It was at this time that he experimented with cannibalism. Although given the infamous reputation of *The Milwaukee Cannibal,* it was a small part of his M.O, as he tried it on only three occasions.

When it came to the crimes, his emotions were completely shut off. He is quoted as saying, "I desensitized myself to it. I trained myself to view people as objects of pleasure instead of living, breathing, human beings." He shared that if he had been acquainted with the men on a personal level he wouldn't have murdered them.

Jeffrey was surprised with how oddly lucky he was in getting away with what he was doing. In one, incident a victim ran out of the apartment and Jeffrey was able to convince the police that the victim was his intoxicated boyfriend. As a result, the cops returned him to Jeffrey without question. Jeffrey later stated that it was as if some darker power was protecting him because no matter what, things always worked out for him and his crimes.

July 22, 1991 was a hot summer evening on the strip. Jeffrey walked the streets of the city as he scanned the crowd through his square framed glasses. At this point, he had been terminated from the chocolate factory for excessive absence. His lease would be up by the end of the month, leaving him with no direction in his mentally disheveled state. Taking swigs from a paper bag, he noticed a young, handsome guy walking in his direction.

He approached him, and the man introduced himself as Tracy Edwards. Jeffrey offered Tracy $50 to take provocative photos, Tracy agreed, and the two went back to apartment 213. While Tracy had had only two beers, Jeffrey was hammered. Jeffrey offered Tracy the drugged whisky and coke. He reluctantly accepted it and took a few sips before setting it aside. Making small talk, Tracy waited patiently to take the photos so he could be on his way. Jeffrey held off for as long as he could, sharing his experiences in the army as he lounged, puffing on a cigarette.

Tracy stood up, walking over to the fish tank to observe it. His compliments were interrupted as he felt a handcuff slapped on his wrist. In confusion, he turned to see the other cuff in one of Jeffrey's hands, a knife in the other. Taken aback and upset, Tracy demanded that Jeffrey let him go and that he would be leaving. Jeffrey's face softened, turning red as tears welled up in his eyes. Tracy looked at him in confusion as he cried, "Everybody leaves me! Nobody cares, nobody gives a shit about me. Now you want to leave too. Why do people always abandon me?"

Tracy took a deep breath, planning his escape. He had a hard time looking into Jeffrey's eyes. "Hey, no, no, I'm not gonna leave you. Look, I'm your friend. Let's just sit down for a while," Tracy said.

"Really? You want to stay?" Jeffrey asked.

Tracy nodded as Jeffrey calmed down, joining him in front of the TV. Piano music started as Jeffrey stared at the opening credits of The Exorcist III tape he had put in. "You know, this is the greatest movie they've ever produced. Best movie out there."

Tracy glanced over and saw that Jeffrey's entire face looked different as his eyes stayed glued to the TV. In a trance-like state he quietly chanted while rocking; he stayed in the same position for most of the two-hour movie. Tracy excused himself to the bathroom, and Jeffrey didn't even notice.

Preparing himself, he stood in the bathroom as he looked into his reflection, "I'm not gonna die like this," he said into the mirror. The flashing light from the horror film blinked on Tracy's face as he crept around the corner of the bathroom. Jeffrey sat infatuated by the movie as Tracy approached from behind. Swiftly, he struck Jeffrey on the back of the head and charged for the door. Jeffrey shot up, grabbing his arm. He briefly looked back as Jeffrey looked him in the eyes with desperation. With a jerk of his arm, he broke free and fled the apartment.

One handcuff dangled from his left wrist as he ran out to the street for help. He looked ahead to see two cops sitting idle in front of the building. Tracy flagged them down, explaining that this "crazy guy" cuffed him, and asked if they could use their key to get the cuffs off. Their keys were not effective as the cuffs were not police standard. Tracy led them to 213 to see if the "crazy guy" had the key.

"Police, open up!" Jeffrey heard at the door. He answered calmly, inviting the three men inside. They walked through a tidy and neatly kept apartment. Everything seemed in order and Jeffrey was cooperative and polite. "We're gonna need the key to these handcuffs," the officer demanded. With blurred vision, Jeffrey pointed to his room to welcome the officer to the key if he could find it.

The cop walked into the bedroom and looked around. Polaroid photos of nude men hung out of the drawer. He chuckled, shaking his head. As he sifted through the Polaroids, his face dropped. "These can't be real," he thought as he looked at the photographs of dismembered bodies. Looking closer, he recognized the black sheets and stained wall from that very room. The officer yelled from the room, "Cuff that motherfucker!"

The cops tackled Jeffrey, attempting to throw him to the floor. He resisted, being so strong that it took the two cops together to hold him down. Once pinned, Jeffrey let out the most inhumane scream that everyone in the apartment building, and passersby outside, heard. Witnesses said the yell was so indescribably miserable that whoever heard it was both frightened and saddened at the same time. After scuffling on the ground for over five minutes, Jeffrey's killing spree was finally put to an end.

Taken into custody around 1a.m., he was interrogated by the main detective, Patrick Kennedy. Jeffrey trembled, crying several times and leaving a literal puddle of tears on the floor by his feet. Detective Kennedy treated him with dignity and respect, speaking to him as if they were pals in order to gain his trust.

Kennedy naively consoled Jeffrey. "Listen, Jeffrey, we all make mistakes. I'm sure that whatever you did can't be too bad. Let's just figure this out together, okay?" He offered Jeffrey a cigarette and coffee. Jeffrey replied, "You're gonna want to kill me once you find out what I've done. This case is going to make you famous." With a long exhale of smoke, Jeffrey began his confession, starting from the first murder in Ohio and on through present day. He didn't hold back, confessing every detail with his head down. Writing at a quick pace, Kennedy took his statement by hand.

Jeffrey was relieved to be caught, admitting he would have never stopped on his own. He is quoted as saying, "The world already has enough misery without my adding to it. It's hard for me to believe that a human being could have done what I've done, but I know that I did it." With a guilty conscience, Detective Patrick Kennedy began to feel genuine sympathy for him, noting how "pitiful and pathetic" he was. Jeffrey was very fond of him, the one person he had ever been able to open up to, and he developed feelings for him. Kennedy's colleagues teased, "Way to go Pat, you got the freak to love you."

Day after day, Detective Kennedy entered the interrogation room with a hot cup of coffee and a pack of cigarettes for him. Jeffrey volunteered the full confession in hopes of helping the police identify all of the victims, and to bring himself to justice for what he'd done. He stated, "It was the least I could do, and even that was hardly anything." Kennedy and Jeffrey would spend the next month together going over the details of his crimes.

The multiple cups of coffee and pack of menthols put Jeffrey at ease as he let out 13 years' worth of guilt. Kennedy said, "Dahmer reminded me of a guy who got caught doing something wrong and was a little embarrassed by it. He became more relaxed as conversations went on…At the beginning there was no eye contact. Toward the end he would look at us and occasionally smile."

Jeffrey made it known that he took full responsibility for what he had done. He stressed that there was nobody, and nothing else to blame but himself.

Angered when the blame shifted to his parents, he stated, "That's not right at all, they had no knowledge of what I was doing and are not responsible for any of it in anyway. The only person to blame is sitting right across from you."

Lionel and Sheri attended the trial and showed up for every court date. Joyce did not once attend. Lionel stated that when he first saw his son it was as if "his soul had dropped out of him." During the trial Jeffrey's lawyer, Gerald Boyle, said that although Jeffrey showed no emotion, he was extremely upset. During court, Jeffrey kept his glasses off because he couldn't stand to see the faces of the victims' families. Jeffrey never knew what it was that caused him to be, in his own words, "so bad and evil," and hoped to get answers through the trial.

To and from the courtroom, Jeffrey wore iron shackles around his ankles and wrists. Because of their weight, Jeffrey would be pushed down the hall in a wheelchair. One morning before trial, a woman walking down the hall recognized him. She shrieked in fear and ran away. "Guess I should've shaved," he said, unfazed.

Jeffrey felt he deserved the death penalty, but that was not legal in the state of Wisconsin at that time. He was deemed sane on all counts of murder, because of the fact that he knew what he was doing was wrong at the time of the crimes. The trial ended with him receiving 15 life sentences without the possibility of parole.

When the trials were over, Jeffrey shared his thoughts with the psychologists assigned to his case. He thought he was an incarnation of the Devil, or equal to the Devil's evil. The psychologists that spoke with him said that they were surprised that he was the one who actually did what he did. Most serial killers are proud of their actions and are almost never sorry for them. Jeffrey, on the other hand, showed remorse. Gerald Boyle is quoted as saying, "Never in a million years would I have ever believed that he was a serial killer. He was just a sick, sick kid. I wouldn't want to live in Dahmer's shoes for one day."

Criminologist Dr. Jack Levin was shocked to find that someone such as Jeffrey Dahmer did not fit the profile of a ritual murderer. He said in an interview, "The very fact that he sedated his victims before he strangled them gives us an indication that he actually felt guilty, and that he did care about his victims, at least to some extent. The fact that he necrophiled his victims is a clue that he felt extremely rejected, abandoned."

Jeffrey seemed to have an awareness of a higher power. When referring to his arrest he stated, "Something stronger than my conscience will made it happen. I think some higher power got good and fed up with my activity and decided to put an end to it. I don't really think there were any coincidences. The way it ended and whether the close calls were warning to me or what, I don't know. If they were, I sure didn't heed them…

How arrogant and stupid of me to think I could do something like this and just go about my life normally as if nothing ever happened. They say you reap what you sow… well, it's true you do, eventually. I've always wondered, from the time that I committed that first horrid mistake, sin, with Hicks, whether this was sort of predestined and there was no way I could have changed it. I wonder just how much predestination controls a person's life and just how much control we have over ourselves."

In prison he was put on 24-hour suicide watch after multiple attempts and self-harming. His cell became a circus cage; the guards taunted and belittled him while on watch. They laughed at him as he urinated and forced him to sleep on the floor in his underwear among the ants. The light in his cell was kept on, with the guards shining flashlights in his face as he slept. In a short amount of time the guards let up on him as they familiarized with him.

Brian Masters, a psychologist, mentioned the recurring dreams Jeffrey experienced at the beginning of his sentence. He was an innocent man, oblivious to any crimes. However, the police dug up bones, incriminating Jeffrey when he wasn't the one responsible. In the dreams, there was always a man wearing a black hooded cape, pointing to him as the guilty one. The other dreams that he continued to experience were very pleasant. These were dreams of being with partners and providing comfort. They were perhaps the only comfort he experienced while incarcerated. Jeffrey recalled that he never had dreams of his victims, and often wondered why.

Being away from temptation lifted a weight off of his shoulders. It was said that Jeffrey was treated like a "rock star" in prison; people often tried to go to the jail to meet him and ask him for his autograph. His special treatment angered many of the prisoners, but he made friends with many others.

As he did in high school, Jeffrey coped with the severity of his situation with humor. As the guards stood around him nervously, he popped up behind them joking, "I bite." Security discovered a "Cannibals Anonymous Meeting" sign that Jeffrey put on the door of his cell and quickly took it down. Shortly after, he spent his first Thanksgiving in prison in solitary confinement for answering an employee call, impersonating the prison guard with the lisp.

He was in his cell for all but one hour of the day, and he occupied his time by going through mail. "I don't get why anyone would have anything nice to say to me after all of this," Jeffrey told Detective Patrick. Alongside love letters from both men and women, he received letters praising him for killing people, specifically people of color. It angered Jeffrey that he was made out to be racist since most of his victims were minorities. He hated that and wanted to make it known that he was sick, not hateful.

After lights out he would lay in his cell and count the ants crawling along the cement wall. Some nights he would hear music echoing from a radio that the guards put on for the inmates. The dancing music reminded him of the clubs. During the day, he would drown out the yelling of other prisoners by listening to his Walkman cassette player. He listened to humpback whale sounds, Gregorian Chants, and classical music.

With desperation for salvation he studied the bible, fully immersing himself in Christianity. He had weekly meetings with pastor Roy Ratliff to discuss readings. He was beside himself that a pastor was willing to help him. He stressed over getting every prayer perfectly right. In May of 1994, Jeffrey proudly walked alongside Ratliff as he told his friends passing by, "I'm going to be baptized today!" on his way to be baptized in the whirlpool in the prison chapel.

One morning, Jeffrey and inmates Jesse Anderson and Christopher Scarver were cleaning the prison bathrooms to earn their daily wage. Jeffrey and Jesse goofed off as Christopher kept his interactions with the notorious inmate and his friend limited. He fixed his eyes to the floor as he scrubbed the tiles with the mop when he felt a finger poke his back. Christopher turned around to them laughing under their breath, mops in hand. "Forreal? Which one of you did it?" he asked. Jeffrey and Jesse continued mopping with straight faces, and Christopher turned back around in annoyance.

The three of them split up, and Christopher followed Jeffrey into the locker room. Christopher waved a newspaper clipping in his face. "Did you really do this shit? Huh?" Christopher shoved Jeffrey into the wall, and he didn't shove back. Christopher held up a barbell, the same item that Jeffrey killed Steven Hicks with. With no expression, Jeffrey said, "I don't care if I live or die, go ahead and kill me."

He bludgeoned Jeffrey with the barbell, striking him repeatedly on top of his head. Jeffrey did not try to fight back and laid on the tiles as Christopher fled the scene. Minutes later, Jeffrey was rushed to the hospital. After efforts to revive him on in the ambulance that day, November 28th, 1994, Jeffrey was pronounced dead at 34 years old.

He told loved ones that when it was his time, he didn't want a funeral or a headstone for people to remember him by. Roy Ratliff, however, still led a ceremony for his passing. Jeffrey's urn sat in the middle of an almost empty chapel. After eulogies from Lionel and David, silence fell throughout the room and the ceremony was considered over.

The news of his crimes rocked the world, and he is now known as one of the most infamous serial killers of our time. To this day, his notoriety is used as inspiration for horror films, books, and TV shows. In 2000, Joyce passed away from breast cancer. David has since changed his name and lives in anonymity to escape the Dahmer reputation. Lionel and Sheri are still happily married, now with grandchildren. To this day, they struggle to move past that dark time in their lives, but the family name will always be tainted with the crimes of their late son, Jeffrey Dahmer.

CHAPTER NINE:
WHISPERS OF VALIDATION

I look through the black as I call to him. Dim grey light appears and forms a faded image, similar to what you see as a projector warms up. Every time now, I see the back of Jeff's head slightly turned to the left side and the rim of his signature aviator glasses. I hold my gaze, wondering why he doesn't simply turn around. Lately, catching a glimpse of him has become effortless. Jeff appears to me in a matter of seconds just by me closing my eyes. The black nothingness is only a screen, shielding the dimension that I am still partially blind to.

My time with him feels like an hourglass, dropping a grain of sand with each passing day. I'm going to miss the daily things that I've grown so used to. There will be a time when I will close my eyes and not be able to find him, a day where this will all become a distant memory. I imagine years down the road when I'm cooking dinner with my kids running around me. In the midst of the chaos I will hear his name on the TV, and it will bring me back to our time in 2018.

With a shake of my head, I shut off my thoughts of the future and relax to the voice of a healing guided meditation. As I sink deep into my subconscious, the voice fades into white noise. I look down at my bare feet in the tall, lush grass. I'm standing in a circular garden, the sun beaming through the spaces between the trees. A piano and the chirping of wildlife caress my ears as I look over the rainbow of multi-colored flower bushes. The light breeze brushes against my cheek and directs my focus to the left. I glance and see a young boy at my side, gazing at the vibrant scenery with wonder. The sun reflects off of his golden hair and kisses his milk-white skin.

My heart is full as his delicate, small hand rests in mine. I feel a tear well up in my eye, overjoyed to guide young Jeff for this session; to heal every part of him and keep him safe under my wing, at least for a little while. He stays tucked to my side as we look down a stone path, each step representing an obstacle from his life. His tiny hand tugs my white dress, apprehensive to step on the first paver. He looks up to me for approval, and I give him a gentle smile. He takes the first step with a concentrated expression. Leaping from stone to stone, his knowledge grows. He doesn't take long on each one, being that spirit time moves much faster than ours. I wish I knew what he was experiencing through those focused eyes of his.

Young Jeff seems wiser as we reach the end of the stone path. I look to my left and see that Jeff's reverted back to the age of thirty-four. As my consciousness dives deeper, the visuals begin creating themselves. I allow the visions to take over, changing from the colorful images in my mind's eye to black and white lava lamp visuals.

Hand in hand, we climb a bright green hill. Over its curve is a fountain; grey and ceramic with two tiers of water trickling into each other and pooling into the bottom. Standing in the clearing of this garden is Joyce. I take a moment to process her appearance, unsure of the significance of her presence here. Instead of radiating bitterness she feels peaceful. She's filled with grace and wisdom, transformed from her time healing in the afterlife. Seeing her feels like a visitation in a dream; I am without a doubt with her here. Her eyes light up as she sees her son next to me and she eagerly walks forward.

I notice Jeff's reaction as she approaches. He leans forward in anticipation, his expression curious. Joyce walks past me and gives an appreciative nod and warm smile. She reaches for Jeff and they hold each other in an extensive embrace. I feel the bridge between them rebuilding, resolving the past as they heal from each other's presence. The feeling of comfort and security overwhelms my senses as I watch.

The scene becomes so vivid that it snaps my awareness back into the room as if an alarm has woken me up. The voice continues through my earbuds as I rub my eyes and stretch my legs on the tan carpet. What an honor it is to have witnessed such a moment. I feel as if I healed a vital part of him, as if I reassembled apart of his soul that was once a shattered fragment.

My phone buzzes twice and I pick it up to see who is texting me. An old friend from high school, River, wants to know if I want to hang out tonight. No way can I go with Jeff in such a fragile state. His energy feels like that of a lost child wandering in a black abyss, and I'm the only one reaching out a hand. When I'm out with friends, I can't help but be sensitive to the fact that Jeff feels he's taking a backseat. I reassure myself that if I do go, I won't let anything happen. If something came of this night with River, Jeff might feel betrayed and abandoned once again. Or maybe he doesn't even care.

I hit send on a message agreeing to come over and instantly feel a shift in Jeff's energy. In the same way that you can smell bacon cooking, I can sense his discontent. My chest dampens as a wave of guilt crashes over me. "Just for this night, you and I are going to go to a friend's house. No matter what, you're always my number one dude. Don't forget that."

I make my vodka and juice, ready up, and head to my car. I put on one of Jeff's favorite songs for the drive, "Paranoid" by Black Sabbath. An electric guitar rings out as the lyrics speak of never feeling happiness because of a sick mind. "As you hear what I'm telling you of what my state of mind is like, I want you to enjoy life the way I never could". I attempt to send Jeff the energy of my words from earlier, but I feel as though they're not reaching him; all I feel is the sadness.

I reach my right hand to the passenger seat and feel a cold nothing. I pull over the gravel and I park beside an oak tree. The music cuts abruptly as I pull the key out of the ignition, and the only sounds are of crickets from the surrounding woods. "You're still my number one dude, Jeff. Come with me." I step out of the car and uneasily approach the door.

After three knocks, I'm blinded by the automatic porch light. The screen door creaks as River greets me. The smell of weed hits me as soon as I step through the door. I sit on the couch with a beer in my hand as I listen to River talk. I lose the thread of what he's saying, wondering if Jeff is still with me. Visiting with River brings back memories from my high school days, when everything was simple. He rambles on about a story from back in the day as my attention shifts to an uneasy feeling on my right leg. I stop my automatic tapping fingers as soon as I notice them.

Hours pass and I stumble over to the kitchen for the wine bottle, tipping the last few drips into my glass. "Oh shit, I drank the whole thing," I laugh. I stumble towards the room and from there, my mind goes foggy.

Some time later I blink my eyes open. We are in River's room and it is pitch black. I feel around for my phone and finally knock into it with my hand. It's 3:30am. What even happened? I think hard as bits and pieces of the night come back to me and my guilt from earlier is increased ten-fold.

Disoriented, I feel for Jeff's density and can't pick up on anything. "This was such a mistake. Jeff, I'm so, so sorry." Careful not to wake River up, I stealthily gather my belongings. My head feels like it's full of water that's tipping from one side to the other as I walk down the hall. I feel around for the couch. My hand grazes the faux leather of my bag and the rubber of my Converse. I glance at River's broken oven clock and notice that it is stuck on 2:13. I stare at it before I walk out the door and go home to sleep.

*

As soon as my eyes blink open I feel a vacancy in my room. Morning rolls into the afternoon, and Jeff is still gone. I clear my thoughts and close my eyes to feel for denseness behind my back, only to feel the empty air. It doesn't feel like he's absent because he is off doing soul work, it feels like he's absent because I betrayed him. I'm really regretting last night.

Sitting cross-legged on the carpet I take three deep breaths in, and three long breaths out. My conscious mind falls away, and my awareness is with my inner self. I sit in silence with my subconscious, waiting for that routine image of the back of Jeff's head to appear. Grey and white swirls left and right, backwards and forwards. "Come on, Jeff…" Nothing appears.

I send a beam of love to him. It shimmers in the void, and I wait for the feeling of connection. I sit for five minutes more, trying to make my light reach him. I push and push, but it feels ineffective. I made him hate me. Awesome. I pull out my earbuds. With a quick exhale, my candle goes dark.

My mind races. I think about how he has probably moved onto someone else. The terrible, devastating feeling that I may not be the only one overwhelms me. It's a hideous feeling, being so selfish for worrying about this. I can't believe how upset I get when this is bound to happen. Maybe it's because, much like Jeff, I feel extremely insecure about my importance to other people.

I need to stop. Setting my phone on the wooden nightstand, I go upstairs.

Hours later, I'm out and about with my family and we make our last stop at the furniture store. Hiding my emotions all day is exhausting, and I can't wait to get home. Anxiety picks at my brain that Jeff left me, maybe for good.

Zig-zagging through tables and couches, my mother and sister agree and disagree on styles. I throw in an occasional opinion so they don't suspect anything is wrong. Catching myself on the arm of a chair, I stumble to the right and Mom quickly reaches for me. "Are you okay, Kris?"

"Yeah I'm good, I just got dizzy for a second."

Taking a pause to gather myself, I grip the leather arm of the chair and notice the song playing overhead. "The call disappears inside you. I'll lift you up, always here beside you. I'm here to comfort you."

That isn't just a song, it's one of our songs. I tune in intently to savor the sign. Walking with my head slightly higher, I catch a flash out of the corner of my eye. Looking over my shoulder, I notice that one of the three spotlights over a couch display malfunctioned as we walked past. It remains flashing as we walk out of the door, giving me the extra validation that I desperately needed.

10/7 Got dizzy/lightheaded feeling right before our song came on in furniture store. A light display started flashing when we walked by.

On the drive home, I'm quiet in the back seat. I rest my head on the cold window as I sit with my eyes closed, watching the grey and white swirls. Before long, the colors zoom closer to me. That familiar turned head appears, and static pops through my headphones just before his image fades. Mom's voice interrupts my visions. "Kris! Look at all of the daisies on that car!" I look ahead lovingly at the sign. Returning home, I see the ectomist twice within an hour. Just like the last time I had anxiety over him, I'm flooded with signs to put me at ease.

I've been tested with cycles of sadness, guilt, and jealousy. I never imagined that I would be thankful for a bad day, but today I am. Without this challenge, the strength of our connection wouldn't have been proven.

*

Even though it's been only a couple of weeks since the 21st, I'm counting down the days until our next session with Denise, just like a child waits for Christmas morning to rip into the beautifully wrapped gifts. I'm interested to see how much progress we can make in his journey before October 15th.

As we return from shopping, I relax in my room. Dusk falls as the world outside settles into a sun-kissed orange. The carpet is fluffed with vacuum tracks and all of my furniture is freshly dusted. *Dahmer* plays in the background. I mouth the lines that I have now memorized as I hang up the clothes heaped on my closet floor, keeping a keen ear for when Kylie walks past so that I know to turn the volume down. I hear the cawing of the crow in the movie. The black crow sits on the counter as Jeffrey stares at it; a symbol of his darkness embodied in a bird.

I fall back onto my bed and watch the scene. Steven Hicks and teenage Jeffrey are goofing off in the kitchen, both high. Steven sits on the counter, sticking his hand in a peanut butter jar. Jeff stares at him with a stink face. "That's kinda gross."

Steven smiles as he shakes his head, "It's excellent."

What should be a mid-western accent from the actor sounds more awkward-Canadian. In a whiny tone he says, "I want some." I laugh, as I do every time.

Turning in for the night, I turn down the volume of the television, making sure I can still hear it as I drift off to sleep. I toss and turn restlessly, dozing off only to wake up ten minutes later. Maybe the TV is too bright for once. I press off on the remote control and the room goes black. The silence quiets me, and I finally feel like I can rest. I am half in and half out of consciousness when I hear an old southern man talking in my ear. I try my best to contain my excitement as I listen to him ramble.

I think I've experienced this before, a few times when I was younger. I always figured it was my imagination. Minutes pass, and he won't stop talking. Being completely lucid, I try to see what will happen if I chime in. "Hello," I say, "What is your name?"

"And then she done ran off on me. I don't even remember where."

"Excuse me, what is your name?"

"Was her name Vanessa? I can't remember. She had an annoying family. Now I know..."

"Stop talking for just one second! What is your name?"

The man falls silent and I feel taken aback, and now badly for shutting him up. "Steve," the voice answers timidly. That old southern man and I hold a conversation for quite some time before I doze off, and I was stunned to find that "Steve" responded to what I was saying. I was disappointed to forget everything that was said by the morning.

In a span of about three weeks, I hear physical talking from the other side twice. Both times it happened as I was going to bed, when my mind was in just the right state.

I could hear an accent from Steve and learned that I can hear the unique voice when it is a ghost's because they're closer to this plane and can speak directly in my ear. When a spirit is on a higher plane I hear their words in my own voice, in my head. They communicate telepathically, using my mind and my words to deliver their message.

*

I wake up for the fourth time in the middle of sleep at night; Jeff has popped into my mind each time. It's probably 3 a.m., but I'm too tired to check. My eyes are half open, my vision hazy without my glasses. The TV is still on, but there's no sound, the frame frozen and glitched out. My eyes lock onto the screen in half-awake confusion until it resumes playing as normal. "Hey, Jeff," I say, dozing back off.

I'm conscious yet again with the twilight sky still behind my blinds. Either Jeff really wants to visit, or I really have to pee. Through the dark I walk to the door, feeling along the cold grey wall for the doorknob.

My mind is in the half conscious, half unconscious state. The door unsticks from the frame as I pull it open. Through the silence, a voice clear as day says in my ear, "*I want some.*" That phrase sends me laughing. I'm so out of it, struggling as I giggle up the stairs for more water. Making my way back to my room, I continue giggling in delirium as I lay under the covers. Finally, I make it to sleep.

*

It is finally October 15th, the day of my Denise reading. I have it scheduled for 3:30, right as I will be getting home from my job's weekly staff meeting. With a half an hour to spare, I sit for meditation. I prefer to meditate during the day, when my room is bright and full of sunlight. Meditating at night makes me uneasy. At night, it's as if I can feel any and all presences around, compelling me to constantly check my surroundings.

Right now, at 2 p.m., my room is perfectly bright. My mind wanders to Alice, the little girl from Jeffrey's childhood. I wonder what he did to affect her, and how it could have been so bad that he's still dwelling on it, even after all he's done.

I relax to a letting go meditation in hopes of releasing both Jeff and Alice from whatever their energetic burden may be. The voice escorts me to the depths of my mind. Bugs click beside a running stream of water. The lush meadow soothes my bare feet and the sun warms my skin. I recognize this field as the creek of my family farm. I try to look around, but there aren't many details around me.

On the sidelines, I see Jeff sitting in a wooden, one-person boat, floating in place on the water. He anchors himself to a tree branch above to keep from drifting with the current. The stream represents his life path, while holding the tree branch represents the event that he can't release himself from.

The voice speaks through my earbuds and I pass along the message to him. "Know that you did what you did in the moment because you didn't know then what you know now. This event was meant to take place for the growth of yourself and others. It is okay to release what no longer serves you." Jeff hesitates, untrusting as he looks down the current and back up to the tree. "It is time to let go of the branch." His hand unclenches the tree branch and descends through the leaves, and the boat flows with the water. He sits straight up and looks only ahead. Drifting further down the creek, there's a sense of restored peace within him and he relaxes back. The music quiets to a silence, and with relief, I wiggle my fingers and toes. Exiting out of the video, I check that the time is at exactly 2:13.

I dive back in for third eye expansion, being one with the black field before me. I could sit here for hours, watching my visuals like a movie. My eyes sparkle as I view a dark ocean shore under a full moon. The visual surprises me, moving instead of staying still like usual. Ripples flow across the navy surface, the white light of the moon reflecting and making the water shimmer.

Two people form in the body of water. I look closer to see that it's me and Jeff, standing side by side. We don't speak as the rippling water tickles the sides of our hips. He turns and kisses me. I snap out of meditative mode, opening my eyes as fast as I can. "Oh. I'm sorry Jeff. I don't know why I saw that." I feel uncomfortable and embarrassed. I close out for the day and get dressed to head out for work.

*

I watch the diner clock, anticipating the phone reading at 3:30. Anxiousness and excitement take my appetite away, and everything being discussed about statistics goes in one ear and out the other. My mind goes off track as I listen. Connecting the dots, I think back to details that now make sense having been affected by Jeff's presence. As a little girl, I had certain quirks that went away when I lost my ability. My head would randomly tick or jerk as I was talking, in the same way that Jeff's did when he spoke. At eight years old, I remember asking the doctor if that was normal, scared that I had something wrong with my nerves.

In the same way Jeff walked, I would walk without moving my arms, keeping them stiff on the sides of my body until Mom corrected me. I was more in touch with the ghostly plane back then, and I wonder if I picked up those habits from Jeff in the same way that I picked up the finger tapping now. The demon incident happened at the same time that I felt reconnected with my ghost. Being told in my first session that my ghost was never a demon makes me wonder if the incident with Beverly was actually Jeff scaring off a bad influence in my life.

During the first reading, Martha kept mentioning "J." Somebody who was a Gemini or Taurus (Jeff's sign is on the cusp of the two). "J" had a tense relationship with their mother in life, but they're closer now since they've both passed on. "J" showed her a wall full of guitars and the man who now lives in Jeff's childhood home is a professional guitarist with a display room in that very house. She also mentioned that there would be a significant move or birthday in the month of April or May.

Cameron and I signed a lease in April and broke up at the end of May on a birthday: Jeff's. Did he influence Cameron to end things on that specific day to foretell our journey together? The apartment complex was cleverly called "The Indigo," also the color of the third eye. The foreshadowing that the universe orchestrated for this connection takes my breath away. I'm blessed with this huge responsibility and can only hope that I'm the right one for it, that I'm doing enough.

The chairs around me scoot out from the table and snap me back into the present moment. I didn't even notice the end of the meeting and look at the clock to see that it's 3:11. I hurry past the staff as we walk to the parking lot and with a quick goodbye I rush to my car.

Fallen leaves crunch under my tires as I zoom down 521 Highway. A new song, "Darkside" by Alan Walker, loads, and I wait with my finger ready to hit the "next" button in case I don't like it. The EDM rhythm accompanies the lyrics about the darkness and the light, reminding me of our journey. The entire song passes, and I don't feel anybody in the car. At a red light I close my eyes and feel the energy in front of me, behind, and to my side. Just like I had the last time before my reading with Denise, I sense that he's gone, maybe to recharge his batteries before our session. I hope.

Arriving home, I shut my bedroom door behind me. I arrange a rainbow of crystals around my crossed legs. Failing to clear my mind, I click my phone repeatedly to check the time. The anticipation of the phone ringing makes my heart pound. With a long exhale, I stare at the small burning flames of my altar candles.

My phone buzzes and I snatch it on the first ring. "Hello, love!" answers Denise. Her giggle instantly brings me back to the 21st. She seems equally excited and begins the session.

"Let's both clear our minds and try to relax. Only beings of a high vibration are allowed to communicate and deliver messages for Kristen's highest and greatest good. I'm now asking any of Kristen's angels, guides, or loved ones that would like to give messages to step forward."

My heart beats out of my chest. Denise begins, "Dreams, dreams, dreams. It's all he wants me to bring up." I think back to that vivid visitation, the one after my breakup that I *thought* was a guardian angel. When I ask Denise about it, she replies, "He took on that form to comfort you, showing himself in a subtle way while also staying somewhat hidden."

"He's visited you in several other dreams that you weren't aware of. *They've always been very poignantly placed* is what he just said. Always at times where you needed comfort… A death in the family, your parents' divorce, times you struggled." I soak that in, realizing he's been helping me longer than I have been helping him. I think back to the hearts that would catch my eye when I felt alone and the dreams I used to have of a deer visiting to comfort me, calming my confused and panicked young mind.

"I'm picking up a vision of you and him in the civil-war era, he was a soldier. Have I talked about this with you before?"

Smiling, I lean forward as if I'm back on the couch in front of her. "Yes! I've been curious about our past. Since we are so tightly bonded in spirit, are there any other lifetimes that we had together?"

"Ye- Nope. None that I can see," Denise answers shortly.

I find her response odd. "Hmm, okay..."

"And your civil war life wasn't romantic. It's not like he was your husband or anything," Denise chuckles. "There might have even been an age gap, like you babysat him just a few times." I ponder that, figuring that we would have been at least closer than acquaintances back then. A little disappointed, my eyes scan my paper in search for my next question.

"Jeff said he's come to me in many forms. What did he mean by that?"

"One way is through the dreams, but he also visits as small animals and butterflies. If you ever looked at one and he came to mind, that was him." I smile, sloppily writing *hummingbird*.

"He's come to you in a reading before, but it was before you knew about him? He wanted you to acknowledge his presence, but didn't know how you would react, and didn't want to scare you." This confirms the Gemini mystery spirit "J."

"He wants to make it known to you that he is taking responsibility for what he has done." I remember being disappointed in him during the last reading, thinking that he felt the crimes weren't his fault. "He keeps stressing, *let her know that I do take responsibility for what happened.*" Jeff knows how I feel and is making it a point to address that incident, to make it right. That's pretty amazing.

"He shows up a pretty significant amount of times to you. You're both so involved with each other, almost too much. His spirit guides and yours have to keep a sort of wall up between you two, because you distract each other from the work you're supposed to be doing in your own planes. They act more like your security guards than guides."

"Really?" I say with my stomach full of butterflies.

"Yeah, they're constantly telling him that he can't keep coming back because he has his work to do, and he has to give you space to do yours. But, *I visit as much as I'm allowed.*"

"He wants to thank you for being so gracious. He likes the way you give compassion. But he's almost like a vampire, and constantly wants to take it."

"I don't mind at all," I venture.

"He's acknowledging the work he needs to do, and I feel like you know when he's doing it because of your bond."

"Does it creep him out with how much I watch him on TV? Does he get tired of re-living that stuff over and over?" I ask.

"No, it's not like that to him. He feels your compassion watching it, and I feel it's how you call him to you. He is, though, worried about you getting too wrapped up in his darkness. I don't want that for you either." I've never been interested in what he did. But it does concern me that he brought that up. Does he know something about my future that I don't?

Denise shares, "He struggles to re-live all that he has done and holds himself back, feeling like he's not worthy of moving past almost any of his life review. When he's unmotivated or can't handle it you light the fire in him. You're like his energy drink." I smile as I jot that down, flattered to be that person for him.

Denise compares Jeff's life review experience to a movie theater. He watches moments from his life play out, then takes a break outside until he is ready to go back in and continue. He bounces around the events out of order, working through the lighter events first, just like a student would answer the easiest questions first on a test.

For over twenty years he's been placed in the shoes of the victim's friends and families, feeling their grief, their pain, and their rage. He's felt himself being hit on the head with a barbell, falling over as his vision goes dark. He's felt the halcyon kicking in as he sits on his own apartment couch, watching his own self approach the body he is in. He's felt the disgust every single American felt as they watched the news of his crimes, and he's felt their paranoia as they locked their doors at night. He has no choice but to face every encounter until he experiences all of it.

I explain that every few days, I connect to a different version of him from a different phase in his life. Sometimes I feel closer to his teenage self, others, his lonely drinking by the bar self. Denise tunes in, explaining that I connect with the version of him in the current phase of life review that he is working through, hence when she told me I feel when he's doing his work.

"How much longer do you think it'll be until he finishes his life review, Denise?"

"I don't know, that is completely up to him. It could take anywhere from a few weeks to a few years."

I swallow a lump, "A few more years? That's a long time…"

Denise chuckles, "He butted in when you said that, *Eh, I got this. I'll be fine.*"

I hear Denise exhale as she pulls for a message. "Is there a song you keep hearing that sounds appreciative, like a big thank you? Kinda catchy? Maybe with trumpets."

Silence falls as I think, "Is it called 'Believing in You'?"

"That's one of them, but I feel like he's talking about another one." I think, but nothing comes to mind.

I see a lot of myself in Jeff, and a lot of him in me. The more I learn of him, the more I find that we're more alike than I originally thought. The way he touches his face when he's being stared at, the way he smacks his lips when he feels uncomfortable—things that I've always done. Our lives seem to mirror each other in ways. For example, at a young age, we both had surgery in the month of March. Our surgeries were both in the groin area, and both were intensely painful and traumatic.

Our high school experiences parallel each other, too, right down to participating in the same activities. The obnoxious changes in our personalities after our parents' divorces; both earning the title of class clown. Wearing the same shade of light pink for senior prom, we both couldn't pin the corsage on our dates and their parent had to step in to do it. In adulthood, single, particular, clean freaks who love fish. The similar way we react in social situations, the awkward politeness yet sense of humor, the loneliness, the longing for friendship yet liking our own space. The same amount of letters in our first, middle, and last names: Kristen Lauren Halder and Jeffrey Lionel Dahmer. We share from the same astrological element, air. Even the significance of my parents getting married on the day he was arrested in 1991 play into the synchronicities of our life events. The list goes on.

I bring myself back to ask, "Are there any other quirks we share that I wouldn't know of?"

"I see Jeffrey tapping his fingers, counting them one by one. I'm not sure if that answers your question. That's something he used to do to calm himself. I see him sitting at his coffee table and just tapping, counting things over and over when he was anxious. He had a lot of OCD tendencies that were never really known, I feel like you have that too." Scribbling *finger tapping*, I look to the next question.

"I want to really know *him*. I want answers to stupid things like what kind of food he liked, the little things that made him happy. I know this is dumb, but do you know what his favorite ice cream flavor was?"

Denise chuckles and tastes her spiritual palate. Her lips smack before she gives her answer, "Hmm it's... vanilla."

"Vanilla? Not even mint chocolate chip?" I chuckle, "He would like vanilla. He is a very vanilla man."

"I know. So boring. I thought he was going to say mint chocolate chip too." Denise laughs.

She takes a moment, "As for food he liked easy stuff, microwaveable, specifically chicken hot pockets. Do you know if that's right? I'm going to look it up."

I chime in, "There's almost nothing personal about him out there. Trust me, if it was online I would have found it by now."

Within seconds, Denise finds an article. "This says in the fridge they found A1 sauce, ketchup, and mustard right next to two heads. So no hot pockets." She laughs, I laugh, Jeff laughs...

"What is one of Jeff's favorite memories? A memorable family vacation? A funny high school story?" I grip the pen waiting for the answer.

She pauses as she takes in an impression, "He's showing you playing as a child... *Watching you grow up*." Gathering myself I ask quietly, "That's his favorite memory?"

"Yes. I can feel his pride as he'd keep an eye on you. Right now we're at your elementary school playground, the one with the giant caterpillar you liked to climb on." I set the phone down, reaching to my face to wipe the free falling tears.

I notice the time is almost up and I wrap up the reading. "Is there anything else Jeff really needs to say?"

"He's thanking you, over and over. For your graciousness, how you see him, how kind you've been towards him. *Just send love and light when you can, but don't feel like you need to do more than you already are.*"

"That's interesting he says that. Well, thank *you* again for everything!" My cheeks hurt from smiling, and my stomach turns with excitement as three beeps end the call. I can feel him right behind me, physically and mentally closer than ever. I happily carry a headache and scoop the crystals into my palm to set them back on the altar.

*

Off after an early morning of work, I shuffle to the car to escape the cold chill in the air. With my key in the ignition and the heat on blast, my cheeks tingle as they thaw. A familiar song starts on the radio as I back my car out of the driveway. I wrap my hands over my mouth in amazement. This is the song he was trying to explain to Denise, and I know exactly what it is: "More than You Know" by Axwell & Ingrosso.

"I'm where you wanted me, praying on my knees so that you can set me free. You have the purest of intentions and they can never put a flame out like yours. I need to get this off my chest that you're the best, more than you know."

I beat my hand on the steering wheel to the trumpets. Adding the song to my playlist, I listen again. As we dig into the heavier and deeper stuff, I really hope he's got this like he says he does. I wonder what would have happened to him if I never stepped in to help.

After picking up lunch I fish for my keys. Looking down, I notice that laying on the asphalt beside my tire is a buckeye butterfly. It is weak and limp, its wings barely moving. I place him in my hand and study the details of his beige colored wings. Another flightless animal with wings, just like the hummingbird. I gently lower myself into the car with my eyes locked on the position of my hand.

During fifteen minutes of one-handed driving, the delicate butterfly rests comfortably in my palm. I'm struck with the fact that Jeffrey is in my presence at this very moment. With the opportunity to heal him up close, my energy can effortlessly flow to this physical form. The vibration of singing bowls hum through the speakers, sending healing energy to the small body. The butterfly perks up more with the passing minutes, but it's still not enough.

Arriving home, I flip on the lamp and set down my things while keeping my eyes on the butterfly. Walking up to my angel altar, I set the butterfly with my crystals. It's surreal, watching him as he slowly makes his way across the wooden stand.

I've been home for almost a half an hour now and decide I should release the butterfly back outside. On my porch, I place him delicately on the flower bush. I take one last look and a picture before walking back inside. I smile at Grandpa watching a baseball game in our living room. It's intermission as I walk past; a snippet of "Bohemian Rhapsody" plays over the field's loudspeakers and through the TV, catching my ear. The abundance of validation makes my heart sing. "That really was you," I think to myself.

Recently, I notice my feelings for him shift. I think I'm beginning to grow feelings and I don't know how to take it. I feel embarrassed that he knows my thoughts. I feel wrong because he is gay, and I don't want to disrespect his sexuality. I think of the night I woke up to someone cuddling me, his jealousy during the night I spent at River's, the visual he showed me of us in the ocean. Cringing, I shoo the thoughts away so he doesn't feel uncomfortable. "It's okay to think of me in that way." I jump and look to my right for the voice that spoke in my ear. Maybe it's mutual.

Chapter Ten:
Uneasy Feelings

I t didn't happen out of nowhere; it's been a gradual process. I can't pinpoint when this started happening, but it hit me like an entire slab of concrete and I can't shake it no matter how hard I try. Days have passed and the feelings won't go away, feelings of absolute dread. Desperately, I turn to meditation to transmute negativity into positivity but feel no different. I sage my room, my house, and myself, but it doesn't change a thing. It's still here. I'm petrified to be around anyone I love, paranoid that these feelings will turn into actions. I am terrified, and terrified of my own self.

What started out as anxiousness slowly turned into worry and guilt. I have nothing to feel guilty or anxious for, so where is this coming from? Day after day, the feelings intensify, turning darker. I feel like I killed someone and am dwelling on it. It burdens me, haunting my thoughts and lingering all day. What am I becoming? Is this what Jeff meant when he said that he was worried about me getting *too wrapped up in the darkness*? Nausea pains my gut as I tightly grip the steering wheel.

I distract my mind from a violent thought as it pops in. "Nope, nope, nope!" I say to myself. Still, I am unable to escape the intrusions. The worst part is that I have no idea what it is that I am feeling or what's causing it, making the problem impossible to resolve. The low bass sounds out to the introduction of "Volcano." I listen to the lyrics. "You used to see as clear as the color of your blue eyes, now your vision is hazy. It's going to land on you". I try to make sense of the piece in the song that I could never figure out.

I interpret it as a warning. Am I going to hurt someone? Is there another reason that Jeffrey is guiding me, in an attempt to steer me away from a violent destiny like his? On the true crime community websites, I read details about crimes and victims every day. I'm sure all of that information in the back of my mind is coming to the surface. It troubles me to think that the horrible things I've read on the message boards can happen to the people I love. That's it. I turn my music louder to drown it all out.

Halloween is coming this weekend, a holiday I anticipate as soon as July hits. For months now, I've planned to go as Dahmer for the bar crawl.

*

A package arrives on my doorstep and I rush upstairs for it, knowing exactly what it is. Ripping open the bubble wrap packaging, I reach in for the two items. I slip into a white beater t-shirt and army green jacket, completing the look with faded jeans and white converse. Adding the finishing touches that came in today, I slide the golden aviators over my nose and grab the "I heart Milwaukee" flask. I study myself in the mirror, impressed by the accuracy of my costume.

The more I look at myself, the more my excitement dims. The crowd will be all superheroes and slutty princesses and then there's going to be me, a serial killer man. I'm also going to look obsessive to the people who know about this. Maybe this is the year to look like everybody else, and not be self-conscious. I order a Wonder Woman costume with my Lara Croft outfit on standby. After a few selfies, I change back out of the short-lived outfit. I hope I'm not hurting his feelings, feeling guilty as I fold up the jacket to abandon on the shelf.

Mom's sweet voice reaching me from the staircase envelops me in guilt. Sheer chills run down my spine as I force myself to interact, sounding burnt out in my responses, distant, and withdrawn. Mom continues our conversation as we unload the dishwasher together. The plates clank as I set them in the cabinet, one by one. Looking down for the basket of silverware, I hold a glance on the steak knife on the verge of tears. With sleepwalking in mind, I hide it under the pile of spoons. I imagine myself dying before I have the opportunity to do any harm. I'm scared of where these thoughts might lead if I don't get rid of them.

I can't even find comfort in simple things. While watching TV with my family, I'm anything but comfortable, the unwanted thoughts latching onto me like a parasite. What should be the sweet escape of sleep only makes things worse. I worry that the dam will break and I will act out in my sleep. I think back to when Jeff killed a man in his sleep, waking with no recollection of what even happened. I feel like I'm going to be sick. Before shutting off the light, I arrange a trail of bulky items on the path to my door, hoping that if I'm sleepwalking, something will trip me and wake me up.

*

For the third time today I sage my space and follow it with a cleansing meditation, but the pit in my gut remains. I have tried everything that I know to do. Jeff and other killers always stressed the point that they struggled with feelings that consumed them, taking over every aspect of their life. That they had compulsive thoughts that would never leave, compulsions that could ultimately ruin a person. I never believed that, thinking it was just an excuse. How does one have something in their own mind that they can't control? In three short days, I have just gotten a taste of living with what they had to live with, and it's a darkness that I wouldn't wish on anybody. You can try doing what you can to distract your mind for a while, but the thoughts will always come back. It is a monster, a terrifying one.

I wake up with a brief glimmer of hope that maybe today will be different. As I come to, I still feel the same. Disoriented, stressed, and mentally exhausted. I stress more, noticing the time. Arriving at a spinal screening five minutes late, I push through the doors, heaving my equipment and food trays. With an apologetic smile, I greet the receptionist. A big haired woman walks past the entrance. "Oh, it's about time," she says. "I thought this lady was going to stand us up. Unbelievable." I pause, anticipating a laugh, but she maintains a straight face. My cheeks turn bright red as I follow her to the room to get set up.

The staff attempts to make up for her approach as I walk by, offering smiles and hellos. We reach the back room when the woman speaks loud enough for the whole office to hear. "I guess do whatever you have to do in the time that's left, my staff's been waiting!" My throat tenses as the door slams shut. As I lay out the display, all I want to do is curl up into a ball and cry. I want everything to go away. The feelings, the unsettling state of mind, the guilt. The next two hours are occupied with screenings and stale conversation as I hide behind a weak smile.

As I leave, the woman who chastised me is nowhere in sight. I thank the front desk for having me. Just as I exit, numbness settles over me. I'm itching to get home and shut myself away. Lugging my gear across the parking lot, my eye catches a daisy charm hanging in the windshield of a hatchback. It feels like the eye in the middle of a storm, a place of calm. A sign that he is here for me, rooting for me to push on.

*

Halloween comes, the day of the year where the veil between the spirit realm and ours is thinnest. Jeff could be within arm's reach. I take advantage of the circumstances, sending an abundance of love to him throughout the day in hopes that it will be extra effective. After healing him, I notice a lift in my own heavy emotions. I almost forgot what it was like not to have negativity pounding at my brain, assuming that was my new normal. The relief feels like a slice of heaven, but as hours pass, waves of extreme anxiousness and worry return. I click on my phone, 5:21 p.m. "Hey, Jeff." I lean my head to my left shoulder, where I feel him standing. The feeling of being watched builds up in me, and I turn around to an empty room.

The half-moon hangs with the stars as night falls. Upstairs, Mom is plugging in orange and purple string lights and eyeing the muffins in the oven. I slump on the couch to watch the Halloween baking competition on TV, even if only to distract my mind for a minute. I sympathize with the bakers' stress as they run across the kitchen in chaos. After the timer buzzes, the first contestant presents her zombie cake. The judge chuckles. "Did you give him a name?"

"Uhhh, I'll name him Jeff." The baker laughs.

Mom pops over the counter. "Do you want me to do your makeup for tonight?" I happily accept. I watch as she applies shades of bronze and gold to my eyes. She takes her time, being sure to get everything just right. Proudly, she hands me a mirror to take a look. I look up at her face, seeing so much love and purity. Then I look in the small circle at my own reflection, one that I can't even recognize. I swallow a lump in my throat as anxiety burns in my chest. I thank Mom, hugging her tightly.

Pouring my ritual vodka and juice, I ready up. Staring into the glass as I pace, I'm reluctant to take a sip. What if the alcohol brings out my intrusive thoughts out even more? With hesitation I close my eyes and take the first swig. I strap on my armor, slip on the skirt and golden headband across my forehead. Looking over myself in the mirror, my body and mind begin to feel a sense of relaxation as the alcohol warms my senses. I notice my worries are... gone? I'm myself again, reunited with normalcy. To quiet what felt like a rock concert of emotions is an absolute miracle. I can see now why Jeff drank so often.

The relief is unreal. This feeling of normality is something that I never want to lose again, and I grip onto it like the edge of a cliff. Heading towards the city, I glance out the window as my eye catches an object on the side of the road. Passing it, I see that it's a beer carton of *Milwaukee's Best Ice*. "Jeff! Thank you, love." I reach my hand for his across the center console.

Stepping out of the car I head towards the bustling streets and wrap my arms in my black cape. A headache and heavy weight accompany me to my destination as my boots click along the littered sidewalk. Music bumps from every pub I walk past, followed by drunk yelling and honking horns. The bar sign shines blue, welcoming me in. Inside, I look to my right, and sitting on the counter next to me is a lonely Pabst Blue Ribbon beer can. The bouncer calls out "Next!" and I snap back to attention. The bouncer straps a paper wristband around my wrist.

I turn as I hear my name being yelled over the crowd. Madison runs up to me in a clown suit, her boyfriend following close behind wearing a yellow rain jacket and a red balloon. "Oh my god. Pennywise and Georgie, I love it,"

I exclaim. It's the last thing I would expect them to go for. Shimmering lights rotate over the crowd, and I observe them as we squeeze our way to the bar.

"Excuse us!" two girls say, brushing past my shoulder in a connected T-shirt, making them look like conjoined twins. To my left is a woman in a giant baby head. What is happening? Of all years, I can't find one normal costume. I totally could have been Jeff.

In the bathroom next to Madison, I look in the dirty mirror under fluorescent lighting. She knows about my situation, having had told her everything over a pitcher of margaritas. "Man. I really wish I dressed as Jeffrey Dahmer," I say, applying a fresh coat of red lipstick.

Madison chuckles. "I was honestly going to suggest that to you, but I didn't know if you'd be offended. I was this close to texting you earlier."

"Really? I would have loved that." The light over me flickers once. I smile as soon as she turns her back.

The night rolls on as we bounce from bar to bar. Most of my conversations begin with a Wonder Woman compliment, but I ruin it with a drunken response about who I wish I was. The awareness of Jeff by my side fades more and more as the night goes on. We stay out until the early hours of the morning, and I return to my house with a beer soaked cape.

*

The next morning, the sun rise peaks through my shades. Before putting on my glasses, I slowly blink my eyes open to a blurry heap on the floor. I'm surprised that I dressed myself for bed when I got back. The room spins as I reach for my phone on the nightstand. I received a text from a new number at 3 a.m. "I have you in my phone as the Dahmer girl." I grunt, throwing my head back onto the pillow. The feelings have begun to come and go in waves, not as persistent as they were a few days ago. I think about how the feelings will eventually come back. Nausea sets in as I worry about losing myself to this feeling. The violent thoughts strangle any hint of joy. I close my eyes to shut everything out.

Quick as lightning, a visual of Jeff's body rushes toward me with open arms as if trying to sneak in a quick hug. My physical arms lift in an attempt to hug him back, but he is whisked away and the void returns. My eyes remain closed in hopes that I'll have that chance to reach him again, but soon, I realize that the opportunity is gone. Why won't our guides let us reach each other?

*

It is 5:30 p.m. and I'm getting ready to give the routine welcome presentation to our new patients of the week. I make small talk as we wait for the last patient to arrive, checking in on how everybody is feeling so far. The door squeaks open, and I'm stopped in my tracks by the person walking through it. In enters a slim man of about 6'1", his arms stiff by his sides. He walks past me smelling like cigarettes. There is no expression on his face; even his eyes droop slightly. With a quick "Hi," he sits in the chair, his ankle over his knee. I stutter as I say hello back and get started with the presentation. My back pocket will not stop buzzing. I'm distracted wondering who could be blowing up my phone so much while I'm at work, and distracted by looking at this man.

As I speak, the man stares at me; he bears an uncanny resemblance to you-know-who. The way he holds himself, the stoic expression. I try my hardest not to smile. I want to laugh and don't even know why. My cheeks rise as I talk, making me wonder how I'm going to make it through the next fifteen minutes. "We're here to make sure you all get back on track, and back to doing the things that you love. Thank you all so much for your time!" I click the monitor off and turn to say goodbye to the group. The man gives a little smile and head nod as he walks out of the door. I stare at him as he walks out, savoring the moment. That was wild. I pull out my phone to see what was so important and unlock a completely empty screen. Not one message or notification.

I race home as fast as I can. I have a reading with Denise in an hour that I scheduled the other day, and I really feel like it's going to be a good one. Butterflies rush through my stomach as I think about it. Then, my excitement turns into nervousness. I am afraid if she'll touch upon the bad feelings I've been experiencing. I pray that she doesn't see anything terrible in my future; I pray that nothing comes of this. Maybe we can catch the problem early enough to change the course if my fate is to take a bad turn.

I sit cross-legged on top of my bed, my heart racing while I wait for the phone call. Right on the hour, I hear the buzz coming from my phone. I feel a sense of relief that I can finally talk about what has been bothering me the most. "Hi, Denise! I'm so excited to talk to you again after two whole weeks." I laugh.

"I know, I'm going to have to cut you off soon," Denise dryly chuckles back. She seems cold. I sit silent on the other line, unsure if she is joking or not.

"Um, before we start, I wanted to ask if you can look into the feelings that I've had. I've been feeling really terrible things...I've tried everything I can to get rid of them but nothing's worked. Do you think anything bad will happen down the road?"

Denise pauses, then suggests that we do a meditation together. "I want you to imagine that coming from your body are chords with TV screens attached to the end of them." I worry as to why she's having me do this. "Each screen represents an aspect in your life. I want you to imagine that the bad ones show up red, the good ones show up blue."

I look at my body hovering in a bright white void. I look down to see that I am lit up red, with only a few blue chords. Denise guides, "Imagine completely cutting the red chords with a pair of large scissors." With the tool in my hand I cut each red chord. One by one, the attachments fall away, and I feel a lift. "Whenever you're ready, you can open your eyes." This feels like magic; the feelings are completely gone.

"So, first of all, those feelings and that guilt that you are having are not yours."

"Really? They're not? Oh, thank God."

"You're actually feeling what Jeffrey feels. You're taking part of the burden for him and sharing the energy, half and half. It takes some of the weight off of him, but it's not good for you. You can feel when he's happy, you can feel when he's sad or angry, kind of like a twin connection. That's why your guides try so hard to keep you two at arm's length, because you're both too close. I put a filter up between you two because there needs to be some separation. And I agree that you should distance yourself from him, too. It's better if you..." Three beeps interrupt the phone call.

What just happened? Was she the one who hung up? I try her back twice with no response. I begin typing to Denise, and my screen is interrupted with a call back from her. I laugh. "Hey! I'm so sorry, I don't know what happened."

Denise nervously chuckles. "I do, Jeffrey hung up the phone to say you're not taking her from me." I feel a rush of adrenaline as I ask if that's true.

I fidget. "How is his life review going?"

"He just said *I'm getting there, just now getting to the meat of it.* He's moved into a much deeper healing, a deeper process of learning. Right now as I'm looking at him, he looks like a drug addict that's going through detox. He looks tired out and horrible, but this is good for him. He keeps telling me he'll be fine."

I ponder on that. "Would it make him feel better if he told us what happened with Alice, talking it out like therapy?"

Denise pauses. "No, he says that this is something that he'll have to deal with on his own, and he'll move on from it when it's time."

Denise inhales and exhales. "He has been stubborn but thanks to you he's at a point where he's telling himself *okay, I'm going to sit here and focus on my work.* I've never seen him so studious. Even as we speak right now, he's doing his work. He looks like he's standing over to the side in a workshop, studying. So from now on, when he visits you, you need to tell him to leave and go back to doing his work."

I think to myself how I don't want to tell him to go away every single time I feel him near. My room is his safe place; the energy of love and healing welcomes him as soon as he enters. I then think about how there is no telling when our chapter will come to an end. But more than anything I want him to reach Heaven, even if that means parting ways.

"Once his work is finished he will be stronger, and I feel like there will be a time when he will be able to connect with you even more than he does now." I forget that he knows my thoughts, baffled that she just brought that up. "He just said thank you for seeing the good in me, because I'm struggling to see the good in myself."

My emotions get the best of me. There is so much that I want to say, but all I'm able to get out is, "Oh, of course."

Looking at the time, I ask, "When he's done with all of this, will he reincarnate?"

"Yes, but if he didn't work through all of this I don't know that he would have been able to. Some souls stay stuck forever in the afterlife, which is how demons form. But, it'll be all thanks to you that he can continue his soul's cycle and come back with some peace." Euphoria stirs in my heart, hearing that I've impacted him in such a way.

The conversation goes quiet, and I peek down at my paper to see what else I have written down. "Well, I think that's all of my questions, it's the end of our session time anyway!" I say.

"Before you go he wants to thank you again." Denise says quietly.

"And try to hold out until at least after Christmas for another reading and then if you really need me, we'll talk again."

"Okay, I'll try." I chuckle. "Thank you so much Denise, I hope you have a good holiday." We end the call.

As I'm brought back to reality, I take notice of the lightness in my heart and mind. There are no intrusions, no worries, no troubling thoughts. It is an incredibly soothing feeling. I have an entirely new appreciation for a healthy mind. I have been so blessed with always feeling happy throughout my life that I didn't realize it's not like that for everybody. I have been shown an alternate reality that I was once blind to. I am lucky that I have spiritual guidance to get myself out of it, and that the feelings were not even mine.

Jeff was not as fortunate. He didn't have a medium to turn to, no one to give him answers or guidance. The dense energy lingers over my left shoulder. In my mind I begin apologizing to Jeff, empathetic of the hell he lived with daily. I will take his sadness, his pain, his anger. The only thing that I cannot do is take on those feelings anymore. He's passed on so he can't hurt anyone anymore, but I'm in this plane where I potentially can, and I see just how dangerous an overpowered mind can become.

The days pass, and I feel much better, knowing what I know now. Bundled in a jacket I step onto my patio under the moonlight. The cold of the concrete radiates through the bottom of my wool socks. I look up at the super blood moon, a rare phenomenon that I have been anticipating for weeks. The moon shines bright, tinted red, its size larger than normal. I stare in awe as it floats in a starry serenity. As I bask in its beauty I feel the power radiating from this rare event. With one earbud in I close my eyes to "Alone" by Alan Walker, drawing him in for a healing.

As the bass in the song drops I channel the power of the moon to his energy through a column of white. The light descends to him. It flushes his troubled mind and soothes his hallowed heart. I feel the shift as the super blood moon dances through his spirit. I feel the lift and open my eyes to watch the moon for fifteen minutes more before going back inside.

*

It's been almost a week since our last reading, and I start to notice a distance between me and Jeff. The signs have come to a halt, and I've barely logged anything in the past three days. I don't like the idea of a filter between us and want it to be taken down. The closeness of our connection was something that I held dear to my heart. Now, since the reading, our distance feels too cold for my comfort. But, I need to trust that this separation will force us to do our individual work. I have to stay patient. There will be a time where we will connect again.

Chapter Eleven:
Homesick

I watch outside of the window as leaves blow past the sill. My hand hovers over the steam of my tea as I listen to Mom talk about work. She stops and takes note of my posture. "What's the matter, Kris? You seem down."

"Nothing's really wrong. I've been in a funk the past few days now, on and off every few hours. I think it's just Jeff's work." A glow comes from below my chin and I look down to see that my phone lit up without me touching it, and no new messages. The time shows 11:11, with my battery on thirty-four percent. I take the minute to wish for Jeff to finish his life review and be at peace.

I pay half attention to Mom, repeating the manifestation in my head until the minute changes. "I've been in a funk too lately. I just feel... I don't know, down," Mom answers. I wonder if she feels him too, being so close by. Minutes pass, and I click my phone to see the time is still stuck at 11:11. I stare at the screen in fascination, only for it to skip right to 11:14 moments later. Maybe Jeff really needed that prayer, or maybe he was attention hungry.

I keep zoning out, forgetting that I'm in a conversation with Mom. My icy gaze at the kitchen wall reflects the numb inside of me. I just wish I could be on the other side, with him. Mom stands from the bar stool. "Well, I need to get on the road for work. I hope you feel better, see you tonight!"

I shake my head. "Oh, it's already past eleven! Drive safe." After she walks out of the door, I sit in lonely silence.

"This is tough, Jeff. I hope you're hanging in there." The wooden floor creaks as I step down from the stool. With bare feet I walk into the garage. I close my eyes, put Jeff in my mind's eye, and sing *Believing in You.* My voice echoes through the hallow garage, ringing out for him to hear. During the second verse I glance over to the steps and see a puff of white mist rise and disappear. Chills run up my arms seeing him come in. I hold onto the moment of peace as I continue singing softly for the presence.

A cold chill surrounds me and my eyes droop from fatigue as I make my way to my room. I yawn, slipping into my oversized t-shirt and fuzzy socks in the middle of the afternoon. I click the lighter and ignite my candle wicks. I lie on my bed, pull up a healing mediation, and close my eyes.

I see Jeff sitting in a black void. He is in the exact state that Denise explained him to be in, looking disheveled and strung out. The pain of 58 years weighs on his face, his body is weak, and his aura illuminates dim grey. The man's voice reaches both of our worlds and calls the golden light of Christ into the space. I take several deep breaths, falling deeper and deeper in. As I do, I see Jeff with closed eyes doing the same. The rise and fall of his chest synchronizes with mine.

Gold mist gathers and floats for Jeff to breathe in. The golden cloud enters his nose as he inhales deeply, filling his head with its light. When he exhales, black energetic fog releases from inside of him. The sky above opens up, and a golden pillar of light cascades down. The energy flows in and around him, bathing his body in the love of Christ. It feels warm and safe as it graces his spirit. The man's voice echoes as he calls in the higher self of the listener, asking its presence to oversee the process of this cleanse. Jeff focuses as he sits with the feeling.

Jeff is guided to a mirror across the black space. He looks up to a reflection that he has a tough time confronting. He looks into his baggy eyes and the shame in his expression, looking at a man that he doesn't want to be. The mirror reflects his light body, displaying his energetic lines and chakras. *"Your mindset and thoughts manifest your reflections and the colors of your aura field. Notice the golden light entering your body and manifesting more radiant colors within you; purifying and elevating your mind to be in alignment with your higher self."*

The particles of light brighten his muted colors, shifting them from grey and brown to multicolored hues. His negative thought forms transmute as his higher self and the man expand his knowledge. The gold melts the energetic sludge from his past, sliding it off of his skin like mud washing off of a tree. His chakras change from diluted dim orbs of light to seven vibrant colors of the rainbow. The man continues as the light heals, telling Jeff to let his fear and judgment dissolve with the light. Every word manifests more color, more balance, and more harmony. The golden pillar remains until negativity is no longer present.

The mirror dissolves and leaves Jeff standing alone. The voice rings out, *"Forgiveness on an energetic level releases us from low vibrational energies of our past. Blame, rage, sorrow, regret. These energies all hold us in the past every day that we experience them. To be free of your past you must first learn from it."* A child begins crying over the sound of the man's voice. Jeff turns around to a little boy at his feet. The boy is his child self of about four years old. He kneels down to be at eye level with his young self. One set of eyes burn bright with a hopeful future, innocently looking back into the ones that have seen the unfathomable.

The child desperately reaches for Jeff. He wipes the boy's tears and holds onto him tightly, clutching onto the part of himself that is still pure. He breaks down, vulnerable in his younger presence. He tells the child how much he loves him, how he accepts him. As they spend time in each other's arms, Jeff speaks to his younger form. Suddenly, they begin glowing together, forming into a white orb and integrating into one. Jeff's aura glows brightly as he feels the energy of self-love.

A bundle of fog manifests in the space, and inside of it appear two lost children. Jeff slowly stands from the kneeling position and rises from the fog covered ground. The boy and girl stand frightened in the distance with tears streaming down their small faces as they look frantically around. Jeff approaches his mother and father in their younger forms, reaching out his arms to comfort them. He hears that what they were looking for was love, just as the boy was before them. He comforts the trembling children and quiets their sobbing as they relax into his arms. He tells them how much he loves them and how he accepts them. *"Tell them that it is okay to make mistakes while learning. Imagine that the children are now feeling safe and loved. We have experiences to learn. Learn forgiveness, learn compassion, learn love. It starts with you."*

A warm glow expands Jeff's heart chakra as the meditation comes to a close. The sounds and images fade out. I sit with my subconscious before opening my eyes. A vision of a Pabst Blue Ribbon sign pops into my mind and excitement runs through my body as I see it. I come back into the room.

A smile warms my face as I blow out the candles. It feels good, like it worked. He feels much better. I take notice of the absence shortly after meditating and a sense of pride envelops me, knowing that he is off again doing his work. I take myself back up to the kitchen to graze in the pantry, and stumble as if I'm drunk as I make my way to the door. I stand for a few seconds to regain my footing as the room sways back and forth. My balance returns, and I'm seeing only one of everything again. I stuff my face, completely indulging in my craving for something salty. Suddenly, I lose my appetite. That familiar anxious pit settles in my gut, and I feel that burning uneasiness in my chest. I begin to feel worried over something that I can't pinpoint, becoming emotional and trying not to cry. This is all a part of his work. This is good. As the sky grows darker, the anxiety dissipates. I'm left feeling cold and tired from the lingering energetic residue.

*

Mom, Kylie, and I occupy a wooden booth in a burger joint. Cigarette smoke, loud talking, and pool cues hitting the ball fill my senses as we share a basket of fried pickles in the corner of the pub. As Kylie and Mom converse about a mutual friend, I remember Jeff and a sickness hits me. Aa devastating feeling falls over me to where I feel like I need to see him. I miss him so unbearably much. But I'll never truly be able to physically see him; flickering lights and feeling him near is the closest I'll ever get. That thought makes me nauseous.

I pull out my phone and scroll to a picture of him. The picture brings a little relief, but the sadness remains. He's completely out of reach, and he always will be. I take a sip of my water and look up directly at a chalkboard sign from across the bar that reads, "Happy Birthday, Jeffrey!" I sneak a picture of it and continue the dinner with renewed confidence in our connection.

My boots crunch over the gravel of the parking lot as we walk out with our to-go boxes in hand. I breathe out, watching my breath as it floats into a white cloud and dissipates into the air. My cheeks are wind chapped from the November chill that blows on my face as we walk. I glance back in front of me, doing a double take as I see paper laying on the ground ahead. "A twenty dollah bill!" I yell from over our car. I pick it up, feeling like it came from spirit, from Jeff as a thank you. I hop into the car and smile at my gift.

We chatter over the radio playing quietly. Kylie turns up the song. "This is the song I was trying to find, I heard it the other day and I loved it." I listen to the melody and find it super catchy.

"I think this is a remake of a Queen song, actually," Mom suggests.

Queen, the band that aided in bringing me and Jeff together, and I barely know any of their music. I look at the radio screen to see that the song is a remake of "Killer Queen," and my automatic thought is of Jeff. I add the song to my playlist and slip my phone back into my coat pocket. "I've never even heard the original before," I say.

Kylie pulls it up and I instantly fall in love with its catchiness. In hearing Freddie's voice, Jeff is all I see. The sound that he carries along with the sound of the guitars reminds me of the beginning, taking me back to when I was still figuring out if this was Jeff. For how many times I've played Bohemian Rhapsody, this feels like a new version of my favorite song.

Returning home the song is still stuck in my head, so I play it while brushing my teeth for bed. I lie exhausted under the comforter and log my signs for the day. As I type I feel someone standing next to my bed. I soak in the denseness of his presence, enjoying the feeling of his brief return.

Suddenly, I jump as the blare of the fire alarm sounds throughout the house. The screeching bounces through the halls. I plug my ears to preserve them from the high pitched wailing. "Who's cooking right now?" I walk out into the dark hallway to see Kylie coming out of her doorway in confusion. Together, we hurry up the stairs to find Mom doing the same. There is no smoke, and no fire.

"What's even happening?" Mom asks with a laugh. I get out the ladder to reach the system. Just as I put my foot on the first step, the alarms silence.

I look over my shoulder and grin at them. "Good ol' Jeff." They shake their heads in amazement and we return to our rooms for the night.

*

I wake up on November 28th, 2018, the 24th anniversary of Jeff's death. The minute I open my eyes, *Killer Queen* begins looping over and over in my mind. Like clockwork, from the minute I first heard the song all the way to the moment after waking, the verses play on and on in my head. I step out of my door at the same time that Kylie does, and she smiles as she says good morning in our goofy voice. "Killer Queen has been stuck in my head all morning," she shares.

"Me too! It won't leave my brain and I love it." I wonder if the song in our heads at the same time is Jeff's doing. I have never had a song in my head overnight and into the morning before. I go to the bathroom to get ready for my day and put on the song, still as catchy as when I first heard it the other night. "Gunpowder and gelatin, dyna… w.. a …aser beam." My eyes light up like a Christmas tree as static overpowers the verse. I'm overjoyed that he is back and log the sign while it's fresh in my mind.

Today, I think of his last moments, what must have been going through his mind at the time. I was expecting to feel especially sad today, but I feel surprisingly neutral. Without passing early, Jeff's life would have been spent staring at grey walls in a prison cell. After sixty-something years of that, he would have had to start this process from scratch. The death jump-started his healing timeline.

Today more than any other is the perfect day for making amends. If there is any reminder of his death on the news today, all people will see is the day where a monster got what he deserved. I have no clue if he can even lighten the weight of that; the world's resentment.

I drop down through layers of consciousness, standing in a blank space. Jeff stands with his back to me. He looks out at the world colored red, symbolic of the anger and hate the public feels towards him.

Jeff ponders in his remorse as he kneels with a bowed head. He shines his own inner light, which, up until recently, he didn't even realize he had in him. A wave of pink coats the world. Rushing over the streets, neighborhoods, and cities, it touches everyone that knows his name. As the energy washes the Earth, it blesses it with love and raises its vibration. Jeff stands empowered, observing the shifts.

A crowd of 17 men appear as the world falls away. They stand on the cloud lined floor, together with completely different backstories but the same end. Jeff stands before them. He drops to his knees, at a loss for the right words. He begs their forgiveness, beaming out all of his energy to each of them. He breaks, and begins sobbing. The men look at him, partially resisting him, partially accepting him. They are much more peaceful and much more evolved than he is, holding their composure as if they understand what he doesn't yet. The men crowd around his feeble body, most placing their hands on his shoulder with a few staying back.

I walk up to them to express my own sorrow. I look upon their faces, going up to each one of the 17, showering them each in the energy of my love and peace. White light dances down to their heads ever so gently and washes them in bliss. One by one, I hug and kiss them on the cheek. I walk up to Anthony Sears, the one I share a birthday with. I look into his deep brown eyes. He is so beautiful, so pure, with so much potential. I speak to the crowd. "Words do not do my feelings justice. It is an absolute shame that there were 17 of you that got caught in the crossfire of such a chaotic fate. You didn't deserve any of this, and your families didn't deserve to lose such special people. You deserved a life full of happiness and memories with your loved ones. Just such beautiful souls… I hope you know how deeply loved you are, and how deeply sorry I am."

The souls accept my words and return to their plane. I feel a sense of relief and reach for my earbud when suddenly the figure of a woman appears in my visions. Her higher self walks closer. I squint and see that it is Rita, the sister of one of the men. During the trial she had an outburst, expressing her pent up anger as she spoke at the podium. She screamed and charged to the defense table. "Jeffrey, I hate you! Motherfucker! I hate you!" Jeffrey sat numb with not even a flinch.

When asked about his reaction, Jeff expressed, "I couldn't blame her one bit. If I was on the family's end of the table I would have done the same thing, and I'm surprised there wasn't more of that."

I look to Rita and Jeff walking to meet each other halfway. Her expression is soft as she so bravely releases resentment. Without words, the two release the past through a brief embrace. The way they hug reminds me of when Jeff hugged Shari in the meeting room for their interview. It is genuine, kind, and healing for them both. Just before they let go of each other's arms, my visual goes black. I emerge from the dream-like state, and for a second, I forget where I am.

*

Heading back home from work, I stop at a gas station with my tank on empty. After filling the tank, I glance up at the total: $21.33. I smirk at the 213 sign on this day. Exhaustion pulls on me as I get in my car. Goosebumps cover my arms; I feel chilled from being so tired. I play "Killer Queen" to satisfy the itch of that song, and as the guitars ring out, I feel Jeff strongly in the backseat. I'm surprised at his quick return. I pull into my garage and make my way out of the car when I hear a bang come from inside the house. I remain still, quiet as I keep my ears open for more sounds. Standing on my tip-toes, I peek out of the small cobweb-covered window at the top of the garage door to see an empty driveway, indicating that nobody else is home. Maybe it was just my cat. My heart skips a beat as another bang pounds the wall.

The garage falls silent and I walk up the wooden steps into the house. I creak open the door leading into the kitchen, and cautiously step in. I'm instantly hit with a strong smell of cigarettes. Jack greets me, seeming to have been lying here for a while.

The blue sunlit sky descends into a twinkling navy. Sitting next to Mom, I fidget with my spoon around the soup bowl. "Today is Jeff's death anniversary, it's been 24 years. I wanna do something for him so I'm going to set off one of the paper lanterns from Brad's memorial that we didn't use, if that's okay."

I pause and wait nervously for a response. Mom perks up. "Oh wow, really? I'll go with you if you want. Where are you going to do it?" My heart lightens at her response.

I zip up my jacket and grab the lighter. I rummage through the plastic packaging of multicolored lanterns, mulling over which color I should choose. I pick the yellow one for him, just like the color of our flowers. We head out to the bare road and drive around the corner, minutes away from my old high school. Our headlights shine through the windows of the school as we pull into its vacant parking lot. I'm flooded with nostalgia and reflect on the phenomenon of bringing my average past together with my abnormal present. The car dings as we open its doors.

I unfold the paper, careful to not make a tear in the lantern. After five minutes and a lot of struggle, the lantern inflates. I close my eyes as I say a prayer, sending Jeff the highest vibration of light with this lantern. I thank him for his presence in my life, and for this journey. The lantern begins to lift from my hands. I give it a push to help it fly, sending it away filled with love energy.

We watch in silence as the yellow floats up to the stars. It looks like a guiding light, showing Jeff the way to Heaven. I wonder if he's watching his lantern float up, too. Watching this reminds me of the golden ball of light, flying into the sky to eventually land on the roof of Jeff's childhood home. The light grows smaller and smaller as it ascends towards the clouds. Mom and I watch until it blends in with the stars, and I take one last look before getting back into the car.

Returning home, I wrap my arms tightly around Mom, thanking her for going with me to something so special. I walk back down to the basement and into my room, shutting the door behind me. I feel a rush of emotion as my happiness turns to mourning. Physically, he's gone forever. I'll never get to meet him in person, despite how close we are now. Homesickness settles over me, and the ache coaxes a tear from my eye. I fall back onto my bed to stare at the ceiling fan, feeling the single tear as it rolls down my cheek.

*

The sun has just risen and I'm staring into the black void. Native music plays through my earbuds while swirls of grey twist and turn to form a butterfly, soon reverting to black. Moments pass, and I see a glimpse of a forest, similar to a wooded area in town, and fades. Jeff's side profile appears in a flash. It dissolves and comes back, showing his entire body. I watch as he raises his arm with a flask in hand to take a hard swig, standing as he chugs. It looks like a vision of his past, possibly a time he's currently working through.

Flutes and drums play on as I strain my eyes to see past the layers of black. I see a door show up and disappear just as quickly. Then, Jeff's face appears right in mine. My heart sinks. "I wish I would just die and be with you." Jeff shakes his head in disagreement and hangs his head low, as if me saying that saddened him. He disappears and I sit for ten more minutes to find that he left in protest. I open my eyes and stare blankly ahead. Anxiety and worry take over, but I know it's not mine.

More than anything, I wish he was here. I go on the true crime community message boards to find a video of Jeff to satisfy the emptiness I feel inside of me. I lock my eyes onto him as he speaks. "Right, right. Not because I was angry with them, not because I hated them, but because I wanted to uh, keep them with me. And as my obsession grew, I was sav... b......parts such... uh, skulls and ....etons." A puff of ectomist floats right before my eyes. I close them and reach out my hand.

"Just touch my hand." I reach before me, waiting. Three knocks on my door interrupt the moment.

"Kris, you wanna watch a movie with us perhaps?" Kylie laughs.

"Yas, I'll be right there." I exhale as I look in the mirror and switch off the light.

After twenty minutes of family time, a serious argument begins between me, Mom and Kylie. Nervously, my fingers tap back and forth as I feel alone and cornered. Before long, something is said that hurts me deeply. Suddenly, our shouting falls silent as we hear a bang come from my room to realize that the door had slammed shut. Mom and Kylie sit in silence on the couch, and an inner pride bursts within me that I won't let show. Through the tears in my eyes I give them both a look of disappointment and rush off to my room. I close and lock the door behind me, crying as quietly as I can.

I grip the pillow beneath my head. Jeff floods my thoughts and keeps them off of the comment that was made. This is why I wish I could just be on the other side with him; he's the one who is there for me in every situation. He's witnessed my pain and my happiness, seen who I've been and who I will become, and knows me better than I know myself.

I hear three knocks at my bedroom door. Mom and Kylie timidly ask for me to let them in. I remain laying without a word as I stare out of the window. "Please, Kristen. We're really sorry." I open the door without words. They wrap me in a hug, and I show little effort to return one. They apologize profusely and join me on my bed to talk things over. After a while, they convince me to come back to the bonus room with them.

We watch the movie in an awkward attempt to pretend that nothing happened. Although I'm acting as if everything is fine, their words linger in my mind and keep me down. The screen shows a snowy mountain scene, the hikers struggling to climb Mount Everest as they head towards the top. A woman in the group falls to her knees in the snow, weak from the journey. "Get up! Keep moving!" shouts the man as he helps her up by her arms.

Mid-scene, the screen goes black and returns to the homepage of the TV. Mom breaks the silence. "Oh no, what happened? This TV is brand new, it shouldn't have issues. I will be so mad."

Kylie adds, "It won't even let me go back." She furiously clicks the remote and I glance up at the time on the TV. It shows 4:34 p.m., when it's actually 8:15 p.m. The snow scene reappears at maximum volume. I laugh as I plug my ears. Kylie and I scramble for the remote to turn it back down and see that it was set on volume 70. I smile, knowing that was his doing.

After the movie I get ready for bed. The white light in the bathroom is bright for my tired eyes. I turn the volume all the way up on my phone to hear a video over the sound of my tooth brushing. My daily PewDiePie video plays to keep me entertained. "Next meme!" Felix claps, and is interrupted by an ad for Milwaukee Pizza. The thirty-second ad plays through, advertising the different specialties, and quickly returns to the video. As it comes back, I catch the first words out of Felix's mouth. "Cannibal! He's a cannibal!" That was especially odd, being that that was supposed to be a local commercial. I log the sign. *11/30: PewDiePie video had words Milwaukee and cannibal all in the span of a few seconds.* Because of Jeffrey's support throughout the night, I go to bed cheered up.

*

It is December 5th. It's been almost a week since I've logged or felt anything, and I'm starting to feel resentment towards our guides and their restrictions between us. I reminisce about the days where I felt his presence anywhere I would go. Work, a friend's house, our cruise: he would find me at any distance. Then I would return home and be with him, feeling him all day and while falling asleep at night. All week my love meditations have been ineffective in reaching him. Frustrated, I work on my own abilities so that I can eventually talk to him myself.

Almost instantly, visuals begin flowing to me. My third eye feels as if someone is pressing on it; my body buzzes as if it is being charged.

Suddenly I am immersed in a scene. Spectating behind him, I see teenage Jeff walking on the side of the road near his Bath, Ohio house. He is wearing a white, long-sleeved puffy shirt, brown vest, and brown corduroy pants; an outfit that I've never seen a picture of before. His hair lays long and shaggy, similar to what he looked like sitting at the dinner table in a family photo. Making his way down the road, he flails his arms up as if to entertain himself and continues walking.

I reach out my arm in an attempt to touch him and before I can, I appear in his old bedroom. The walls are a dark turquoise with white molding halfway up the middle. The room is empty, only occupied by a window to my left and below it, a tall wooden dresser. I'm floating in the room feeling very on edge, as if something bad is about to happen. Slowly, my astral self gravitates towards the corner of the room and descends down onto the hardwood floor. I feel like a balloon without helium, bouncing uncontrollably with the draft. Sitting on the floor is a Raggedy Anne doll, perfectly accurate with her triangle nose and spiky red hair. The doll stares vacantly at the wall behind me as I get closer. It feels evil; looking at it makes my skin crawl. Frightened, I return to the awareness of the backs of my eyelids after being in the scene for only 2 seconds.

I return to a relaxed state, take a few deep breaths, and dive back in. A glimpse of Jeff looking stressed, sitting with his back to the wall, quickly fades to black. I search for images through the dark veil. There is a muffled but alarming noise coming from far away, and I listen intently to identify the sound. A woman screaming rings out from the distance, getting louder as I become more aware of it. Over ten women scream so loudly in agony and fright that it drowns out the third eye reiki music. My nerves rise in confusion as I listen. A woman shrieks, "He's here!" In front of my eyes, a flash of another face appears; A brunette man with bushy eyebrows and dark eyes. Ted Bundy. The screaming silences as my eyes fly open.

I come back to my quiet room, dampened in sweat. Overwhelmed, I rub my hands over my face. I tap my phone to see one minute remaining on the video. I was only in there for seven minutes and have never had a stranger experience in meditation. Why was Ted Bundy present? Is he also seeking my help?

My mind races with thoughts of that meditation as the day rolls on. Into the evening, all I can wonder about is Ted Bundy. Was that my subconscious throwing an image at me, or was that really him? In the darkness of my room, I watch on my TV as Gerald Boyle grips the sides of the podium, speaking before the court. "Ladies and gentlemen of the court, we now begin an odyssey. As to whether or not Jeffrey Dahmer was, at the time he committed these horrific murders to which he has plead guilty, suffering from a mental disease." My console controller lets out buzz after buzz, like a cell phone vibrating. I look over and it stops.

Jeff sits in the swivel chair at the defense table. He stares ahead, emotionless. My controller buzzes on its own once more. My heavy eyelids lower to rest while my mind remains awake and I listen to the court footage. As my eyes are closed a visual appears of perfectly symmetrical daisy petals, followed by a vivid image of Jeff's face. The details are sharp. I see every pore and every follicle of facial hair, getting the chance to look into his crystal blue eyes. I sit up as if to get a grasp onto him so that he can't slip away. He disappears and it saddens me. I have to stay patient and remember this distance is only temporary. More images flash to me, only for me to doze off, forgetting what they are by the time I fall into sleep.

I lay on a field of grass, effortlessly flowing with him. I stare above and watch as a giant infinity symbol traces itself over the blue sky, like a golden firework. Jeff, laying to my right, watches with me in pure joy. Nothing else matters in this moment. For once, the feeling is satisfied; that feeling that I crave when I listen to our music, when I'm out in public and suddenly remember him. I hear the words "twin flame" spoken in a woman's voice. *Oh yeah, that's what me and Jeff are*, I think. I begin to gravitate towards the glass door and Jeff sits up in the grass, looking back at me as I return to Michael. I resist, not wanting to leave. I try to ground myself.

I wake up on my bed, bummed that it was only a dream. It was so good to see him again. Stretching my arms, I remember the words "twin flame." I've heard the term somewhere before, but I'm not exactly sure of it meaning. If it means what it sounds like, it makes sense for our bond. If anyone on this Earth is like my other half, it's my ghost, the one who has been with me since I was put here. We share the same feelings, and we're inseparable.

I reach for my glasses to start another day. I really don't want to be back. I close my eyes to send him a message. "I'm so proud of you, and how far you have come with your healing. Whenever you feel like you can't make it, I want you to take my earth angel wings and wear them like armor." In my mind's eye I rip white feathered wings from my shoulder blades and hand them to him so that he can wrap himself in my love and support when I cannot be there. "Our time will come again," I remind myself.

Chapter Twelve:
White Winter Hymnal

I make myself a cup of matcha tea, ready to decorate my room for Christmas. Grabbing a snowflake cookie from the kitchen, I prance back down the stairs. "Baby Please Come Home" by Darlene Love serenades throughout my room as I string multicolored bulbs over my curtain rod. The scent of Fraser Fir fills my senses and reminds me of nostalgic times.

I pull the Christmas tree out of its box. Section by section I stack the three parts, acquiring scrapes on my forearms from its fake branches. It is a pencil tree that I decorate with simple and old-fashioned ornaments, inspired by the 1950's, my favorite decade. I delicately open each box to reveal the sentimental decoration inside. I look down to the bottom of the plastic bin to see a single ornament that I must have forgotten.

I dangle it in front of my face, trying to recognize it. It is half the size of my palm, silver, and heavy for its size. The picture on it is of an angel feeding a deer with the word "kindness" printed at the bottom of her dress. I'm curious, finding this in my box that I go through every year, never having seen this one before. I ask Kylie and Mom if they know where it came from. They've never seen it before, either. I hold it tightly in my hand, feeling like it is a gift from my squad on the other side.

I set the ornament on the top branch next to angel wings. I wish that I could give Jeff the gift of spending Christmas in Heaven this year. Maybe it will take us both by surprise and happen right before the 25th. I reach over the shelves to hang lighted garland above my TV and plug in the lights. For the finishing touch, I place white candles in each windowsill and stand back to enjoy the tranquility.

I feel at peace surrounded by the twinkling decorations around our haven. I shut and lock my door. Closing my eyes, I take five deep breaths in and out. My heart rate steadies and my mind empties. I see a flash of Michael, boldly holding his sword with his large wings outstretched. I feel love well up in my heart and send it to him in appreciation. In the swirls of black, another visual appears, this one of a man wearing wings. It is Jeff, wearing my wings just like I told him to. He struggles to stand as tall as he can. "That's right! Wear my wings!" I exclaim.

His back faces me as the wings fan out, extending past his arm length. In this moment he reminds me of a phoenix, rising from the ashes. The visual fades, and a golden symbol of infinity shines in front of me before disappearing, reminding me of my dream lying in the grass. I close out the meditation and see that my phone is at thirty-four percent, with the time being 4:34, giving me even more validation.

The sun rises and sets for three more days. I've found myself at work, home, and out in public feeling completely on my own. My emotions are steady, my energy, light. Today feels significant—it's 12/13—and Jeff is still MIA. I stand on the mountain top, walking over the gravel in my bare feet to see the cliff's edge occupied by a lonely barren tree. The instructor guides me to visualize the person that I want to send love to, and all my brain can produce is a forced, blurry image of him that feels imaginary. I try to surround Jeff in a pink, healing glow, but this also feels forced, and unsuccessful.

I become tired after several attempts to give him this energy, and switch over the video. I put everything I have into the golden ball of healing, connecting to every fond memory, every time he has showed his support, every time I've felt my heart flutter. As I push these feelings into the orb, I send it up to wherever he may be. The orb gets close but will not reach him. For one last try I push the ball further but without success. I tug on each wire of my earbuds and close out.

*

"That's kinda gross. I want some." Jeffrey catches the jar mid-air. I watch as he walks near the sink, laughing with peanut butter in his mouth. I blink my eyes open and shut. Hours later I open them to a pitch-black room; the TV shut off after hours of inactivity. I check the time on my phone—it's 3:00 a.m. Emptiness settles in the air as I stare into the dark. I really, really miss him. I wrap my arms tightly around the pillow, wondering if he is okay with no way of knowing. I drift back off as I think about him.

*

I'm conscious in my room yet again in what feels like the longest night ever, and I have to pee. I click the lamp switch to find that it won't turn on. I click it twice more and get up, dragging my feet over to the switch on the wall to find that it doesn't work, either. Right as I go for the doorknob, something blue grows on the wall next to me. I can hear it inflating with a rubbery texture. Another one appears, yellow this time. Then a red one, a white one, then purple. I look at the wall of colored balloons in confusion and happiness. A loud pop surprises me as the blue one bursts, and then the yellow. One by one they pop, and I notice that a dart is being thrown at them from behind me.

Demonic laughter comes from the back corner of my room. I turn around to see the girl with long black hair standing in the back of my room. My heart sinks to my stomach and shivers run down my back. The entity's voice echoes in multiple inflections. I duck next to my fish tank, realizing that I'm in another lucid dream. My eyes struggle to stay open as I try to awaken my sleeping body to escape the nightmare. I peek back over my bed to see where she went. I look down at my legs. A red balloon has stuck to me, and more appear as I continue to look. The demon's laughter gets louder, heightening my stress as I shake the expanding balloons off of me.

My eyes won't stay open, and I begin to panic. I can't see where I am or what's around me. Suddenly, I'm back on my bed. I feel the comforter beneath my suddenly paralyzed body, finding that I now can't move. I yell for Jeff at the top of my lungs; his name is the only thing I can think of in my panicked state. My eyelids are still stuck shut, but I can feel someone beside my bed. Hazily, I pry my eyelids halfway open to see Jeff's figure looking down at me. The filter prevents him from interfering.

I look over to my open bedroom door and see my black cat, Jack, standing outside the boundaries of my room. I feel that this is actually Jack on this plane to guide me, as cats live in multiple dimensions. Jeff and Jack disappear, and the girl reappears, her head twitching at the foot of my bed. My eyes close firmly and I imagine a column of golden light descending around the demon's aura. I fill it with God, watching as the light sparkles around the demon's black core. Her laughing stops and she begins to fade. The girl disappears, and I wake up. My eyes open easily, and I know that I am back. I reach for my phone: 5:05 a.m. I fight to stay awake for at least ten minutes instead of falling back into the nightmare.

My alarm blares at 7:30 a.m. I yawn the whole way down 521 Highway, feeling too burnt out for work today. I want to reach out my hand for his, but he is still gone. At a stoplight I close my eyes to try and catch a visual of him, but he does not appear. I turn on my music and run through our playlist, and still feel no presence.

I arrive at the office and shuffle in the door. Kelci peaks her head over the counter to see who walked in. "Heyo!" She smiles as she realizes it is me.

"Well, howdy," I reply.

As I walk down the hall, my notebook slides out from under my arm and my papers scatter. The incident makes me irritable. I grip onto the pages unnecessarily tightly to gather them. As I'm trying to pick up the pages, my phone won't stop buzzing! I stop everything just to answer a spam call. In a huff, I tuck my phone away into my back pocket. I make my way down the hall, my stuff finally together. A child begins to scream from the waiting room. She continues and the sound of it makes my blood boil. I shut the door behind me in the bathroom, escaping the noise. Where is all of this rage coming from?

Under the dim lighting I look at my reflection in the mirror. I close my eyes, taking a few deep breaths in hopes of re-centering myself. I inhale for the count of four... exhale for the count of four. Inhale... exhale. I still feel like I could punch a wall. Quickly, I grab the needed supplies from the front and leave as soon as I'm able.

My anger calms by the time I get to the store. I walk through the aisles, one of the wheels of my cart squeaking against the tile floor. So far I have my protein bars, oatmeal, and green tea. Glancing down at my shopping list, I notice that I need to go back for chia seeds. The carts tires skid as I turn it around and reach for the bag.

I toss the bag into the cart right as a feeling hits my core, one of immense sadness. My eyelids feel like they're attached to a paperweight; then comes the fatigue. I mosey over to self-checkout, listening to each beep as I scan the items. I become more alert. What was a small pit in my stomach has transformed into full-fledged worry and anxiety. It is like mild acid is in my solar plexus and I can't stop fidgeting. I tap my fingers one at a time pinky to thumb, thumb to pinky as the payment screen loads. Then it hits me that I haven't lost him. That chord between our souls is still there, and we remain connected even though we're apart. After the realization, these feelings become a relief, because it is me feeling him. In my mind I tell him, "Keep pushing on, it's going to be okay. I love you."

As I return home I go into meditative mode. Wasting no time, I aim my light ahead at a blurry image of Jeff and stretch the column the farthest that I possibly can to get it to him. The light does nothing. An underwhelming result of this meditation is the same as it has been every day this week: ineffective.

My mind won't even allow me to envision Jeff. I revert back to my neutral space, my black void. I call upon Archangel Michael. In my mind's eye, he stands before me mightily. His hair is a clean blonde, his armor silver and blue. "Please let me reach him, please. Just this once." Michael stands guarding the space with his head tilted down, reluctant to allow me in.

"I just need to reach him, just let me for today. I really think it will help him along even faster." Michael looks at me as I plead. He sighs, and I feel as if he briefly lifted the veil for me. My eyes light up as I step through an iron gate. I walk into a pitch black dungeon; the only source of light is from a small, castle-looking window, less than a foot in width. In the middle of the cell, Jeff sits in front of a vintage box TV. I look at the screen to see static as he watches what I cannot see. I rush up, grabbing onto him as if letting go meant he would slip away. Jeff holds me tightly with a muffled, "Hey, Kris."

His energy feels depleted, like a fighter in the corner of a boxing ring before the final round. He's rung out, barely an ounce of fight left in him. Rushed for time, I hold the sides of his face and ramble, "Have you been okay? Can I help? What can I do?" He offers no verbal responses. I hand him a white candle of peace and harmony, infused with Reiki energy so that as the flame burns, it will emit my love. I exchange the thought with him, suggesting that just like my wings, he can burn this light so that he'll still have my support.

Michael opens the gate. The light coming in reveals the dingey stone walls. I grab onto Jeff for one last embrace, allowing him to feel all of my love and pride for him. My head rests over his shoulder. "Remember to wear my wings." He doesn't let go, gripping onto me as if it is the last time we'll see each other. Michael takes my hand escorting me out of this scene, and I return to my own mind. A lava lamp visual of Jeff holding a candle validates that we've connected. Another visual appears of Jeff as a child, laughing hard with his hands on his knees. A sudden bolt of lightning strikes the sky to his left. My sight goes black. I can hear the music again, and I open my eyes.

*

A few days have passed and I put on "I am the Walrus," feeling connected to the teenage version of him today. As the music plays, all I can see in my mind's eye is him; the way he looked in a picture taken of him in school with his long hair and glasses, making a duck face. The song statics and skips, and my natural reaction is to look at my phone.

The time of the static is exactly 12:13. 1 is the number of purification. Maybe the 1 before 213 is a validation that the man that once identified with that number is being purified. Happiness floods my mind at the first sign from him in what feels like forever. The song is almost at its end, and I close my eyes to connect. He is here.

Directly after, I see a flash of Ted Bundy's eyes once again. Since that first day I saw Ted, I haven't given him much thought. Did word spread around the spirit realm that I'm helping a serial killer to Heaven, and now there are others here? Do Ted and Jeff currently hang around each other because of their similar notoriety? Or did Jeff guide other lost souls to me?

I check on my chameleon for one last time before heading to Allison's for our Christmas gift exchange. I reach my hand in to turn off the humidifier and Leaf hisses. "I love you too, my son," I whisper, zipping up his cage. Leaf glares at me with one eye, the other looking towards the ceiling.

I stop at the grocery store for a bottle of a red blend and sit in my car before leaving the parking lot. I can feel Jeff, but not because he is present. I'm still connecting to his teenage version, currently feeling his low self-worth. Whatever he is working through at this moment is definitely something that he has been putting off, and I can feel why. I allow myself to cry to release the energy.

My spirit feels dimmed to a low glow as I drive. I'm tired and numb, wondering how he made it through anything always feeling this way. Wiping my cheek with the back of my hand, I pull myself together and walk up to the front door. Allison's greeting feels ingenuine, like forced excitement. As I walk into her home, the familiar smell takes me back to high school. Together, we head upstairs.

The night rolls on as she gossips about her old roommate and vents about her relationship. On and off she cries as she explains her situation. I pour a glass of wine to the rim and hold back my own emotions. Allison stops mid-sentence and asks, "Are you okay?"

I smile as I shake my head, "Yeah, I'm all right…It's actually a Jeff thing." A seal breaks as I bring up his name; my tears start. After explaining our bond, I'm overwhelmed by sadness. "Alli, if you could feel the sadness that he feels, you wouldn't be able to function. It is unbearable. He's just so sad!"

She watches as I sob and awkwardly tries to console me. I sniffle. "I'm sorry, I know this is weird. I wasn't going to bring it up."

"No, this is so cool, Kris, this is a celebrity!" She smirks to herself. "I tell

literally everybody at my work about how you're connected to Jeffrey Dahmer."
Silence envelops the room.

I shift with unease. "You do? Well, how do you word it to them?" I respond,
unsure of whether to be flattered or self-conscious. I act happy about it but
feel mortified with how it probably comes across. Allison's response is short
and unsympathetic, and I quickly realize her motive behind telling them. This
wouldn't be the first time she's shared my secrets, and I know she is only telling
me all of this because she has been drinking. I worry about what those people
might think; some of them are people we went to school with. I'm already
embarrassed by how I used to act in high school. Sounding delusional gives no
chance of redemption, and she knows that. I have a bad taste in my mouth for
the rest of the night, seeing her true colors. After a couple of hours I go back
home, realizing just how different the two of us have become.

*

I wake up on December 24th, childlike excitement warming me as I join my
family upstairs. "I had a dream about Jeff last night," Kylie shares. I had a dream
about him last night too, and I feel pride that she was the one who brought
him up. But my mood soon changes, and I'm anxious, cold, and tired into the
evening, and all the way through our Christmas Eve dinner with the family. I
can feel him working through his rollercoaster of emotions. I hold my hand
out to my side, offering him comfort. My spirit perks up as Kylie points out a
man carrying a case of Pabst Blue Ribbon in the hallway. I wonder why she's all
of a sudden talking about Jeff, but I'm not complaining. Sitting at the table, I
run my fingers nervously through my hair. I pull at one strand that feels coarse
and hold it up closer to see that it is a single grey hair. My first and only grey
hair at twenty-one; the effects of Jeff's life review in a nutshell.

Arriving back home, the three of us sit in the living room to open one present
before the morning. The fireplace crackles as we sit on the couch together. Kylie
reaches for a small box. "Okay, so, I want to give you this present early before
everyone gets here tomorrow so I can tell you about it." I smile in wonder. I can
tell this is a present that correlates with *him*. I feel a rush of happiness, not only
about the gift itself, but that she thought of something like this.

Kylie hands me the small green box, wrapped perfectly with a sparkly ribbon. I tear open the paper and take off the lid. Lying on a thin foam pad inside is a silver daisy necklace. It is dainty with two other charms on the chain. I hold it before my eyes to admire. My bottom lip puckers out as I reach for a hug.

"Okay, but look at what the charms are," Mom says with eagerness. I see that one charm is a garnet gemstone, my January birthstone, and the other charm is a K for my first initial.

Kylie explains, "I was looking online wanting to get you a really pretty daisy necklace. An expensive, nice looking one, and this specific one is all that kept popping up. I couldn't get away from it, it followed me on every website. And that's exactly how it came, I didn't customize it at all." Kylie hesitates, "It's like he picked it out for you and made sure I bought it."

I look at in amazement, a gift from him in my very own palms. With a warm smile I place the daisy over my neck. I give Kylie another hug. "This is the most special gift I've ever gotten. Thank you so much." Later in the evening, I search "Daisy Necklace" on my phone. I have a hard time finding the one she got me, when to her it came so easily. I look at the necklace, my tangible item from him. I add the charms from my golden saint's pendant cross necklace to it and hold it tightly between my fingers.

CHAPTER THIRTEEN:
2019

I'm dressed up in sparkles and fringe for the ball to drop tonight. I feel at home in my vintage look, standing in front of the mirror to evaluate myself. I bought this dress for the occasion a few days ago; it's a black flapper slip that I've paired with fishnet tights. I've pinned a feather in my curled hair for the 20's themed New Year's Eve party uptown. I take selfies with my Polaroid as I wait for Kylie and her friends. As I wait I look back at my notes from this year, pages full of memories from our journey. I reflect on just the past few days, reading the logs of things falling over on their own, random gusts of wind inside my house, and :34s almost every hour. I'm happy to have my signs back, and happy that our separation is over. He didn't get to Heaven this year, but I'm hoping 2019 will be it.

Hours later, we leave the house too late to make the party, and decide to make it a night at the restaurant/bar where Kylie and her friends work. I sit at the table with a drink in hand as the girls hang with their boyfriends. There's no place I'd rather be than in the space that made my year what it is, with him. I imagine how good it would feel to sit there just me and Jeff, entering the new year together. I click the side of my phone at 11:34 and look around for someone to talk to. I tap my fingers on the side of my glass as I watch the TV over the bar. I check the time again at 11:45 and request an Uber home. At five minutes before midnight, I'm dropped off in front of my driveway and rush inside to turn on the TV.

I spill a little wine, quickly pouring it into a fancy glass. I sip my wine as the ear-muffed announcer talks about the performance coming up next. My phone buzzes twice and I see that Mom sent me a video. A live band is playing the venue where Mom is celebrating her evening. Her text reads, "'Bohemian Rhapsody' just came on!" I turn the volume up and hold the phone closer to my ear. As I listen to the sign he sent through her in perfect timing, filled with the energy of love and happiness to start the new year. I chug the glass of red blend as the countdown is announced. His presence lingers densely behind my back, and for a second I swear I feel a double tap on my shoulder. I stand with the feeling of him behind me as the announcers count from ten. "Three… two… one… Happy new year!" The confetti falls on the screen and I feel good about the year to come. "Happy new year, Jeff. Thanks for always being there." The room spins as I tuck myself into bed for the first time this year.

*

Water trickles over my skin as I rinse bubbles out of my hair, my eyes squinted closed to keep shampoo from getting in. I feel someone standing directly behind me and keep my eyes closed to hold the feeling. My headache booms as I turn around to face him, and stumble from feeling like I'm going to bump into somebody. I open my eyes, hoping to catch a glimpse of a figure. In front of me is an empty white background; I find myself standing alone.

I play Jeff's documentary as I get dressed. From my closet I can hear his monotone, northwestern voice. "Your honor, it is over now. I know society will never be able to forgive me. I know the families of the victims will never be able to forgive me for what I have done." I straighten out my Def Leppard t-shirt as I walk through the beads hanging in the door frame. I look up at the screen for the intro as a low beat plays and photos of Jeff's apartment flash across the screen. A white strip pops up, obstructing the view on the bottom of the screen, and a pop comes through the speakers.

"Woah." I rewind it back to see if it does that again. The low beat plays, making it through the apartment photos and into the beginning of narration. I rewind it again just for good measure, finding no malfunctions. With a grin I add the sign to my new 2019 list. There are a little over two weeks until my 22nd birthday, and I want to hear from him as a gift to myself.

Opening my phone, I navigate to Denise's website to book an appointment, finding the best time: 2:30 on January 21st, right after my staff meeting. With excitement, I click "book appointment" and write in the notes section "Dahmer Day," a name we joked about calling our readings.

I feel something in my eye and close it to rub my eyelid. Instantly, a visual pops in. Jeff and I are hugging. Through that hug I see two souls rejoining as if it they had been separated for a lifetime. My heart skips a beat from seeing it, but I automatically repress any romantic feelings that surface within me. I shake my head in discomfort and say, "I'm sorry." In my right ear a voice speaks, "Don't apologize, I miss that." Physically hearing that snaps me out of my meditative state.

*

I arrive at the cafe right at 1:00 for our Monday staff meeting. The hour passes by as we go over statistics and plans, and I continuously check the time. 2:00 strikes and I hop up and into my car with excitement running through my gut. I play "Good Old Fashioned Lover-boy" by Queen on the way home and sing the chorus, getting most of the lyrics wrong. "Oooh, love. Oooh, loverboy! It's all alright, hold on tight, trust me because I'm a good old fashioned lover boy."

I can't stop smiling, looking forward to a reading with Denise after waiting for over two months. I set up my space, my multicolored crystals in a half circle around me and my candles lit for serenity. My phone is charged, my paper and pen ready. I look down at my list of questions that I have been waiting to ask. I sit in near-silence, listening to my own heartbeat and heavy breath. My hand shakes as I pick up the ringing phone. "Denise! Hey!" My voice squeaks.

"Hi!" Denise chuckles.

"Are you proud of me? I stuck it out over two months!" I laugh.

She gets right to business, beginning with the guided protection and connection meditation. Anticipation sets in as she calls forth my loved ones and pauses for a moment. "Hmm, he seems cranky with us today, like he doesn't wanna talk. His back is facing me and he's just pesky and irrita...." Three beeps end the phone call.

"Um." I look down and wait for her to call me back. Cranky with *us*? Did I do something to upset him? My phone buzzes with Denise's call. "It happened again," I laugh.

"Yeah, he's not up for this today." Denise chuckles. I hold back, slightly embarrassed. I feel like I'm bothering him and offer to reschedule. "No, it's fine. What do you want to know?" Denise answers.

I look down at my page to read the first question. "Well, we were separated for a while and he's come back recently, but sometimes I don't know if I feel him as often as I..."

Denise cuts in with a snicker. "Because he's not around! That's why."

My voice quiets. "Oh, really?"

That hurt, as if our friendship is not a mutual exchange. I write down her answer and go to my next question. "I want to know what he truly thinks of me and our connection. Does he care about me how I care about him?" I smile, ready for the answer that I know will be a sweet one.

"He's not genuine. He's actually manipulating you to get what he wants. He's been giving off these romantic vibes to you lately? That's him manipulating you too, because he knows that's how you feel towards him. What he is doing is kind of like being extra nice to your mom, so she'll give you money, or let you go somewhere." She giggles. My chest weighs heavy at her response. This "bond" apparently isn't at all what I thought it was. The whole beginning of our conversation makes me feel like shit. I don't know what to say next, crossing out my next few questions in embarrassment.

"He hangs around me a lot, isn't it because he feels like we have a friendship?"

"Well, he uses you as a distraction. He's like, well, I don't feel like doing my work so I'm going to go hang out with this girl to procrastinate," Denise harshly explains.

"So, he doesn't really care, he's just sort of using me?"

"That's what it feels like, yeah. You're teaching him how to have relationships for when he crosses over or eventually reincarnates, and then he'll appreciate you more, but right now he's just kind of using you for his advantage. It could be too that you have so much love for him and he doesn't know how to handle it, because he was never shown that much affection in life." I feel stupid.

Denise waits quietly on the other line, and I go to an emotionally safe question. "I've had this recurring lucid nightmare with a demon after me in my room, and I know you said that our guides keep us to where can only interact so much. In these nightmares I can feel Jeff's presence, and I saw him once too, but he was standing beside my bed and couldn't do anything to help. Was that actually him?"

"I don't think so. Why would you think that a serial killer cares about you or would try to help you?" Denise laughs.

"Oh, I don't know…" I fidget with the pen, neglecting to write that answer down.

For once, I just want this phone call to end. I don't even feel like crying, I feel betrayed and angry. I scratch out, *"In between 1994 and 1997 when we were both spirits, were we together?"* and *"Being that we're so connected now, was I watching over him as his ghost in his lifetime, like how he is in mine?"* and *"What were some ways that he has affected my life that I didn't know it was him?"*.

"Well, since he's being a dick, I guess I'll have time to ask you some other questions I had. I did this intuition Reiki meditation and long story short, I saw Ted Bundy's eyes by the end of it. Since then he's popped up two more times. A few other killers have come through to me too, Richard Ramirez, he was another serial killer in the 80's, Eric Harris, and Dylan Klebold, they were… school shooters. Obviously, I'm not even thinking about them because my interest isn't in killers, so I thought it's interesting that their faces pop up on their own. It's only ever them, and it's only happened a few times. Is this my brain associating with serial killers, or is that really them visiting?"

"Nope, it's not them. No more serial killers for you, missy!" She laughs. More disappointment settles in me, and I chuckle back with the little positivity I have left. Her responses become shorter with every question. I notice how after each answer, she stays quiet on the other line until I break the silence.

I feel a little humiliated in front of them both, like I'm a pest that won't leave them alone. I ask about my recent health issue that I'm having checked out tomorrow, and it seems to be the only question she wants to answer.

"So... he really doesn't actually care about me, at all? Like, he couldn't give two shits." She tells me that that is correct, and I decide not to ask anymore. I draw a line through the remaining questions I had. "Well, thank you Denise. You were awesome, as always. I, um… yeah, I guess that's it. I'll probably talk to you in a few months."

"Good luck with your appointment tomorrow. I hope you feel better. Bye." The call ends. I sit motionless on my bed. I want to throw away the papers and forget everything that was just said. I gather up and return everything back to its place.

I walk into the bonus room and join Kylie to watch a movie. Kylie sits on the couch with a bowl of popcorn. "How did your reading go, Kris?"

"It was shitty." I grab onto my fuzzy blanket and make myself comfortable on the couch.

"Is everything okay?" she asks.

"No, I'm mad at him. He's an asshole." I rest my head on my fist as I explain what Denise told me. "I don't know how I could have been so stupid." I continue as Mom joins us on the couch. They look at me with consolation, chiming in to justify what may be the case. Their words would have meant a lot to me if it were any other day, but now I just look at him differently. The conversation calms down, and I sit on the couch feeling worthless.

Kylie clears her throat. "I know it's not a good time, but I was just stalking Derek on Facebook and look at the most recent meme he reposted, I thought you'd appreciate it." She flashes me her phone; Jeffrey Dahmer wearing a chef's apron and sunglasses. I just snicker it off. He's already reaching out, trying to manipulate me right back in. "Kris, you have to understand, he had mental issues. Psychopaths can't get close to people, it's not in their DNA."

"He wasn't a psychopath," I respond. "They just labeled him as that to stereotype him."

"Ok, well… this is probably just how he is, it's nothing against you. And maybe this is the closest he can get to a person because he's incapable of making a genuine connection." It makes sense and doesn't make the hurt any better, because that's probably true. The weight of betrayal exhausts me. After dozing off multiple times during the show, I go to bed for the night, TV off.

*

It is the morning of my appointment and I wake up feeling just as low as I did when I went to sleep last night. Knowing I've been unwanted and used sucks me into the same funk that I felt during my breakup in May. Everything feels different. I feel alone.

As I drive down 521 I feel drained. My anxiety is so high that I feel like I'm going to be sick. I guess he really is a master manipulator. I was so dumb to think that he is anything different than what they portrayed him to be. The song volume goes out and slowly fades back in, and my head pounds from his presence. "Leave me alone for a while, Jeff." Emptiness remains in the air for the rest of the car ride.

I walk into the doctor's office and sign in. "What's the point of keeping myself going and healthy? It's not like anyone cares anyway," I think as I find a seat in the waiting room.

The heavy wooden door creaks open and the assistant looks over her clipboard. "Kristen Halder?" I force a smile and follow her back to the room. The assistant asks about my medical history, symptoms, and current medications. I answer each question with more and more vacancy as I feel my face flush. I begin to slur my words and she looks up at me. "Are you okay?"

"Yeah, yeah. Just kinda weak." Suddenly, everything goes black.

My eyes are closed, and my body feels fuzzy. I'm coughing from the back of my throat. There is a horrible, strong smell in my nose, and I open my eyes to three women huddled around me, holding cloths and vials. "Yeah, she's back. There she is."

One of the nurses holds a pack of crackers in front of me. "Kristen? Will you eat some of these?"

I reach for the bottle of water sitting next to my arm. "Did I faint?"

"Yeah, you went out on us for about a minute. Those were smelling salts, sorry about that. We're going to run some tests just to make sure everything's okay, but this happens with some patients when talking about blood and things like that."

"No, no, that's not what bothered me. I think I'm fine." I push myself up.

The nurse puts her hand on my shoulder. "You should sit for another few minutes, we're in no rush."

I sit and gather my strength, baffled that I am so upset over this that I blacked out. After a few minutes pass, I make my way back to the car. I try to put on my music app, but it won't load. I try online music, which won't load either. It's whatever, I just want to get home. I put on the radio for background noise. "Darkhorse" by Katy Perry comes on, specifically the verse that mentions Jeffrey Dahmer. I glare over at the dashboard. Now I see why my music wasn't working: so that I could hear this sign. But I'm not falling for it. I reach for the power button and drive home in silence.

Shuffling through the door of my house, Mom notices my clammy skin and the sweat on my hairline. I explain my upset as I reach down for my boots. "How do you know that Denise was even telling you the truth? It kind of sounds to me like she doesn't want to read you anymore, for whatever reason. I've been thinking it's weird that she's been telling you to not schedule for months at a time," Mom says. I look up from untying my laces, realizing a point that I haven't yet considered.

"I wouldn't look into what she said with too much thought, I'm not convinced that's the way things are." Mom's voice softens. "I don't know. That's just what I've been thinking of her for a while."

I put so much faith and trust into Denise that I overlooked the possibility that she may have ulterior motives lately. But what would her reasoning be? "Yeah, you might be right. What she was explaining didn't even really make sense." My heart drops. "What if this has never been Jeff at all, and she didn't have the heart to tell me so instead she pushed me away?"

"Hmm, I don't know. Why don't you try talking to someone else?" she suggests. I agree that may not be such a bad idea.

At night, I try to ease my mind to sleep. Instead, I'm bombarded with Jeff's face and daisies behind my eyelids as soon as I shut them. I shed a few tears, wanting so badly to believe in his goodness again. Panic sets in that this may not really be him, but I shut it out. It's too much think of that right now.

I wake up with Jeff in mind, my shirt soaked from sweat. I rub my face and check the time: it's 3:34 a.m. I roll over the side of my bed grossed out, making my way over to the shower because I can never stand feeling unclean. In and out in five minutes, I walk back to bed and doze off to sleep. I awake again with Jeff in my head, checking the time, 4:34 a.m., and fall back asleep. What feels like ten minutes have passed and I awake again, 5:34 a.m. I check my phone to distract my mind for a while. I view social media stories, first viewing Courtney's. Someone yells as two girls chug a wine bag in the middle of a small dorm kitchen. I exit out and view Ronni's story. Her and her friends sit in the back of an Uber, drunkenly singing along to "Bohemian Rhapsody." I close my eyes, not sure of what to believe about his genuineness.

I awake to a sunrise through my blinds: 8:34 a.m. I walk to the bathroom, chilled by the cool tiles under my bare feet. Instead of a PewDiePie video, I feel like hearing what's on the radio while I go through my morning routine. A slow alternative song hums through the radio. I know this one. I listen to how the lyrics reflect our current situation as it sings about misunderstandings and not wanting to accept distance between two people. I feel him, right over my shoulder. I try to sing without losing it. I close my eyes to feel him more strongly. As I sense him directly behind me, static interrupts the music and overwhelms my emotions. I pause, realizing that my own intuition is pulling me towards a different truth than what Denise led me to believe.

I reach for my phone and stroll out of the bathroom. A lawnmower sounds from outside of my bedroom window as I search, "best psychic mediums in Charlotte, NC." A page of results pop up. I scroll past the ads for $1 per minute phone readings, and past Martha and Denise.

My eye catches to a picture next to a five-star rating. "Psychic Medium Ed Team." I keep scrolling to investigate, seeing his name mentioned in all of the top lists. I remember coming across Psychic Ed while looking for a medium before. I click on the link, taking me to his homepage. Below the greeting is a picture of him, displaying a warm smile and deep blue eyes.

I scroll further to read testimonies. *"Spot on." "Specific details without me saying a word." "A gentle, kind soul with genuine God given talent." "Mind-blowing."* I get lost in the reviews, reading these experiences the way a child would read a fairytale. As I realize how long I have been scrolling, I'm convinced that he's the real deal. Hesitantly, I book the thirty minute slot for February 1st. There's still the chance that I will walk out of there crushed, finding that I've been wrong this whole time. If it's not Jeff, I hope he's nice about it. If it is Jeff, I hope he doesn't judge us. Then there's the chance that Denise was right about his manipulations. I'll figure this out, but for now I just have to breathe.

*

It's January 28th, my 22nd birthday. I wake up to a lock screen full of notifications and find balloons, breakfast, and flowers upstairs. My boss pops into my head as I eat birthday pancakes. One minute later a Happy Birthday text from her pops up on my phone. Within the same time frame, I suddenly remember my old friend from high school. Minutes after, she tags me in a birthday post online. I realize that these odd moments are a result of my surfacing psychic abilities. Maybe my birthday is empowering them.

I feel complete bliss in my natural state of being, my mind and body still as I tap in for a quick birthday meditation. Everything is black, until my lava lamp screen warms up. An old woman hands me a golden moon and stars pin, placing it in my palm before fading away. It feels like a spiritual medal, holding massive significance.

Static pops through the music, and I hear the boom of muskets shooting in the background. Jeff is dancing with me in a wooden ball room. He is wearing a tux with white fabric tucked up to his neck, and I'm in a red gown with my hair pin-curled. The visual lasts less than two seconds, and I try to gather everything I just saw. Was that a memory of our civil war life that he was trying to remind me of? Was he trying to show me that we actually did share a relationship then? I snap out of meditation to write it all in my log before forgetting what I saw.

I drive to the grocery store to get snacks and chasers for tonight. As I stroll down the chip aisle with a noisy cart, a man walks past me in a letter jacket. He brushes past and I look at the number on the back of his jacket: 34. I smile at my birthday gift, a sign. The self-checkout scanner beeps as I ring up each bag. I glance up at the registers in front of me to a young boy, probably still in high school. His hair is long and blonde around his glasses, his shoulders hunched, and his face expressionless. I try not to stare yet can't help but eye the resemblance. My scanner beeps three times and lights up red. "Help is on the way," the machine voices.

"What? No. I don't need help." I repeatedly touch the screen with my finger.

"Do you need help with something?" I jump and turn around. It's knock off Jeff.

"I don't know why the machine did that, sorry." I laugh. I watch as he punches in a code on the screen.

"There, it should be fine now." He walks away stiffly.

"I'm sorry, thank you!" I reach over for the last item in my basket, a bottle of wine, which needs an ID. My face crinkles as I scan it, summoning him over again. He approaches with a shy smile, reassuring me that it's fine. He scans my license and punches in another code. "Have a good one" He walks away again.

"Thanks, sorry! You too… Sorry." I catch his glance as he walks away, feeling that Jeff influenced the interaction.

*

Music blares through the Bluetooth speaker in the hotel room as we cram in to pregame. I take another birthday cake shot with Kylie when a text pops up on my phone from an old coworker, Chris, saying that he'll meet us out. Butterflies rush up my stomach, knowing that he's going to make it. It's been awhile since that night after my breakup when we all went uptown and I saw him last. I remember sitting in the back of Ben's car, talking with Chris and feeling drawn to him because of how he resembled Jeff. The shape of his nose, the way his upper lip slightly overlaps the bottom, the dimple in his chin. I remember feeling like I was confiding in Jeff that night as I spoke to Chris about my breakup. Jeff was comforting me even then, before I knew of his presence.

I walk into the Roxbury with my group, feeling like I'm home. The disco ball twinkles on the dance floor to "I Wanna Dance with Somebody."

The room is packed so we yell in each other's ears to communicate. TV screens around the walls play 80's workout routines. I try to follow along with Kelci and Logan, reaching side to side in time with the music. Chris buys all of my drinks and I start to forget how many I've had. I excuse myself to the bathroom and run through the graffiti filled door to kneel down in front of the dirty porcelain seat. "Blue Monday" booms from outside of the door, covering the sounds of me puking up four whisky and cokes. Suddenly, the lights over the mirror flicker three times. "Oh thank you, Jeff." I flush and look over to a daisy drawing on the wall. I smile and stagger back out. Chris and I stay glued to each other all night and I enjoy it, feeling like I have Jeff by my side for my birthday.

*

I wake up on February 1st, the day of my reading with Ed. My hands shake as I put the key in the ignition. After typing in the address, I see that his office is exactly thirty-four minutes from my house. Anxiety pumps through me as I think of everything that could go wrong, and I close my eyes to relax. The back of Jeff's head slowly fades in. I keep my gaze on it, hoping that he will be present in about an hour.

As I pull into the parking lot, I find a spot front and center. Killer Queen stops and I cautiously step out of my car and look up at the building. Approaching it, I notice a single plaque on the concrete wall, *Suites 200-213*. I click a photo of the sign and make my way up the staircase. I reach the top step and walk through the glass door, facing a long corridor. I swallow a lump as I walk down the hall. I approach a white door with a sign, "Psychic Medium Ed." I can't find the strength to walk in. I go to the bathroom down the hall to buy some time.

I come back and slowly turn the knob. A bell chimes as I enter. It smells of essential oils, as these offices always do. Ed walks in from the other room to introduce himself, and I can feel his radiant energy as he offers me a smile.

I follow behind him to the reading room. As I walk in I observe the dim and calming atmosphere.

I warn him as I take my seat. "I'm sorry, this is going to be a weird reading."

Ed laughs, assuming it won't be. "Okay! Let me just kind of tune in and see who is around you." Ed closes his eyes and inhales deeply. My heart pounds as I close my eyes too. I focus on my breathing, controlling my nerves in the silence.

Ed breathes in and out as he sketches down on a notepad. "Whew, you got a lot in that head of yours, huh?"

"Mhmm, yeah." I chuckle back.

Ed quietly speaks. "There is a man here. He feels like he could have been a love of yours?"

He begins touching the top right side of his head, mumbling about pressure there. He continues sketching. "There's a little bit of worry, hmm. Some of the family, not being able to talk about him. There's a lot of relationship energy between you two, and I'm getting the sense that you over think it too much. Also, your family doesn't fully accept your bond." My heart flutters as I listen.

"What is the person's name?" Ed holds his pen and looks for my answer.

I fidget with the fabric of my shirt. "Um, Jeff. We do have a bond, but I've never met him when he was alive so I'm trying to make sure he is who he says he is. I believe he is the ghost of somebody well known."

Ed sketches as I explain. "It's very, very, natural to question your spiritual awakening and your own abilities. Especially when you're new, it's easy to be skeptical. I feel like with your situation, you kind of ask, *Why me?* But you need to ask, *Why not me?* It's important that you know that." He channels with an expression of intrigue.

"When it comes to how he passed, I'm getting a lot of pressure in the head, and also in the chest area. There is something in the throat, a tube? I don't know what that is there... It might have been CPR...There's some heaviness, almost liquid or fluid filling the head."

Ed holds his stomach. "I'm feeling nauseous, too. Did he pass from a concussion?"

I for some reason agree with little enthusiasm. It is as if I'm in a daze during this session, unphased by the information I am receiving.

Ed senses my distrust in my situation. "Let me just start by saying, I would not have gotten any of these symptoms if you were not connected to this person. I would not have felt anything or seen any kind of connection." I look up to Ed, afraid to open up.

"Then to pull just from that first name and get the symptoms confirms you have the connection. If there wasn't one, I would have felt nothing. I have had people before you think that they've had celebrities present."

Intrigued, I ask, "So you've met somebody connected to a famous spirit before?"

"In my career, I have only read for one person where that was the case. However, there have been multiple that have come to me believing they were. Besides that one person, I've had to apologize and tell them it's not really them. It can be very, very devastating news to some. I don't know if breaking the news to them is harder for them or me." I sink with discouragement.

"It is not common to be hit in that exact spot on the head and to die during CPR. I would not have known the details of this man's death if he wasn't here."

I nod as I soak that in and brace myself to the answer of my next question. "Is it possible that someone is…catfishing me? Pretending to be him?"

"Um, you can be catfished, I've seen that too, but you're not. In time you would have felt something wasn't right. Being that you've worked with Jeff for this long, you would have realized it was a lie by now. For example, have you been in a relationship?"

"Yes, only one."

"Okay, so, towards the end, it started to get weird. You knew it didn't feel right. When a spirit tries to lie about who they are, it feels the same way. This is not the case with you."

Ed closes his eyes to channel. "He kept people at arm's length, he didn't trust many people. He feels very intelligent. He is very mental and so are you… you're both thinkers."

"He's pretty quiet, a little too shy to talk yet. He shows me a library, studying books." I flash back to when Denise said the same thing, him studying in his life review. She'd see flashes of him holding books, learning, and now he's showing Ed the same.

I lean forward in enthusiasm. "Actually, if this is him he might be hard to reach because-"

Ed butts in. "He's not a very social person. He's not good with people or communicating. He has a curious mind, much like I do. I would really like to pick at him. The odder the person is, the more I like to learn about them." He laughs.

Ed rubs his hands together as he looks down at the floor. "I'd really like to get to know him but he's...socially awkward a little bit."

"He also might not want to show himself because we've scared mediums away before. He's just kinda harder to read I think."

Ed quietly says, "Even you took a long time for him to warm up to. Trust is very hard for him, but he's grown a strong bond with you. Like I said, he keeps people very much at arm's length, because he felt very judged by a lot of people, very judged... He's awkward and odd, you know. But once he finds somebody that he likes it's like, too much! He clings deeply onto people he likes. He's very, very loyal." I add that to my mental list of similarities we share.

Ed continues to draw as he channels. I stare at the pencil lead as he outlines a symbol. He takes in a few deep breaths and shifts in his seat. "I will be honest with you; I don't know if he's crossed over. He feels ghostly. But I feel since he's appeared to you he's been becoming lighter, transitioning..."

My eyes light up as I validate that Ed is correct. "He's deeper in his healing, and I haven't felt him as much. I wasn't even sure if you could pick up on him because I don't know if he's around."

"He is around, almost constantly. Spirits who are in what we call heaven feel very light and fluffy, ghosts are very heavy energy. Someone who passes over feels like silk. Ghosts feel like wool, and he was that dense when you first encountered him but now he feels like linen. As he's going into that linen, he's getting harder to feel, so then you'll really have to quiet the mind and meditate to sense him, because he is transitioning up to a further world. Ghosts have stronger energy, ghosts are like, HEY!" he says as he nudges the entire tissue box towards me. "With him, now that he's more at peace he's more like, hey." Ed says throwing a single tissue.

Ed rubs his hands again, refocusing. "Now I'm really getting him, knowing which plane he's in. I think he's getting a little more comfortable with me, too."

"Oh good, good." I smile.

Ed emphasizes, "He is very, very, very connected with you. Even right now he's clung behind your left side."

I lean towards it, as if to try to feel him standing there. "Really? That's where I always feel him." I speak softly as I admit, "Our last medium said that he was just kind of taking advantage and doesn't really care about me."

Ed lowers his brows in protest. "Oh no, no, no. This is a bond. There is no way he is using you. He's actually almost co-dependent on you. It's almost like he's a shy child. For this session, he's so afraid and timid, standoffish. He's still standing behind you, as if you're his protection. So as long as you're here, he's okay. And if you're okay with this, he's okay with it."

The feeling of love and comfort washes over me. "That is so sweet. That's awesome to know…" I look down at my feet as I embrace the moment. I feel like I can breathe again.

"There is going to be a time where he is going to be so dependent on you, that…" Ed stares me in the eyes, trying to phrase it correctly. "…Saying this actually hurts my heart. It's like fostering a puppy, you don't want him to go. There's going to be a time where it has to happen for the best. He hears you, and he feels you. So like a mother bird, you will have to push him out of the nest."

I grip onto my sleeve, holding back my emotions. I don't know if I can ever let him go, fully. "His heart is very hurt and there was very much of a disconnect with him." He stops and sits back for a moment, processing. "I think this is why he does like you, and why I feel him as a child symbolically. It has a lot to do with a mother energy, he's making me feel as if he was negatively impacted by his. This is why you're in his life as a female healer, working with his heart energy. He needs to heal his heart towards women, a mother energy."

Ed continues sketching, penciling in shapes and patterns before losing his grasp on the visions. "I'm seeing a school, kinda lab thing. I see a microscope."

"Lab thing makes sense. That's not what he was famous for, but that had a lot to do with-" Ed finishes the sentence, "That's what he loved. Biology."

My confidence rebuilds as I think of the scenery from *My Friend Dahmer.*

"I don't know how to articulate this, and he's laughing at me because I don't get it." Ed chuckles. "He's explaining his life like, if he was in a wheelchair, he's showing himself as a racecar driver in a wheelchair. Weird sense of humor. He's what we would call, an um...idiot savant."

I whisper with a smile. "A what?"

"Idiot savant? A super genius but having some form of a mental disorder."

I grin, "Oh, yep. That makes sense." If only Ed knew.

"Society would consider him some form of disabled is what I keep getting. So he's referring to it saying he has a disorder which represents this wheelchair, but he's a *fast* wheelchair." Ed laughs, throwing his hands up in the air in confusion. "He really wants me to tell you that he's tapping his fingers back and forth at the moment, I think." I toss my head back in a chuckle. Ed looks at me, unsure if he just got the information right or wrong.

"I wish he would tell you something to prove who he is."

"These messages are not for the medium to understand, they're for you to understand." The timer dings and cuts off our time. Ed mutes the sound and turns back to me.

"I have no idea who this person is, but me knowing who it is isn't what is important. It's important that *you* know you are correct. Everything relates to him, that means it relates to you. There is no doubt that you have this connection with this person. Absolutely no doubt. I have no idea who he is, but if it all makes sense to you, that is 100% proof. I would bet my career that you have this connection."

Ed stands to hug me. He talks over my shoulder, "Don't doubt yourself. You 100% have this with him."

We release from the hug and walk towards the white door. "Thank you so much, Ed," I say with a smile. "You put my mind at ease, I was so nervous all day, week."

Right before I walk out of the door, I turn for one last word of gratitude. As I do, Ed reminds me, "And just know, he is not using you. He doesn't understand emotional things, but he cares for you. Very deeply. He's very, very loyal to you."

I go back for one more hug. "Thank you so much for that."

The bells chime as I walk out of the door. I walk down the hall, uplifted. Jeff's energy is strongly behind me, and this feels like the beginning again. The excitement, the rush of finding out it's him, the strengthened bond of knowing I've just spoken with him. My boots patter down each concrete step, and I glance at the 213 sign once more before getting into my car. I sit behind the wheel, processing all of this information in my mind. Jeff cares for me deeply and feels that I'm his protector. He hides behind my back, trusting *me*. I crank up Queen on the radio and head home.

Chapter Fourteen: Letting Go and Coming Together

2/8: Since Ed's reading I've felt Jeff every day, haven't logged because I don't need the proof of his presence lately/Seeing all of the numbers constantly in random places, 34, 213, 1213, 521/Song messed up today at 6:34 right when I felt Jeff/Going to bed feeling glad to have him back, watching documentary and the volume turned up on its own, I felt him right by me.

"A twin flame is a soul divided into two, separated at the beginning of consciousness. The masculine and feminine parts of the soul incarnate in two separate lineages and become individuals. Through each individuals' multiple human incarnations, they will go through trials, tribulations, and suffering. But also joy, love, and bliss. With our world consciousness shifting, many twin flames are reuniting at this time. This will complete the fulfillment of returning our world to a state of oneness.

Twin flames can be met in the physical world, but often it's through the ethereal dimension. You will know it is them when you experience their energy, there will be a pull towards each other. You both will feel complete, unconditional love like you've never experienced before. There will be strong telepathy and comfort, an all knowing within yourself, within your heart chakra. Your twin flame will most often feel like the piece of you that has been gone for a very long time. Often there is a huge gap between the two, a distance that creates an obstacle.

The reunion will fulfill a spiritual service for the world, as your origin energies contracted to come together for the greater good. The twin flame reunions are now so frequently taking place to help ease the world into this next age of enlightenment and being. And so we begin."

He walks towards me dressed in white, with a serene smile on his face. I am having a hard time being able to keep focus on him, seeing what human eyes should not. In between two veils pushing the boundaries, my physical face actually twitches. Tears of joy form in both my physical and astral eyes as I watch him walk closer. The imagery switches to a lava lamp visual, a real vision of him and I walking up to each other. I watch as two light bodies join one another. There is an immature humor between us each time we meet, like two kids that can't help but laugh when they are together. It becomes a try-not-to-laugh challenge as we stare into each other's eyes. The voice guides us with a serious tone, while our cheeks hurt from containing our smiles.

We hug, taking advantage of the time that we can. We don't speak as we hold each other, basking in one another's energy. Holding him makes me feel complete, an indescribable feeling that my soul knows only from touching his energy. Time falls away along with the world; my only awareness is my head on his glowing chest, right at home.

"Now, offer something to your twin flame that they need from you at this time." I gather the feeling from this moment, forming it into a bright orb of light over my chest. I send it directly to his heart, filling his body with my love. The voice asks, "Now, what do you need from them?"

"Just this," I reply in his shirt, holding him tightly.

With every inhale, we breathe more life into our connective chord. "Now, give your twin flame a gift. It can be anything. It will serve as a reminder of this eternal devotion to one another." Without thinking, I reach my arm through my chest. As casually as taking something off of a shelf, I hand him my heart. He takes it delicately in his hands and holds it close to his own chest, guarding it like a fragile baby. Once again my imagery turns to a vision as he hands me a single flower, and I see that it's actually a daisy. My physical hand covers my mouth in surprise of what I just saw.

My mind goes on autopilot after the guided meditation ends, and I spectate visuals. Jeff takes on the form of a bird, blinking one eye repeatedly from something being in it. I look closer to the problem: a single thread across the bird's eye. My consciousness speaks for me without my thinking it, and tells him, "You are always loved and protected." Raising my hand, I remove the thread, allowing him to see clearly again. I watch as he flies away; snap out of the meditation; and doodle the images I've just received in a nearby sketchpad.

Minutes pass and I notice that for quite some time, "The Phantom of the Opera" theme song has been looping in my head. It's funny how I've never made the connection between the phantom and Christine, and Jeff and myself, until now.

I secure my ear buds and zip up my jacket as I pace down the sidewalk. "Sing Me to Sleep" by Alan Walker starts out my run on this chilly winter morning. I'm winded as the road inclines towards the highway, the cold wind chapping my cheeks. "California Dreaming" by The Mamas and the Papas plays in my ears. The song makes me think of Jeff as a teen, walking on the wooded road to his home. Just as I realize how strongly I've been feeling him, static pops through my left earbud. The sign serves as a burst of positivity, motivating me to run faster.

I return home, walking through the door short-winded. Unzipping my jacket as I make my way down the hall I hear a familiar tune coming from the living room TV and walk towards the sound. Kylie turns around on the couch. "Kris! Look what's on!" she says with enthusiasm.

I stare at the TV in disbelief. "Phantom of the Opera… I haven't watched this since I was what, ten?" This theme song has been stuck in my head for an entire day, and now the movie has appeared on TV. What are the odds of that? I carry that sign with me, flattered that he compares that beautiful story to our own.

*

Since my birthday, Chris has been asking when we can catch up. I brushed him off for weeks before finally agreeing, and now I regret it. Jeff and I have grown so close. "It's just for tonight, Jeff," I tell him before going out. "Don't forget why I'm interested in him in the first place…"

On my way to Charlotte I glance longingly at the exit to Ed Carlton's, wishing that's where I was heading. I feel guilty for what Jeff has to go through when I just get to have fun. I can feel him at this moment, his sadness and grief. His worry, his guilt, his anger. Tears escape from my eyes as the tight grip on the wheel aids in releasing my emotions.

I arrive and walk up the concrete path to the front door. Ringing the bell, I hold Jeff's energy with me, reminding him of his importance. Chris greets me with a hug and we walk inside. I sip on cabernet as he talks about his current job. As he talks, I can't help but watch the way his expressions move in the same way that Jeff's do. The way that Chris's features resemble so closely to his. An hour passes and this thought lingers in the back of my mind. The person who I want more than anything to do this with, to simply talk and enjoy a drink, is not here and never will be. Setting in is the harsh reality of an emptiness that I'll never be able to fill. It will always have to be with someone else.

My fingers tap against my leg, pressuring me to go home. Chris interrupts my gaze on my hand. "I saw that Snapchat you posted of the orb in your selfie. It's cool, I didn't know you were into paranormal stuff. How'd you get interested in it?" he asks, swirling the wine in his glass.

I'm taken aback by somebody bringing up my interest in the paranormal on their own. I feel open, having had a glass of cabernet already, and lean forward. "Dude, do I have a story for you." I toss back the last sip before telling him about my childhood ghost, leaving out the name. As I finish up the story, a frightened look comes across Chris' expression. "You okay?" I ask, looking at his pale face.

"Yeah, I um…It's just weird, when you were just talking about it I swear I felt like, a breeze or something. It was probably the air kicking on."

I smile. "Maybe."

For a second time, I notice tapping fingers occupying my hand that isn't holding the wine glass. Even though it's still early, I suggest I should start driving home. The porch light blinds me as I step outside. I reach back for a hug and a goodbye.

My phone restarts entirely just as I open my map for directions. It takes its time recovering from the glitch. I fix an empty stare onto the road as I drive home. A phrase in the song skips, validating his presence. I lean my head to the right, wanting to lean on his shoulder, instead leaning on my own.

*

The next morning, I arrive at the office bright and early. Kelci perks up as I walk in. "Ma'am, do you see what is sitting on the counter? And who is Nick?" she says with an impressed smile.

Confused, I walk around to the front desk and look at a fresh bouquet resting next to the sign-in sheet. "No way, are those flowers for me?" I peak at the card on the stem. "Nick? He's been messaging me for a few days on Instagram, but I haven't been replying. Now I feel bad." I pick up the vase to smell the pink blossoms. "This is the sweetest thing ever; I've never been sent flowers before!"

"Are you going to let him take you out?" Kelci asks giddily from behind her computer.

"I think I have to now!" I giggle. "I can't get over how nice this is."

A pit settles in my stomach, knowing that the right thing to do would be to accept a date from Nick since he made this sweet gesture. I haven't been on a date since I was with Cameron, and I didn't want to go on one until Jeff's crossed over. I feel Jeff fading into the background. I don't know what to do.

Reserved, I take the vase in my arms and head out to take greeting baskets around town. Carefully, I set the flowers in the passenger seat and start the car. As it turns on, the dash clock flashes 12:13. I stare at the time, wishing circumstances were different.

After making my rounds I end up at the last stop, a local plasma center. On the way there it crosses my mind that Jeff used to be a phlebotomist, working at a similar place. After giving the manager our office's gift, I sneak off to the bathroom. I walk through a heavy wooden door and under fluorescent lighting towards the stall. I look down at the small, dark blue and white floor tiles. I imagine them covered with my own blood. The tiles trigger sheer panic in me, as though something bad is about to happen. I rush into the stall with my adrenaline pumping and my heart beating out of my chest. What the hell was that? Paranoia? A memory from a past life? But then I remember. Jeff was attacked from behind in the bathroom of the prison. It's like I felt his fear from that moment, incredible. I wonder if the tiles looked the same in that prison bathroom, being that I got the sensation from looking at the floor.

I arrive home, looking at the oven clock at 2:13. Vase in hand, I show Mom and Kylie what showed up at work today. They are over the moon, making a big deal at the thought of me dating again. I put on my fake smile, acting excited for them as I share what a surprise this is. I take the flowers downstairs to my room. As I walk up to my doorway I notice the brightness in my room. I reach for the light switch and notice that the lamp is already turned on. Strange, being that I always make sure it's off when I leave. On my angel altar sits Jeff's yellow roses in the middle of my crystals and candles. I set the Nick vase on the dresser in the far corner of my room, away from Jeff's spot.

My phone buzzes with a reply from Nick. "Of course, I'm glad you liked them! It's no biggie, you deserve them. Are you free next week?" I set the phone down and sit on my bed, holding my hands over my eyes. I'm not ready to let go of this time with Jeff. I don't know if I will ever be, but especially not now. I sob into my hands, mourning what I can't have, grieving the thought of eventually letting him go. My sobs are interrupted by a tone ringing in my ear. It's not as low as I've heard before and not as high as an angel pitch—somewhere right in the middle. The beep stays in my ear for almost thirty seconds before stopping. That frequency had to have been Jeff, transitioned to a higher plane than when I heard from him last.

*

It is the third of March, and as I have the past few days, I wake up to a vacancy. I go back to my notes and notice that I haven't logged anything since the day I got the flowers. I don't feel rage or anger in Jeff's energy because of this, I feel sadness; sadness that it can't always be just the two of us, and sadness to accept that our time is soon coming to an end.

I conclude a healing meditation, watching the end result as white-hot light intensifies in Jeff. Tears fall from his chin as he embraces his importance, pushing his darkness out to replace with light. The scene fades out, and I open my eyes to exit out of the video. Funny, my phone is at thirty-four percent. I feel light and free, catching the denseness of Jeff for a moment.

I close my eyes to channel him. I squeeze my eyes as tightly as my emotions are and repeat in my mind, "I love you. I love you. I love you. I love you. I love y-*I love you too.*" Chills run over my arms in hearing such a clear and articulate response.

I grip onto my pillow and lay with my thoughts. I don't want to let Nick down, but I can't lead him on, either. It would be giving him false hope to give any indication that our date tonight can turn into anything beyond one dinner. The idea of our date fills me with guilt, towards both him and Jeff. What I look forward to is another session with Ed on Wednesday, when Nick will already be fizzled out and we can go back to the way things were.

Jeff's interview plays from my TV as I get ready for my date with Nick. As I plump up my lashes with mascara, I attempt to shake off the headache and fatigue that has been hanging on me for a few hours now. I fasten the back of my earrings and tighten the straps on my heels, stepping back to look at myself in the mirror. The doorbell rings and I glance up at Jeff once more before shutting off the TV. With a click of the remote, I head upstairs. I inspect myself in the hallway mirror before opening the door. On the other side of the door stands a slim guy with long brown hair and dark eyes. Nick leans forward. "Should I come in and meet everyone?" he asks shyly. I appreciate that he would like to but hesitate before saying yes.

Together, we walk down the arched corridor of my front hallway and into the kitchen. I peak my head through Mom's door. "Help. He wants to meet you." Mom jumps up and I walk back to him, making small talk before she steps out.

"Hello ma'am, my name is Nick," he says, extending his hand to Mom's.

"Hi, it's nice to finally meet you. Those flowers you sent Kristen were beautiful!" She smiles warmly. Kylie walks up and introduces herself, and I can tell she likes him for me. The three of them seem to click well. If it were at any other point in my life, I would be thrilled at the first impression.

I give Mom and Kylie hugs before heading out to make it to our reservation on time. He opens the passenger door and waves me in. As I lower into the seat, I get a sinking feeling. Nick turns on the music, pulling me back into the present moment. The very first song taunts me, and I recognize the tune as soon as it begins: "Somebody to Love" by Queen. The rest of the car ride is a mix of sweet and awkward between Nick and me. My impression is that he is soft spoken and very kind. He seems to have a unique and creative energy. I notice that his face resembles Brad's, which could work in my favor: an excuse not to be into him.

The candle flame wavers between our glasses of water and illuminates the dimly lit booth. Italian music plays softly and fills in the moments when we're not talking. Nick apologizes for yawning. "This is weird, it's like, since I picked you up and I just got so sleepy. I'm never like this, I'm so sorry." He laughs as he yawns again. I can feel Jeff hanging on Nick's energy, sizing him up. I smirk to myself.

"I'm always tired, it probably just rubbed off on you," I reply. I listen to him talk about his background as I slurp my spaghetti, not caring how much sauce I get on my face; the more unattractive, the better. As we exchange stories, I'm surprised to find that I'm actually having a nice time. As it gets later, we head out. He makes sure to hold every door that I walk through.

I dread the anticipated kiss as we approach my driveway. I turn to him with an uptight posture. I thank him for the amazing dinner and rush for the door handle. I notice he reaches for his as well. Shit. We walk to the front door and he reaches in for a hug. "Have a good night, Kristen. I had a great time with you." He releases his arms and walks back to his car, no attempt at a kiss. I stand on the porch and give him a wave goodbye before walking inside.

My heels click down my hallway, relieved that it didn't happen. Mom and

Kylie sit waiting for me in the kitchen, ready to hear all about it. "Kris! He's so cute!"

I smile in agreement and share how well the evening went, but I still feel like I'm just not there yet. "The only thing is his features kind of remind me of Brad. I don't know if I can get past that." I laugh.

Mom tilts her head to the side in contemplation. "Yeah, I can see that." She chuckles.

Kylie smiles. "I really like him for you, Kris. He seemed so sweet! Do you think you guys will go on another date soon?"

"Maybe, he said he would like to again. I actually really liked him." I set down my jacket with discontent towards what I just caught myself saying.

I unhook my shoe straps and mumble over my shoulder, "I'm just going to change into my bum clothes, and I'll meet you guys in the bonus room." I walk down to the basement. As soon as I get far enough from them, I break. I shut the bedroom door behind me to release a single tear, allowing it to roll freely down my cheek. Walking past my altar, my heart skips a beat as I notice something odd with Jeff's roses. A single yellow rose lies unattached next to the vase, the rest of the flowers stand intact. I look closer and find the stem that the flower fell from. It looks like it had been snipped clean off with a pair of scissors. The cut flower lays helpless on the wooden stand as I stand in amazement. It is as if Jeff snipped the flower as a symbol for his pain.

I rush to the quietness of my closet and fall to the carpeted floor. Sitting up against the wall I sob into my hands, careful not to let anyone hear me grieve. My telling Mom and Kylie that I actually like him loops over and over in my mind. This night feels like the beginning of the end of something I never wanted to say goodbye to. I feel him here, standing by my side as I'm having a moment. I apologize to him. I remind him of his importance to me, and how I so desperately wish things were different. I tell him how sorry I am for taking the first step in possibly moving on. Before getting back up, I quickly check the true crime community feed. I scroll past videos of Bundy, Klebold and Harris, and Kemper, looking for Jeff content. I scroll to one last post before exiting out; a gif of Freddie Mercury singing "Somebody to Love," the same song I'd heard in the car hours earlier. I let the wave of grief pass and compose myself to rejoin Mom and Kylie.

*

My heartbeat gets more intense as I approach Psychic Medium Ed's door. The familiar bells chime as I walk in more comfortable and confident than I was the first time. Ed graces me with his mystical presence; the lightness in his energy helps me to lower my guard as I follow him to the reading room.

Ed rubs his hands together, concentrating on the realm beyond as he centers his breathing. I sit upright in my seat, attempting to relax as Ed feels spirits' presence in the room. He closes his eyes and sketches on the notepad, and I watch as he illustrates a square with inner boxes. "Did you lose your love? Or is it a love 'friend' because it keeps going back and forth?"

I smile, relieved that he showed up. "I can't say I really I *lost* him, I didn't know him while he was alive. It's interesting he came across that way to you." My stomach flutters before asking, "Is it on his side, the love part, romantic?"

"Mhmm, yeah, of course," he replies with certainty. "It feels like the vibes bounce back and forth from romantic to best friend, you both aren't really sure of where the relationship stands."

"I've always felt that, but it's hard to know because he was-" I look at Ed as he sits flamboyantly across from me, and carefully choose my words. "He wasn't... into women."

Ed claps his hands together with enthusiasm. "Oh my gosh, I remember! What was the name?"

I smile, "Jeff!"

"Famous Jeff, that's right! I remember going home that night going 'Gosh, who are you?' He sort of just hung out with me; he wouldn't identify himself. I don't think he wants me to know him, at least not yet." Ed clasps his palms together and focuses on the floor. "Back to the romantic aspect between you two, the soul knows no gender. Although he was gay in life, you two obviously have a soul tie that attracts you to one another." Just like last time, I feel dazed as he reads our energies.

"It's unique, the way your abilities have surfaced. It feels like he manifested them to you; Jeff woke you up." Ed mumbles as he shades in a symbol. He pauses, "He's getting a little overpowering. I would like to bring the reading focus to *you,* but I feel like he's used to being the center of your attention. He was offended when I even mentioned not focusing on him for a minute like, *excuse you, it's always about me.*" Ed and I chuckle with amusement at the matter. A smile tugs at my lips even after our laughter goes silent.

Ed shifts his focus around the notepad. "He's telling me you work at a sort of doctor's office?" I brightly nod my head in confirmation. "He's at a point where he is going to make sure he gets what he wants in life. Jeff wanted that job for you because he knew it would be good for you, so he made it happen."

My eyes widen. "That is amazing. The practice has always reminded me of his interests. Come to think of it, I got the call for an interview while watching his movie. Also, the name of the clinic is also the maiden name of his grandmother, the only family member he really loved. There's always a connection in his signs, always." I fidget with the daisy charm of my necklace as I ponder the correlations.

"Yeah, he wanted that for you. You're taking care of him so he's making sure you're taken care of. He needs you to know that." That statement warms my soul. I rest back in my seat, thinking about how someone so feared, so violent, can have such a soft spot. Ed continues scribbling and concentrating, then stops abruptly. "You really need to write the book." I tilt my head in doubt and let out a little chuckle. I think to myself how about a month ago I began writing about our journey, just to have for myself and maybe my future kids. Never in a million years would I get it officially published for the world to see. I would look delusional, and it would embarrass my family. Our journey will always remain a magnificent secret.

"No, he wants you to publish it."

"Oh god, really? I just don't know how people would take it."

"Yes. Enjoy the journey of writing and retelling, but he's like, *you're going to publish this, it has a bigger meaning than only re-living our memories.* Whether you realize it or not, he's going to push you to publish it. It would be a very interesting story, and I feel it will serve a purpose of awakening for others.

When he's crossed over and you're done with your book, please let me know and I will send it to my publisher. He's telling me you won't have a problem with getting it out there," Ed says, sipping from his giant tea mug.

"Oh wow, thank you so much," I say, brushing it off, knowing I'll never take the time to be an author. I take another sip of my water as Ed re-centers himself.

"You are very good with the ghostly plane, helping them cross over. You can feel ghosts really easily. Lighter frequencies are harder for you, while I can feel passed loved ones really easily. You're the opposite of me. You're meant to help not only him, but others trying to transition."

I ponder the faces of the other killers that I have seen. "Somebody else came through, but it's… I don't know, maybe I won't bring that up."

Ed butts in, "You would be very, very, VERY good with paranormal activity. Haunted houses, restless places, and helping the spirits cross over to peace. Jeff was not settled, like, *I'm not going until I am ready to*. Now, you're helping him, but I don't think he would have felt it was okay if you didn't tell him."

I take the opportunity to ask, "Is he done with life review?"

Ed sighs as he closes his eyes, "Not quite, he's still reviewing… but he's getting close to being done." He taps his chin. "He keeps reminding me of Freddie Mercury."

"No way!" I exclaim, burying my face in my hands. That simple mention, that validation, overwhelms me and robs me of my words. Never have I brought up "Bohemian Rhapsody" in front of Ed; I have been waiting for Jeff to tell him.

Ed hands over the tissue box as I attempt to explain the significance of Queen. He giggles. "I keep trying to give messages and he keeps showing me Freddie so I thought I should say something."

I shake my head in disbelief as I wipe my tears. "I'm sorry, I can't believe that affected me so much." I laugh.

"No, it's wonderful. It validates you, and it shows you that you should not question this because it is a very, very strong connection. It is funny, every time I ask him to unmask, he tries to tell me he's Freddie Mercury. He does it to kid with me, trying to make light of all this." Ed chuckles.

Ed takes the pencil in his hand as I dab my running mascara with a tissue. "You had a friend that wasn't the best influence for you… Jeff didn't like that. He's giving me the impression as if he scared her out of your life, knowing you wouldn't have cut her out on your own." My jaw drops as I go back to the moment in 2014. Astounded, I gather my words and explain the "demon" that Beverly caught watching me sleep.

"This is wild. I was always so afraid of that demon… I've wondered if that was him." Ed puts his pencil down. "Jeff is honestly… he's a little possessive over you. But he has genuinely always had your best interest at heart. I don't know his talent or profession, but I feel it was not accepted or misunderstood in a lot of ways? No matter how he was in life, I know that Jeff would never hurt you. The perfect display of his care for you; getting your bad news boyfriend to break up with you, getting you that job you love, distancing bad friends from you, these are all proof to you that he is and has been taking care of you, even if you weren't aware."

"Well, I just went on my first date the other day, and I don't really feel him now. Did I hurt his feelings?" I sit upright in the seat with angst.

Ed breathes in, looking in the space beside me. "He's trying to understand the relationship, his part in it, and how it affects the bond between him and you. This is where he feels ghostly, because when you pass over you don't have that… possession kinda thing. The whole, 'she's mine' jealousy, but he still does."

I respond, nodding slowly as I comprehend. My heart hurts as Ed taps in. Ed looks at me intently. "He's still very, very strongly around you. I very much encourage you to keep dating. You should not stop your own personal life; he will get used to this. That's why he's kind of like a child because you have to explain these things to him. So talk to him. Remind him of the special connection you both will always share no matter who you meet." Knowing I will still pick this time with him over anybody else, I nod my head in agreement.

Ed pauses, then continues. "At some point in his life he stopped his own social development, cutting himself off from everyone. He really is not used to allowing people into his life, but he's now allowed you." I soak in the feeling of

Jeff standing behind me and Ed's pencil scratches across the notepad.

All of a sudden, he jumps up, "Have you ever worked with a pendulum?" Before I can say no, Ed is out of the room. I hear shuffling from outside of the door as he scrambles to look for something. With a smile he comes back in holding a silver chain. Ed places it in my palm for me to see. I admire the pendulum, decorated with beads that represent the seven colors of the chakras. A clear, pointed crystal weighs one end of the pendulum, with an angel charm on the other end, where it is supposed to be held.

His eyes light up as he explains how to use it. I keep my hand perfectly still, watching for movement as I hold the pendulum over my palm. It begins to shake and wiggle, eventually forming a small circular motion. I hold my gaze on it as the circle grows wider. "That's so cool…"

"This is a good way of really being able to talk to him and receive valid answers. So, clear your mind," Ed instructs me as I close my eyes. I take three breaths in and out until I feel relaxed. The pendulum stays still, dangling over my palm. "Ask it, Jeff, are you here?"

I close my eyes to concentrate and feel the slightest tug between my fingertips. I squint one eye open to see if it really is moving and see it swinging in a circle for yes. "Look at that!" I exclaim.

"Now ask him, did I upset you when I went on a date?" He looks at me, hoping that it will say no. I still the chain and close my eyes to send Jeff the energy of the question. I feel it shift, and open my eyes to a swinging circle, *yes*.

"Yes. That makes me wanna cry."

Ed chuckles at my sad puppy dog face. "Well, this is my gift for you and Jeff, now you can ask him anything you'd like."

"No way… Thank you so much, Ed," I say, inspecting the beads on the pendulum.

"Going back to you, you need to date. It's good for you and he knows you need that. If you go on a date, you know, just talk to him about it because he is a big part of who you are. Let him know that it is not an act of you replacing him in any way, because he can be sensitive to that." Ed pauses and looks up at me. "You're his. I don't know how else to put that." Wonderstruck at his adoration for me, I cover my mouth with my hands.

"I think it's very sweet and romantic, too," Ed says. "Unfortunately, you have to have a life, you're still young and he has to understand this."

Ed sits puzzled as he interprets a message. "I can't say for sure, but you're either soulmates or twin flames. I just wonder why you wouldn't have met in this life… I take that back. You had to learn things without him so you could meet another soul, and he had things he had to learn without you, too. You two needed to break the co-dependency on one another, to be separated so that you'll be on the same level of knowledge for your next life together." He says it so casually, but that phrase changes everything for me.

"So, we're going to have our other lifetimes… together?"

"Absolutely, you've already had *many* lives with him which is why you are so attached. As luxurious as you would think a celebrity life would be, his Jeff life seemed very difficult. He's showing me that because of how his life went, it was something he didn't want you to have to deal with. He was protecting you by making you stay back instead of coming to Earth when it was his time." I sit speechless. All that I can manage out of my mouth is a few short words, doing the opposite justice of what my emotions hold. As a kid I would comment on how I didn't like my own time or generation. It all clicks now with how much I've always loved the 80's, a longing from my soul to be where it was meant to. How different my life would have been if I was by his side back then…

Ed eagerly picks up his pencil, "There is someone else in the background. Earlier, you mentioned seeing someone else in a meditation and I feel like this is him. Tell me this person's name, just the first, though."

I hesitate. "Ted," I say. Ed mumbles, looking for a connection associated with a "Ted."

Ed opens his eyes to share his visions. "That's him. Immediately, there was some heaviness in the head, but it's split, almost like there's two different personalities. Tingling all over my body… It feels almost like electricity, but he might be indicating he had a problem with his nerves…He feels very likeable."

I throw my hands in my lap, completely blown away. I sit across from Ed in astonishment, not saying a word about who the Ted is that he is communicating with. "I feel like Jeff is keeping everyone in line and you have to really focus to work with other spirits because he cuts them off in a sense. I feel like Ted's here because it's something to do with your gift, your soul's purpose."

Ed's eyes slightly squint, "Does he have blue eyes?"

I gasp, "Yes! Do you see what he looks like?"

Ed's eyes remain shut as he rubs his hands together in concentration, "He's kinda handsome. He likes women, too much. He's extremely smart, was he a famous lawyer? He's showing me... law books?"

I laugh, "He studied to become a lawyer, but he was not famous for that!" Under my breath I mention how wild this all is.

"I think that you should first focus on helping Jeff, the lawyer guy is going to have to be patient. Don't do research on Ted, meditate with him and see how much information you can pick up on your own, and then look it up and see if you were right. Like Jeff, he's going to enhance your own abilities. All of that affirmation will wipe away your doubt." I've tried watching Ted's documentaries and lose interest every time only minutes in. Maybe the purpose of me getting distracted is so that I can validate this presence myself, or maybe it is Jeff's influence.

Just before I can ask more questions of Ted's presence, the timer chimes gently and indicates that the hour is up. Ed continues, "Ghost Counselor, that's what you should name your book!" He laughs. "But seriously, I feel that book is a big part of your purpose. Don't write it with judgment in mind, write it for you." I find it interesting that he keeps bringing up this book I'm supposed to write; maybe I should consider it.

My expression feels shut off from the intensity of my emotions. I sling the leather strap of my purse over my shoulder and come back from my "reading daze."

"You are incredible. Thank you for everything, and for our pendulum!" I reach for a hug.

"Of course, Kristen. Keep in mind everything I told you, embrace your connections and believe in them. You're doing so well." I hold the pendulum tightly in my hand, careful not to drop it on the way to my car. I can't stop thinking about everything that was revealed. This day feels unreal, like a lucid dream.

Evening falls and I relax into my bed. A text from Ed Carlton lights up my phone screen. Surprised, I open it to read, "I hope I am not bothering you this late. Ted showed his face and I recognized it; he was very open about himself. Was Ted... Ted Bundy? So is Jeff... Jeffrey Dahmer?"

My heart races as I respond. I can't help but smile, thrilled at the validation.

"I think it is wonderful what you are doing! Once I figured it out, Jeffrey was more open because I didn't think it was a big deal...he was worried about me judging him. But he is definitely okay with me knowing now, FYI. I think everyone needs a little guidance and he is lucky he has you. It's interesting because from what I thought I knew about his story I would've assumed he would be emotionless, but Jeff is actually very kind and has a lot of emotions. Thank you for trusting in me...you are doing a wonderful thing." I feel uplifted and encouraged by Ed.

I press play on *Dahmer*, staying awake to watch him from this new perspective. Jeff stands with his Polaroid in front of the TV, smiling as he flashes a picture of the guy on the couch.

I've never noticed what movie was on behind him. Curiously, I glance at the corner of my TV screen to the old black and white film, the scene of a man wearing the *Phantom of the Opera* mask. I rewind it over and over just to convince my brain that that is indeed what I saw. I see the same mask with every viewing; an Easter egg of our connection in his movie for me to find years later.

CHAPTER FIFTEEN:
LILY

I kneel on the carpet in front of my angel altar as the pendulum dangles in front of my face. "Is your favorite ice cream flavor actually vanilla?" The chain shakes before rotating in a circle for yes. "Ew." I close my eyes to refresh the energy. "…Do you like Denise?" The pendulum swings back and forth for no and makes me chuckle. "For healing today, would you like me to do a meditation with imagery of moving on from the past?" The crystal struggles before swinging side to side. "Would you like me to send you love energy today?" The crystal's direction shifts to a small circle.

Density falls over the right part of my back, creating a crowded room. "Ted, are you here?" The pendulum fights direction, ending up swinging back and forth for no. Well, Jeff can answer my questions about him. "Has Ted been around me my whole life like you have?" The pointed crystal answers no. "Can I help Ted the same way that I help you?" The pendulum hesitates before answering yes. All of my other questions about Ted remain unanswered as the pendulum stays still after every question.

"Jeff, will it be within this year that you finish life review?" The pendulum answers yes. Testing the accuracy, I ask, "Will it be two years before you finish life review?" The chain wavers and swings from side to side. Impressed, I ask,

"Will you finish your life review sooner than later?" Yes. "Will it be within 6 months?" Yes. "Will it be within 3 months?" Yes. "Will it be in 2 years?" No. I smile in amazement, "Will you finish life review this month?" The chain struggles and trembles, making its way to form a circle.

I beam with eagerness at the idea of our time coming close. "So, you will finish life review by the end of this month?" Circle. I look at the date, March 8th, and start narrowing down the three weeks that are left. According to his answers he should finish within about two weeks, around the 20th of this month. "Are you nervous about crossing over?" The chain shakes and swings from side to side for no. "Are you excited about crossing over?" The pendulum swings in a big circle for yes. My headache becomes unbearable and I set the pendulum down, laying it over the neck of my Archangel Michael statue.

I cross my left leg over my right and lay my hands delicately on each knee. I close my eyes, centering myself with controlled breaths. Here it is, my first time healing Ted Bundy, and I better make it a good one. A video with love frequency bounces through my ear, and I gather up the feeling that I get when I think about Jeff. The warmness builds in my heart, filling until I am ready to send it out. I imagine Ted before me, wearing his black turtleneck and brown slacks.

The hot pink column of energy beams out of my chest, on its way to him. I keep a laser focus, my intent and thoughts purely on Ted. He stands in a deep black void. He knows he needs the help but is still ignorant to the magnitude of what he has done. It is unlike when I found Jeff: weak, down on himself, and desperate. Ted stands as the light draws closer, ready for it to fill his soul. The flow of the light stops right before him. Maybe that's just my mind. I push harder to reach Ted but feel resistance, a block. A visual of aviators disrupts my concentration, and I understand what is going on. I send the love to Jeff first. Jeff accepts it, then steps aside..

I restart with gathering my light and envelop Ted in the energy. With eyes closed, he tilts his head towards the sky. Black smoke releases from the top of his head; the energy of obsession and dark thoughts. I feel an immense lift, like cutting a rope that was supporting a sack of bricks. The feeling brings me back to last summer, that first time that I sent love to Jeff. Feeling satisfied, I close out the scene.

I open my eyes to the bouquet of roses and the single fallen one that I never threw out. I notice browning edges of each yellow petal and the murky water. If Jeff is going to cross over soon, I want to make sure I have a nice arrangement for the day. Without hesitation, I slip into a hoodie and sneakers and head to the grocery store.

I stand over the wooden crates and plastic buckets, looking over my options. There are bouquets vibrant with oranges, blues, and purples, but they have to be yellow. I slouch as I realize there are no daisies, and only one bunch of yellow flowers: lilies. I figure the lilies might be a nice change, and being my only yellow option, I go home with them.

*

I breathe deeply as I jog along my neighborhood sidewalk. My favorite scent of fresh cut grass and the light feeling of spring air fills my senses as I listen to an Alan Walker station. A song of his that I haven't heard begins: "I Don't Wanna Go". A chill, other-worldly beat echoes through my headphones, the electronic rhythm setting the pace of the song. The lyrics tell of two people being in two different worlds; one person has to leave but they don't want to "just yet."

I envision teenage Jeff as I listen to this song, as I have the past few days, feeling connected to that version of him. I wonder if he's saved the toughest part of his review for last, facing the time with Steven Hicks. Hearing this song's message makes me sad. It hasn't fully hit me that this journey is almost over. But as much as I'd love to hang onto this forever, or even just a little longer, this was always the goal.

-3/11 Music skipped twice today on the way to store/Saw JLD license plate, then 311 license plate. With Saint Patrick's day coming up Sunday, Kylie's found a Celtic festival going on at a historic plantation only thirty minutes from us. Time period costumes are encouraged, so, like two children, we excitedly go to the costume shop together. It smells of stale air and old fabric and a man with a beard welcomes us in. From behind the desk he explains that each row is a different theme or century and tells us to let him know if we need help with anything before going back to his phone.

I brush my hand against velvet gowns, cotton pants, and silky dresses as we search for 1800's attire. My eye catches a golden yellow ball gown with white lace flowing from the sleeves. I throw it over my arm to try on in the fitting room. The next dress I pull is a simple design, dull grey, with a line of buttons running down the middle. It looks to be inspired from the civil war era. Without hesitating, I throw it over my shoulder.

With our arms full of dresses, we make our way to the fitting rooms in the back corner of the store. In the middle of the two dressing rooms hangs a *Phantom of the Opera* poster with a mannequin modeling the phantom's jacket underneath it. I point it out, taking a picture of it before going in the room. Trying on the ball gowns inspires a childlike excitement but trying on that civil war dress with it brings in a faint sense of nostalgia. I wish I could remember that life with Jeff. I wonder which side he fought for. One thing I know is that we shared a much closer connection than what Denise had let on.

*

In the darkness of my room, the TV screen flashes on my face. In a home video, Jeff sits in a dim living room with his left foot over his right knee, flipping through a magazine and talking to Lionel. He laughs in response to Lionel's compliment of his spotless apartment. My eyes slowly close as I lay on my side. Suddenly, I feel the pressure of a hand in mine, just for a moment. I open my eyes wide to look down at my hand. Of course, I see nothing, but my palm draped over the cotton sheets. I wish I could experience these touches for longer than three seconds. My hand rests where his was, and I close my eyes.

Deep in my headspace, I work on pulling voices from the other realm. I squint my eyes with concentration, my nose crinkled as I listen for an outer voice. I pick up on words and phrases that make no sense, just like stumbling into a conversation without being filled in on its context. "Bird… Her mom… Can't get…. Grey color…"

Telepathically I say to the voices, "Jeff? Can I talk to Jeff?" The memory of the conversation is hazy, like experiencing a dream only to forget it upon waking. I'm in conversation with Jeff. I experience the strange occurrence of my subconscious speaking for me without my thinking the words. It tells him, "You, just like anybody else, deserve whatever it is you want."

Loud and vividly his voice responds, "I want my wife."

Surprised and intrigued at that phrase, I stay tapped in to ask him why he said that. After a few moments, I return to my own consciousness and my mind blanks immediately. I sit up in desperation, trying to remember what just happened. I can't recall one thing that he told me or what I even said to him. I would give anything to remember that talk.

I head out the front door, locking it behind me. I step out under the spring sun and press play once again on the Alan Walker station. I head towards the stop sign, jogging once I hit the corner. The energy of adolescent Jeff is strongly with me as I envision him to the music. A sense of relief sets in as I realize a bittersweet reality. Although this time is coming to a close, there will soon be peace for that broken boy.

I look down to the title of a new song, "Lily." by the best, Alan Walker. The beat begins simply and the words bounce to a sing-songy tune. I can tell there is going to be an amazing beat drop. I take note of the words as they tell the story of a child lost in the woods. A creature comes from the void, telling the child to follow it over the mountains and valleys. As I hear these lines, I imagine the scenery from the unconditional love meditation. The creature will guide the child out of the dark and give her anything she wants, if she only accompanies him. The electronic bass booms through my earbuds as I run past the sprinklers. I save the song to my playlist and rewind to listen again, loving it even more the second time.

Noticing the time, I head back to the house to get ready for the Celtic festival. Bagpipes echo through the plantation as we walk up to get our wristbands. I shield my eyes from the sun and look up at the historic white home surrounded by acres of lush, green grass. We step into the gift shop for registration. A wooden stand in the middle of the store is filled with bugle horns, toy muskets, and drums. Next to it is a display of mini confederate flags and kepi hats. "Kye, this is all Civil War stuff!" I exclaim as I pick up a mini cannon. I smile at his gentle reminder that we had a past in this era, apparently a significant one. A man in highland dress offers us a free shot of whisky for our walk around the grounds. We happily accept. I toss it back as we walk under an archway, choking on the after-burn.

Over the dirt trail we see a small village; a chicken coop next to livestock, an old church, and wooden cabins. It feels like I've been caught in a time warp. I notice a campground, complete with white tents and horses tied to the wooden fence. I eagerly make my way over to a firepit for a closer look. As I approach, I see that there are men dressed in confederate uniforms, standing in a circle by the tents to converse; I study their grey felt uniforms. If Jeff was a soldier back then, this is what his life probably looked like. I stay for a while to appreciate the scenery.

We walk up the steps of a cabin and through the wooden threshold. Inside is an older woman and a little girl, demonstrating how to make an apple pie from scratch with the freshly picked fruit. I watch in fascination and lose track of time. I find that in each of these places always end in Kylie asking, "Kris, are you ready to go yet?" With a beer in hand and a buzz coming on, I get the feeling of longing as we walk back out to the grounds.

Over the fiddles and bagpipes, I hear the boom of a cannon. I grab Kylie's sleeve, urging her to follow the direction of the sound with me. In a clearing, a group of soldiers huddle around a cannon and fire it into a hay target. I plug my ears, grinning as I watch. "Oh, sorry for stepping on you!" I say to the person behind me. I turn around to an empty space. I turn back around with warmth in my chest, thrilled that Jeff's presence is here to share this with me.

Before leaving, we go to one last cabin that we seemed to miss the first time around. I take a sip of my beer as I walk up the stone steps. A couple makes their way out as we enter, leaving us by ourselves, able to enjoy this one final visit without any disruption. The wooden planks creak as we step onto them; the house smells of must from standing for over a hundred years. The inside of the cabin is almost empty, housing a stone fireplace with a wooden bench in front of it. I take a seat and something about it feels like home to me. It is evocative, as if I miss being here.

My throat tightens as I feel like I'm mourning. I don't want to leave and take the longest time possible to finish my beer. Twenty minutes pass as I look into the crackling fire. "Are you ready, Kris?" Kylie asks. With hesitation, I get up. Reconnecting with that distant part of myself was a true gift, and the last thing I expected on Saint Patrick's Day.

*

-3/18 A lot of visions of him reading and of daisies while meditating the past few days, not many obvious signs but I feel very connected and close to him/Today workout video stopped by itself at 2:13.

I'm in the middle of third eye meditation. I lean forward as I keep my eyes shut, attempting to see the images more clearly. The visuals are beginning to gain momentum, coming in faster and more vividly with each passing day. Grey light dances into a tree and shifts into a Victorian house, then fades. A crisp black and white vision of a forest surrounds a clearing in a meadow, and the scene disappears as soon as I move my eyes. Music hums in my ears as I wait for the next image to form, enjoying this weightless state of mind.

Jeff slowly places his footing on the cloud's surface. A path illuminates with his every step. I look about fifty yards ahead for where the glowing steppingstones end and notice a metal railing in the distance. I follow behind Jeff as he approaches the structure. It's massive, with double gold metal doors, surrounded by clouds in the purest shade of white. I realize we are looking at the golden gates. Its energy is completely freeing, filling me with joy just by looking at it.

I stay submerged in the meditation as I feel a real squeeze on my physical hand, a nervous, "This is it" from Jeff. "Is it time, Jeff? Go ahead!" I urge, but he doesn't go forward. He looks at the entrance as if it would be a sin for him to walk through. Jeff steps away, taking me out of the dream-state. I strain my eyes to look past the void and go back into the visual, but I can't. I don't think it happened yet. I don't feel any different, and neither does he. That was a preview of what is soon to come, a sign that he is close.

My mind feels burnt out, urging me to call it a day. I extinguish my candles, click on the lamp, and drape a large t-shirt over my dark hair. With ease I tuck myself under the fuzzy blankets of my bed and turn on the TV. I guide the remote control over to YouTube and see a "recommended for you" video. Intrigued, I press select and read its description; a rendition of Killer Queen, dubbed to sound like it is being performed acapella in an empty cathedral. This was uploaded months ago, and of all times, I am shown this on the week of Jeff's crossing.

The image that fills my screen is an elegant ceiling, white with gold trim. There are details everywhere I look and angels built into the molding. The ceiling is painted with a mural of Heaven with over twenty angels interacting in light pink clouds over a baby blue sky. Freddie's voice rings out, echoing through my room like a private concert celebrating Jeff's anticipated arrival. I close my eyes as I listen to Freddie's heavenly voice. I feel moved by such an ethereal version of our song. Chills creep over my body as I imagine this being what Jeff will experience when he arrives. After the video ends, I select the next one on the playlist.

It opens to the aisle of a cathedral, lit orange from the candelabras around the space. Flower arrangements and candles adorn the walkway. I wait in the silence to hear what acapella Queen song will be next. The song surprises me, turning out to be "Lovely" by Billie Eilish, the song that I imagine Jeff entering the light to. This is unreal; two songs from completely different genres, but both from our journey, and both delivering such a heavenly sound. I feel like it's a reward for our hard work, allowing us to reminisce on our journey before it comes to an end.

I am in complete bliss, blasting heavenly versions of "Bohemian Rhapsody," "Don't Stop Me Now," and "We are the Champions." I look at the time. It's 2 a.m., and I have to be up for work in six hours. I shut off the TV so that I can practice talking to the other side but end up falling asleep instead.

*

My tires bounce over the pothole filled roads as I drive around for work. "Welcome to Historic Downtown Chester" greets the small town. At a red light I look to my back seat to see how many stops I have left; all that is left is one lonely fruit basket. Having already been to every place in town, I decide to call it a day and keep the last one for myself. I gaze out of the window to appreciate the original architecture and memorial statues as I pass by.

I take the back way out of Chester, over the railroad tracks and through a side street. I slow down as a building catches my eye: a three-story, all-white concrete building with barred windows. In rusted letters, the center of the building reads, "Chester County Jail 1814." "No way, how cool." I say, looking at the museum's signpost on the lawn.

The wooden door creaks as I step onto the original hardwood flooring, the smell of musty artifacts filling the room. The room is silent as I stand with the gift, waiting for an employee to hand it to. My eyes can't help but wander along the wooden display cases. I scan over damaged ammunition pellets, rifles, and arrow heads, when I hear a woman's voice greet me. I turn around with a smile to introduce myself. I clear my throat before giving my spiel and hand her the basket. Her eyes crinkle as she smiles. "Yes, I remember you from our car show last June!" It hits me that their event was one of the first times I heard "Bohemian Rhapsody," before I noticed it following me.

"I'm sorry I'm here right now, I just noticed you close at 3 on Thursdays so I'll let you lock up! This looks amazing in here, by the way. This time period fascinates me."

"It fascinates me too; I can't get enough of it." She reaches for a dusty brown book and slides her spectacles over her nose. "Right before you came in, I was looking over this log that an older gentleman just gave to me. Generations ago, his family owned a general store and this log is how they would keep record of the purchases. See, it says their name, what they bought, and for how much." A landline rings from the other room and interrupts her explanation. "Excuse me, feel free to keep looking if you'd like!"

I thank her with a smile and glance down to the faded pages. *Emily Smith, 1 pound of sugar, total of 0.08 cents on March 23, 1859. Hunter Lincoln, 2 pounds of coffee, total of 0.18 on May 26, 1859. Teddy Smith, 2 pounds of rice, 2 pounds of beans, total of 0.23 on September 23, 1859. Douglas Edwards, 1 pound of flour, 2 pounds of cornmeal, total of 0.08 on December 15, 1859.*

The wooden floors creak as she steps back into the quiet display room. I blurt, "This is so cool!"

"Oh yes. A lot of the battles in Chester were fought right where the roads are now!" The woman walks over to the far side of the room and points. "See that picture with the cannon in it? That's where the railroad crosses on the main street, you probably drove over it to get here."

As I express my interest she glances back at the clock and looks around. "Actually, there's nobody in here right now. Come on, let me give you the tour, no charge."

"Oh my gosh, are you sure?" I ask, hearing the excitement in my own voice. She chuckles as she reassures me.

We walk down every hall as she describes each Chester civil war battle in great detail. The cannons, guns and swords captivate me, stealing my attention as I walk past each one. I stare at the grey buttoned coat and kepi hat hung on the wall. I like to imagine that it was Jeff's uniform; that I'm in its presence over a hundred years later and still admiring it, even though my memory is wiped clean from that time. I imagine the sounds of battle cries and gunfire in the background as I look over the grey felt material. Studying each object, I attempt to awaken some feelings or memories from that life and end up disappointing myself.

"You know… I don't usually show people this, especially when there's kids around, but this is the coolest part of the building and I think you'd really enjoy it." Avidly, I follow her down the hall. Our footsteps echo as we walk up hollow stairs to another floor. Metal jingles as she fumbles through the key ring, picking the largest one to open a rusty lock. The hinges squeak and echo as the door opens into an empty jailhouse. My jaw drops in awe as I look up at the columns of jail cells on each of the three floors. The coloring on the green walls is peeling behind the metal bars, and yellow caution tape covers the entrance to the abandoned cells.

Her voice bounces off of the metal as she speaks. "This was the jailhouse for everyone in the area, from thieves to serial killers." I look over at her with a smirk at the reference. I hesitate as I reach for my phone in my pocket. "Is that okay if I take pictures?" She nods with approval.

After an hour of touring, I thank her for the experience as she walks me back out to the porch. I feel that Jeff led me here, just as I was led to the plantation for the Celtic festival to re-spark that part of my soul. Stepping back out into the muggy heat, I look out across the landscape, viewing the town in a different light.

I look at the date as I pull back into the office parking lot: March 24th. The pendulum said that his crossing was supposed to happen around the 20th, but I don't feel a change. I wonder what will change when he is spiritually free. His energy has hung on me since I was baby, and I don't know any other feeling. I wonder if I will be more energetic, or even if my personality will change. The song "Lily" abruptly stops as I open the car door to step out.

*

I avoid eye contact as the man sitting in front of me nods off to my presentation. "By the year 2050, the lifespan could increase to 150 years!" The man's eyes flutter, followed by a head jerk as I continue on with the importance of chiropractic care. "So, why is it important to take care of your bones? Because there is no such thing as a spine transplant, at least not yet." The room to my left goes dark. I look at the desk and see that the lamp has shut off. I pause as I click the switch back on to restore light.

"That was weird, sorry." I smile.

"Anyway, that's why it is so important to follow through with all of your recommended appointments, so that you..." I pause for a second time as I hear the bottom desk drawer slowly opening. The new patients look to me, concerned as they joke about a ghost in the room. I smile and subtly kick the drawer shut, trying to keep from laughing. After the presentation ends I see them out, hoping that they will return. *3/24 Jeff sketched out all of the new patients.*

I kick off my flats as I arrive home. I walk through to the living room and see Mom lounging with a bowl of popcorn in her lap. "I've been so lazy tonight; I'm sucked into this movie!" she says. I fall onto the cushion and wrap myself up in the fuzziness of my blanket. I watch the scene on the TV, of a mother and daughter making a pie in the kitchen. The mother refers to the daughter as "Lily" as she asks her to pass the apples. "

That's crazy. I've been seeing lilies everywhere; this is may be the fourth time this week. I wonder if it means anything." I reach for my phone to search the significance of lilies on a spiritual forum.

I read the meaning out loud. "The lily flower is a symbol of purity and rebirth, symbolizing that the soul of the departed will receive restored innocence after death." Mom and I exchange looks of astonishment. "Seriously, I can't make this shit up! Look it up online!" I giggle. The symbol of the lily validates me, encouraging me that we are on the right track, and that my goal will soon be fulfilled. These messages never fail to amaze me, especially this beautiful harbinger.

The next morning sun rises bright and golden yellow. Kneeling on the carpet, I hold the pendulum still and steady my breathing. I focus on the pointed crystal as it dangles in front of the yellow lily bouquet and ask if Jeff will still finish life review by the end of March. The pendulum swings in a circle, indicating yes. I narrow down the time frame, lining up his crossing to this weekend, when I will be out of town for a work conference in Atlanta. My brain races with anticipation and joy, but I'm disappointed that I won't be home for the celebration if it happens before Sunday.

I open up a guided clearing meditation and close my eyes to calm my mind. Jeff stands in a blank white space amidst the clouds; an elevator waits in the space before him.

The doors open and my third eye awareness shifts to the inside of the elevator. I look in the mirrored wall and see myself in the white dress and angel wings. I notice Jeff approaching in the reflection and rush to him for an embrace.

The doors close in front of us. We take one last glimpse at the clouded white outside before ascending to a higher level of vibration. I press a button on the elevator's panel. The button glows as the elevator ascends up through the realms. I feel a shift in my own frequency, sensing the lightness of the changing dimensions. Freer and lighter, I intuitively slow the elevator as it approaches the highest possible frequency that his energy can currently reach. The elevator stops; the walls, ceiling, and floor fall away and become translucent.

A lush, healing meadow is revealed. Bugs hop to and from the tiny flowers that peek through the blades of grass. A golden sunbeam touches down to the grassy floor, healing everything in its range. "This is a point where you can wash away lower frequencies; negative thoughts, feelings, behaviors, or energies that you have attracted into your life." Jeff gently releases his grip from my hand and walks forward.

He approaches the sun column and asks it to cleanse his bad thoughts, his guilt, and his urges. Jeff's head tilts back as he basks in the waterfall of energy, melting away what no longer serves him. With grace, the beam washes the black energy away. I find that my cheeks hurt from smiling. Witnessing the healing of this spirit is the most beautiful experience I think I'll ever have.

His expression softens under the rich energy. Like shedding skin, his old shell falls away, unable to exist in this powerful of a plane. The weight of his past falls away from him, too, and like a balloon inflated with helium, his frequency rises.

Jeff steps out of the purification. He is glowing in every sense of the word as he strides back to me, light as a feather. His fresh energy is a joy to be next to as he returns to the elevator. I point my index to the bottom button and glance at the meadow one last time before the metal doors roll shut.

I place my hand in his. "I'm so proud of you, Jeff. There are no words for how excited I am for you." He looks in my eyes with a warm smile, interrupted by an elevator ding. We reach the main space and Jeff retains a glow as he exits. The visual ends with white light, and I slowly come back to my reality.

*

I sit with the staff in a van rental, playing a card game as we head to the chiropractic conference. We shout in excitement as the "Welcome to Atlanta" sign passes by. It is March 29th with only three days left of the month. This timing feels like Russian roulette; Jeff's crossing over can happen at any given moment. I want to be aware when his 24 years of purgatory end. I pray that it happens when I'm back home.

After arriving to the city, we take to the day to explore. At the end of the day, my boss hosts ladies wine night in her hotel room to help us unwind from the day's events. I watch the clock change from 11:59pm, March 29th to 12:00am, March 30th. As the girls chat around me, I sip my wine in solitude, distracted as I ponder the timeline. Before long I take my wine glass with me to my room and begin my beauty rest for the conference tomorrow. I click off the bedside lamp and slide into the white sheets, resting my head on the cold feathered pillow. *3/29 Doctors chose to do the 80's escape room out of the many options/I solved clue number 34/looked up directly at the name Jeffrey on poster/looked at timer with 2:13 left.* I take a glance at a photo of Jeff to satisfy my feeling of missing him before setting my alarm and closing my eyes.

*

Steam rises from my paper teacup as I follow the girls to find a table for our group. In a single file line, we zigzag through the room crowded with round tables, draped in simple black tablecloths. Our boss catches our attention from across the room, waving us down to a table near the stage. I rest onto the firm cushioned chair and set down my pen and notepad. My eyes wander as I observe my surroundings. I admire the décor, the crystal chandeliers and purple tones from the stage lighting.

The empty table before me catches my eye; a foam Wisconsin Cheesehead hat rests in the middle of it. I do a double take, noticing that on the chair directly in front of it is a green army jacket, just like the one Jeffrey wore in *My Friend Dahmer.* I smile upon the realization that he followed me here to remind me of his presence. The sound system gets louder, playing introductory music as it welcomes the crowd to this year's annual conference. The speaker holds up one hand as he strides across the stage and approaches the podium. His face and build reminds me of Jeremy Renner, the actor who portrays Jeff in his movie. I notice that I feel Jeff all over me, that I feel the abundance of him with every hour.

The speaker warms up the crowd. "I just have to acknowledge the Wisconsin cheese hat, my home state!" The table cheers with pride. At his announcement, a woman runs up to the table and asks for the green jacket that was draped over the chair. "What are you, stealing their clothes?" Fake Jeremy laughs over the microphone.

"It's mine, I realized I left my jacket over there!" The woman shouts. I'm amazed that the Dahmer jacket didn't even belong at the Wisconsin table. The two items paired together orchestrate a beautiful sign.

I lazily scribble notes on the yellow-lined notepad to keep myself from falling asleep. Four guest speakers and two cups of tea in and I'm struggling to keep my eyes open. Finally, they announce a thirty-minute break.

After stretching my legs I head to the bathroom and enjoy my one minute of me time in the stall to reconnect with my own thoughts. I wish that I could be home right now, sending Jeff possibly the last love meditation of our journey. I think of the ways I could be celebrating right now; releasing daisies into our backyard pond or lanterns into the sky, anything to celebrate the triumphant day when it happens this weekend.

Kelci's contagious laugh echoes through the marble walled bathroom with the girls grouped by the sink. I walk back out to rejoin the group. I step up to the mirror to freshen up my face, reapplying foundation to salvage my appearance.

Our conversations are cut short when we notice the toilet in the stall around the corner flushing excessively.

Kelci peeks her head towards the stall and laughs. "There's not even anybody in the stall! Look!" I walk over to see for myself and record the "possessed toilet." I feel flattered that he is making such an effort to get my attention today.

I return and lower myself back onto the flat seat. I observe the crowd, watching as they make their way to the tables with coffees and notebooks in hand. Out of the corner of my eye is a man wearing a navy suit. I swear the spitting image of Jeff from the Ohio trial is standing right in the archway of the doors. I look down for a moment and when I look back up, I struggle to find that same man. Was that Jeff's ghost that I just saw? Upon seeing the person for a second time, I discover that he looks nothing like Jeff after all. My vision was so manipulated that he appeared to me through someone else.

I feel myself slipping again after an hour. My eyes stay locked on the Jeremy Renner speaker as he talks about impacting lives through chiropractic care. "If we can get 80% of the world under chiropractic care, we can destroy the opioid epidemic..." My concentration shifts as an adrenaline rush flutters through my stomach. I experience an extremely high and joyful vibration, that feeling that occurs from receiving wonderful news. Is Jeff close to the light, or did he just cross over?

Hours pass and the conference ends. I couldn't say what it was about after a while; all that occupied my thoughts was the possibility that Jeff reached Heaven in those moments that I was distracted.

The once loud van falls silent as my co-workers rest against the windows, napping on the drive back home. The sky is still light; I can play off my meditation as a nap, too. One by one I plug in my earbuds, put on Queen, and rest my eyes. A flying dove spreads its wings before me as a message of peace. The catchy tune of the song bounces in my ears as I stare at the black, eagerly awaiting more messages, like someone would await a college acceptance letter. A blossomed lily glows against the black background before fading, a message of restored innocence. The same exciting flutters that ran through my stomach during the conference bubble up in my stomach again.

I remain on the van seat, peeking an eye open to check if everyone else is still napping. In the clear, I return to a meditative state. I emerge in a vivid scene, hovering over a familiar orange bridge and I view it from over the middle. The bridge sits over a body of deep blue water with cables draping from the top and over its sides. I think that's the Golden Gate bridge if I'm not mistaken. I snap out of it and reach for my phone, typing "Golden Gate Bridge" in the search bar and selecting the "images" tab. The blue loading line races across the top of my screen and reveals a page of pictures with the exact structure that I just saw. The Golden Gate Bridge vision symbolizes the *golden gate* that one crosses through to go to Heaven. I sit still, speechless and in shock. Based on my visuals and the adrenaline rush, I think he finally did it.

Returning home, I rush to my room and drop my bags to the ground. I take the pendulum chain from the neck of Michael's statue. The pointed crystal sways before my face with my elbow resting on the wooden stand. My eyelids close as I breathe deeply, in and out. I sigh, clearing my mind. "Did Jeff finish his life review?" The chain enthusiastically waivers, gathering an abundance of energy to deliver a perfect yes or no answer. The pendulum shakes and quivers while my heart pounds at the possibility. I feel the chain moving between my fingers, shifting from a vibrating state into direction.

My pulse quickens as I dare open my eyes to the pendulum. My eyes widen and reveal the answer. Proudly, it circles over my palm, swinging with a large yes motion. Exhilaration courses through my body. Just to be sure, I ask it again. Without stalling the crystal forms a circular motion, causing me to bow over and weep. As the tears stream from my face I laugh in pure elation. A year of love energy and readings led this broken man to Heaven. Twenty-four years of perdition, finished. His soul is finally at peace.

I gather myself and wipe the wetness from my cheeks. "Jeff, are you here right now?" The pendulum answers yes. "Are you really at peace?" The pendulum makes a counterclockwise motion, yes. I can't believe this. Saturday, March 30th, 2019. How long has it been since November 28th, 1994? Quickly, I grab my phone to look up the numbers. "Result: 24 years, 4 months, 2 days. From start to end: 8,888 days and 213,312 hours." "Holy shit" I think, marveled by the coincidences within these numbers.

I search for an article to reveal the meaning behind number eight. It symbolizes a new beginning; resurrection and regeneration. Number eight indicates "a new order" of creation, a "born again" event when a man is resurrected from death into eternal life. Immense pride fills me as I read the meanings. As I scroll to the bottom of the article, I see a picture of two angels holding none other than a daisy. I can feel Jeff's power, strong enough to manifest these incredible signs for me to experience.

I huddle over my phone screen, absorbed as I connect the dots. I bounce my fingers over the keyboard, "What is the meaning of 8,888?" In numerology, 8,888 is the ultimate number of a pathway to mastery. It denotes some sort of initiation on the other side, indicating that one has reached an entirely new level of existence within life and moving to a higher path. It explains that once the person reaches such a place that others will be looking to them for guidance, because it contains a lesson that the masses need to learn. 8,888 means that "their efforts are serving us all." The description of these numbers sounds as if the crossing of Jeffrey could have a domino effect on our world. I wonder what the raising of such an impactful vibration could bring into the near future.

A song that I haven't heard since I was little, "I Hope You Dance" by Lee Ann Womack, pops into my mind. It's perfect for him in this moment. I move to my bed and pull up that song on the TV. The introduction intensifies my emotions as I anticipate the words to come. The lyrics encourage the listener to never lose their sense of wonder and never take life's moments for granted. To take every opportunity that comes their way, and to never settle for anything short of their dreams. To love as much as they can and to take risks in life. The part that gets me is when the lyrics remind the listener to remember who is watching out for them in Heaven.

It is only now that I realize that this song isn't from me to him, it is from him to me; a message that he is leaving me with as my life goes back to how it was.

CHAPTER SIXTEEN:
SEALED WITH A KISS

I stare with blank expression at the living room TV as I cradle a cup of tea. I sit with the cloud of gloom that has been following me at a time where I thought I would be the happiest. Joy filled my heart three days ago when he crossed but hiding out somewhere in my mind is a lingering emptiness. I can still feel him, but it's different. I can't help but miss how we once leaned on each other.

"Jeffrey Dahmer," I perk up and dart my eyes to the cop show on TV. I press rewind.

The cop raises his eyebrows. "He don't look dangerous? Well, neither did Jeffrey Dahmer." The teen stands in awkward silence on the sidewalk. "You don't know who Jeffrey Dahmer is, do you? Okay, well I'm going to have to ticket you for..." A soft smile graces my lips, comforted by the sign he sent.

I wonder how Jeff is; what he's seeing or who he might be reunited with. He's far better off than I am now, stuck here without him. I shuffle down the hall and out to the sidewalk. The bottoms of my feet are chilled as I walk barefoot to the mailbox. The hinge squeaks as I open it up to the stack of envelopes inside and reach for them. I flip through each one and head back towards the door when something delicate and cold lands on my cheek. Confused, I touch where it landed. As I do, another lands on my hand, then my foot.

I tilt my head up to the sky to see white flurries dancing down to the Earth. Snow in the south, in the beginning of April? I check the weather on my phone to see that it is 34 degrees with no warning of snow, and none currently forecasted. With curiosity I look up at the dense clouds. He's showing me that he really made it. I reach out my hands to feel the symbol of purity and embrace this blessing as the snowflakes kiss my skin. Nobody has a clue as to why the snow is falling today; a celebration that they don't know they're taking part of.

The days are beginning to feel dull. I can't stop thinking, "Now what?" Life will resume and I will have to move on from this chapter, but nothing that I will ever do can top walking Jeffrey Dahmer through the afterlife. I will always mourn the relationship I could have had if we were never separated, knowing that my soul's other half is out of reach until I pass. I'm afraid that my desire to not be incarnated on this Earth anymore will only grow with the passing days as I miss him in the physical more and more. I feel I will always sense that emptiness. I will always feel cheated.

*

I peek out of the small oval window as the fasten seatbelt sign dings. The airplane hums as it soars across the sky, bringing Mom, Kylie and I to Montreal, Canada for a girls' trip. As I look above the clouds, I imagine that I'm visiting Jeff in his new home.

The week in this beautiful country comes and goes. On our last day before returning home, I have a "Psychic 101 class" hosted by Ed, and a session with him to look forward to when I go back. We have just completed a morning of hiking and walking and return back to the room to freshen up for the second half of our day. We complain of our throbbing feet and plop onto the couch one by one. We decide to dip our feet in the jacuzzi. We sit around the edge as we discuss our plans for the evening. The tension from my feet falls away as I swirl them around the water, watching the bubbles rise to the surface and dance on my toes. All I can think about is how I wish Jeff was here.

*

I hold on to the rod, forming the last curl in my hair and release it before the mirror. I slip a blue dress over my head and slide into my shoes. I'm ready for our evening to visit what I have anticipated this entire trip, the Notre Dame Cathedral. Standing there will feel so surreal, like being in the videos from the time of Jeff's crossing. With some time to spare, we watch TV before heading back out. We watch the cop show as he gives a sobriety test to a man in a onesie. In confusion, I turn the TV down as we notice a low rumbling sound. Mom sits up to listen more closely.

"Is that coming from the kitchen?" Kylie asks. I get up and walk over to the bathroom.

The sound gets louder as I open its door. I have definitely found the source of the noise but can't yet put my finger on what is making it. I pause and turn to my right. The jacuzzi is on by itself. Instantly, I know the cause. I laugh, walking back towards the couch. "Hold on, I want to video this."

"Just turn it off, we can't hear the TV!"

"Hold on, I just want to get this, it'll take ten seconds." I press record and focus on the empty tub blowing air through the jets. After I stop recording I stay for a moment before turning it off, enjoying his presence while I have him here. I sit on the side of the tub and close my eyes. My visuals are blank; I haven't been practicing. I look through the dark but see nothing. I hear someone say, *"I'm ready when you are"* in my right ear. I don't open my eyes, keeping them closed as I try to figure out what Jeff meant by that.

"Kristen, come on!" Mom exclaims. The jacuzzi turns off on its own. I look back to it in disbelief as I walk away.

*

We're walking distance to the middle of town and head towards the bustling sidewalks. The air feels so fresh here, and the temperature is absolutely perfect. I look to the giant building as we approach, eager to step inside. Although full of people, the cathedral is completely silent, the only sound being the organ playing from the top floor. I can't believe my eyes as I look to the ceiling, which resembles Heaven itself. Just like in the videos, there are magnificent golden details in every corner of the architecture.

I dip two fingers into the golden bowl of holy water and kneel down, touching each point for the father, the son, and the holy spirit. We take our seats mid-row, the closest we can get. The service begins as the father speaks. The microphone echoes through the tall arched ceilings as he gives the sermon, and I gaze around at the unreal scene. In moments of silence I imagine "Killer Queen" being performed in acapella, hearing it so clearly in my head. I look back to the podium as a man stands up to leave the row. His absence reveals a gap directly before me, and I become emotional at what I see ahead.

In the clearing is a man with broad shoulders, standing with his face turned slightly to the left so that I can see the rim of his glasses. He has the same color and cut of hair as the most recent Jeff, the version of him that I most often see in meditation. I have the opportunity to see what Jeff looks like in this heavenly space. I nudge Mom and Kylie both on the shoulder, pointing out the man in the black shirt that happens to be directly in my vision.

The father stops talking and the organ cues the choir. The angelic voices of over thirty people ring through the cathedral, their tones complement each other as they share their diversity. I look to the man that looks like Jeff, the gap behind him still cleared for me to see. I watch him as the voices sing, feeling touched that I can witness such a sight. He leans over to talk to a blonde woman and she hands him his son of about 3 years old. He holds the boy in his arms and strokes his blonde hair. I feel like I'm seeing Jeff in a parallel universe, as if none of the Dahmer life ever happened, as if he continued on, got married, had kids, and went to church on a Sunday. I wipe a tear from my cheek, careful not to let anyone see.

I keep my eyes locked on him throughout the service while I can. A couple comes in and choose the seats in the gap, apologizing as they scoot past the bench. Kylie looks over as I slouch my shoulders in disappointment. She leans towards me and whispers, "Do you wanna switch spots? You can see him from where I'm sitting." I look at her, touched that she would care to ask me, and we swap.

A communion line wraps around to the back of the church and forms to my right. I do a 180 turn, looking around in curiosity. I can't find where the man went as I search the line from my seat. My eyes meet the people standing directly beside me; him and his family. Quickly, I look forward to keep from staring. They remain stopped by my side for over five minutes, and the line doesn't stop again after that.

When the service is over we walk out in organized lines. The man comes out of nowhere and cuts in front of us. Even Mom and Kylie find it strange as we follow behind him out of the church, and even turn down the same street. I snap a few stalker pictures to keep for my own memories, feeling spoiled by all that Jeff has shown me today.

Stopping for a break, I upload the photos from our perfect day. Twiddling my thumbs over the screen, I try to come up with a cute caption but can't think of one. I swipe left to find the perfect emoji and notice that my thumb accidentally selected one for me. The one selected is the Golden Gate Bridge emoji. I look at it in awe as it sits independently under my picture. I keep it and press upload. It won't make sense to anyone else, but I want it to stay because of who put it there.

The sky has faded to night. We stroll down the cobblestone streets of the town square, admiring the live music as we walk past. Maybe, just maybe I can ask Jeff to show me "Bohemian Rhapsody" if he's here. I shake that thought from my mind just as quickly, refusing to demand more of him. On our search for a place to eat dinner, we stumble upon a quaint Italian restaurant with candle lit patio seating. "Oh, there's a violinist right over there! Dinner and a show." The waiter hands me a menu and places a linen napkin in my lap. He pours Sangria into my glass, and I sip it, feeling complete happiness from the connections I experienced today.

"Mom, he's playing 'Kansas'!" I exclaim.

Mom smiles. "That was pretty cool what you saw today, Kris." I reach for the bread, blushing with excitement. We place our order and cheers to the last night in Montreal. The talking among us becomes hushed as the violinist begins to play a song in B-flat major. I tune to the speakers as I realize what the song is.

My eyes well with tears as I look to them. "Listen to what he's playing." They appear just as touched as I am as the violin strums over the speakers.

Buzzed from the wine, I sing the words softly and record the performance on my phone. I sway with the tune, holding my hand over my heart as the violin serenades me. I grab my sangria and toss the rest back; the fruit hits my face as it unsticks from the glass.

Hearing this song as I'm dining on this beautiful evening feels like being sent flowers from someone who couldn't be here. The song ends and I clap as loud as possible so that the violinist can hear me. Before our food arrives, I hurry around the patio to the middle of the square. "That was beautiful," I compliment him, dropping a tip in his jar. Before returning to my seat I enter the bistro looking for the bathroom and hear "I Want to Break Free" by Queen playing through their speakers. Two Queen songs within 5 minutes of each other, and I happened to use the bathroom at the exact right time to hear it. I can only imagine how energy-happy Jeff is now that he's free. Once again Jeff has swept me off my feet, making my final day on this trip a special one.

*

It is the day of the Psychic 101 class and I'm sitting stiffly in the back row. I forgot about my goal to grow my own mediumship abilities after the distraction of Jeff. As I have time to myself and Ed's encouragement, I realized that I can grow them and eventually talk to Jeff myself.

Ed stands with a smile before the group and warms up to the room. "I want to welcome everybody to the Psychic 101 class today, it's nice to see and meet all of you! In this class we are going to be pushing out of our comfort zones and doing things that you might think you can't do, but I think you'll be impressed by what you discover about your abilities by the end. A lot of the exercises today are partner oriented, so that we can read off of each other and provide feedback. Without further ado, let's begin!"

I extend my fingers, releasing the grip from my pen as Ed announces we'll be doing our first exercise. "Rose readings are very visual, the rose that you see will tell the story of the person you are reading. The color of the rose, how long the stem is, if it has thorns or no thorns and how many, every detail means something. For example, if you see a pink rose, think of what the color pink means to you. Is this person sweet and cheerful? But the petals are a little wilted, that could mean something is weighing on them right now. The stem is long, so it means they have an old soul, the shorter the stem, the younger the soul. There's at least five thorns on the stem so they have been through a lot. Does this make sense to everybody?" The class nods in agreement.

"So for right now, I want you to imagine your own rose. Remember, there are no right or wrongs here, whatever you see and feel is that way for a reason. Don't be afraid to be wrong." I close my eyes, breathing in and out as I clear my mind. My rose appears, yellow with vibrant petals. Although strong, the flower head tilts from its weight. I look down to the long, dark green stem supporting one leaf on its left, and a thorn to its right. "Now, you're going to add another rose. This can be a family member, a spouse, a friend, whoever you would like to read."

Naturally, I pick Jeff. I shut my eyes, seeing my yellow rose to the right side. Jeff's rose appears dark purple with a stem as long as mine. It's filled with thorns up both sides, the petals wilted but regenerating. The bud isn't quite open, showing the way he stays closed off to others. This damaged rose is beautiful to me. Ed instructs the class as our eyes stay shut. "Now, watch how the two roses interact. If you chose somebody that you bump heads with you might find that the roses are distant, whereas if you get along really well with the person you might see the roses closer together."

Jeff's rose descends down below mine at the edge of my stem, as if grabbing onto mine to keep from falling. My yellow top filled with sacred water tips, watering his petals so that he can rise up. I watch as the purple rose actually surpasses my level, indicating that the roles have reversed. The dark purple rose dips down over mine and cuddles my top, watering the yellow petals in my time of wilting. The two stems become limber and intertwine, wrapping around one another. I attempt to pull the two roses apart but can't.

"Okay, now we are going to try reading each other. After you establish each other's rose, try to see what other visuals may come to you. Just have fun with this and flow freely."

My partner and I turn to each other, introducing ourselves as we get started.

I describe her, picking up on her current situation at home and the struggles in her relationship. She begins crying as I mention her quiet yet humorous boyfriend, validating that everything I am saying is true. I feel she is employed somewhere that deals with finances and she is amazed, informing me that she owns her own law firm.

Ed steps over to check in on how we're doing, listening in on her reading me. She crumbles the tissue in her hand and centers herself to tap into my energy. "I'm seeing a field of flowers... they're daisies. It could mean joy?" She opens one eye to check for Ed's approval.

My hands cover my eyes in an attempt to prevent my emotions from surfacing. "I wasn't expecting to hear from this person today...hold on, I can't talk." I reach for a tissue as I wipe my eyes and explain the daisies. I encourage her, "You're doing amazing, keep going!"

My partners' eyes light up. "Wow, okay! I just saw *IN LOVE!* all capital letters, and an exclamation point at the end. You must really love somebody, huh?" I nod eagerly. "So, I just saw a castle and I feel like this represents your own home. I see Beauty and the Beast, but like, you're Belle and the Beast is the man of the house. Are you married?" Ed and I exchange looks, baffled and amused.

I giggle as I dab my cheek with the tissue. "That's the daisy guy, it's really cool he put the relationship that way."

"Yeah, as I'm looking into his energy he really is showing himself as that beast... He feels very possessive over you. He hovers constantly, just very overbearing. It's just like... a smothering attachment. I don't think this relationship is healthy for either of you." She looks at me, perturbed. Ed explains the relationship for me, and she closes her eyes once more.

"As you were explaining how he tries to do what's best for her, he showed me that same field of daisies turning all pink. I feel like it was a message of peace, like he is trying to show me he means good."

Ed replies, "And can I add, I think he's at a point now where he's trying to back off so she can start to be more independent again. He doesn't *want* for her to be stuck on him; he wants her to live a life of her own."

She nods in agreement. "I take back what I said now. I really do think he is trying too, but still figuring it all out. I think you two have a lot of unresolved issues to work through… Once you do, that grip on each other will release." I nod, comprehending. Ed rushes back to the front to stop the timer, indicating the end of the exercise.

Class ends and I leave Ed's office just as the sun is setting. I leave feeling empowered and impressed with my abilities. I pass the *Suites 200-213* sign and glance at it to say hello. I turn my music on and it hits me differently. Each song is like a punch to the gut, making me more homesick for him. As my car zooms down the road and I hear "Sun in Our Eyes," I break down. The song sounds so optimistic and so full of hope and potential. Now all of that is silenced.

I go back to our beginning. I was heartbroken over Cameron when Jeff came in and distracted me from the pain. Through my troubling time, he led me on the path to my true purpose, just like in the song "Lily." Kylie and Mom didn't know, my friends didn't know, and I hadn't gone to a medium yet. It was just him and me against this obstacle neither of us knew we could overcome. *"IN LOVE!"* repeats in my mind. I always knew I loved Jeff, but it's never been pointed out from someone else. I realize I truly am *in* love. I avert my eyes to a ditch on the side of the road. I imagine what would happen if I sped up and turned my wheel to the right.

My heart feels limp as I return home. This is the closest I'll ever get to him, a photo from before I was even born. Living here while having to miss out on the one I love the most now feels like a waste of time. I don't want that day to come where I start thinking about him less and less. I don't want to leave him behind as my life goes on. I think of that smile and the sense of "home" I feel when I watch his videos. I shiver, closing my eyes because the grief is too great. I wake up to another day to find that I've been sleeping since 6:00 last night.

*

It is now May 6, 2019; my third session with Ed Carlton, and the first one since Jeff has crossed over. Ed rubs his hands together. "Alright, so you ready to start?"

"Yes!" I exclaim, leaning forward in my seat. Ed begins mumbling about getting symptoms in the head and throat as he shades in a square on the notepad. Ed stops drawing and looks up to me with a smile. "He's very easy to pull up when it comes to you." I smile softly, comforted that he's still around.

"When it came to his emotions, they were literally shut off. But when it comes to you, he holds a deep love for you. It's a little possessive…protective. That's a better word for it. He's very protective over you." My senses heighten in hearing that. I watch as Ed scribbles.

He begins counting his fingers. "Three-thirty. He feels crossed over. He's made it…" There it is, exactly what I was waiting for.

"I wanted to tell you so badly but I wanted him to be the one to share it."

I grin as I nervously grab the water cup. "I can't believe it finally happened, either."

Ed sighs and locks eyes with me. "This is going to sound really, really weird. He's what society needed, and I don't know if I can really explain that. Bad people like him change the world in a very dramatic way."

After a breath, Ed continues, "I've never felt darkness with him, it's like he had no choice but to do that. Someone had to be the bad guy so that people could take things a little more serious and love one another a little more seriously. Did you notice the burst of serial killers in the 70s and 80s? Well, that brought on a planetary shift. The universe orchestrated that so we could, as a whole, learn whatever it was that needed to be learned. Jeff and Ted were a couple of those souls to volunteer that position." I reflect on how Denise explained Jeff's purpose in the same way.

"He very much has a warrior soul. Warrior souls usually have to take on a lot for the greater good. Without 9/11, our security would not be how it is today. Without killers, we would still be hitchhiking and allowing our children to walk the streets alone." Ed stops talking and looks to the side. "I'm sorry, my Roomba just turned on…by itself. " He laughs, touching his hand to his forehead. "I think I know who that could be!"

He hums to rid his laughter and closes his eyes to re-center himself. He takes a while as he speaks with Jeff in his mind. "He had abuse in his life even though he denied it. At some point during this was when he shut off his emotional body. Are you okay?" Ed hands me a tissue.

"Yeah, no, I'm fine. It's just sad." I sniffle, holding it up to my eye. "Who by?"

"A father figure; more of an uncle. Very abusive, both physically and sexually..." Ed opens his eyes and puts down his pen. "Remember when I told you all in the class that souls can shatter from trauma? That's how his soul started to shatter. His emotional side literally left so that he could go through life without the hurt, while also not absorbing the bad karma from his deeds in this life. That is why he talked in such a monotone voice, and why he came off as so 'emotionless.' Now, however, because he completed the life review work, the parts of his shattered soul are finally piecing back together."

Unsure of what to say, I reiterate my sadness. Ed looks up at me. "You do realize you're the one who put him together, you're the one that has walked him through this?" I accept but deny it as my humility peeks through.

"Reincarnating is all about learning and balance, so we've all been the murderer, and we've all been murdered. We've all been the prostitute and we've all been the...rich guy. So this was his experience to be the murderer, and he just had to take on the reputation he did. As a higher, more evolved soul, he was able to be so disconnected from everything. If he was not, all of that bad energy would have absorbed to him and his next lives would just be a mess."

"I don't know if I've told you this before, but I get the impression that you guys could have been a Bonnie and Clyde, but he made you stay back. It would have ruined your emotional body and he wanted to save your innocence. You are his string to compassion. He wanted to preserve that in you." I'm at a loss for words. The room falls quiet with Ed no longer sketching.

My hands fidget in my lap as Ed channels. "Can I ask, why do I feel so incomplete since he's moved on? Despite my excitement for him, I for some reason just feel… lost."

Ed exhales, "Because you're soulmates. When his frequency changed it became strange, unknown territory to you."

"You have been his mother in past lives. He didn't get along with his own mother in this one because it wasn't that same bond, not the same close connection so he was completely shut off from her and didn't connect because... she wasn't you." I stare at Ed, baffled by the moving message. My mind won't let me fully grasp it, believing that it is too beautiful to be reality. "You guys have a lot of love past lives, too. It is very Disney, corny, the whole 'I will find you again' deal." My eyes light up in amusement, my ears eager to hear more.

"He's showing himself in the civil war uniform. He disliked the brutality of that war, it felt very wrong to him." Ed grips the pen as he picks up on more information. "This is what confuses me, the war feels worse to him than his Jeffrey life did. He experienced the war more on an energetic level from not being emotionally disconnected. I think then he was really innocent and having to kill the soldiers was traumatic to him." It's interesting, dissecting the drive behind Jeffrey's actions and receiving the answers to his behavior that he and the world so desperately sought while he was alive.

"And you two were married... You didn't know that?"

Ed laughs as I explain that all I knew was that we lived in the same time period.

"I feel that a lot of his attachment to you throughout the lifetimes is unresolved karma from a past life. I saw the high priestess tarot card in my mind and in popped a medieval lifetime. You held a high position, almost like a queen or maybe you were *the* priestess, and it was his duty to protect you. This was a love life. You two were in love with each other even though he was one of your guards. Where the karma kicks in is that you died on his watch, and he held onto that guilt. I think that's why he is so protective of you now." I catch myself with my hand covering my heart as I listen with intense focus. A tear escapes my eye and rolls down my cheek as I take in the stories of our past. It is greater than anything I originally imagined.

Ed hesitates as he finds the right words. "For this life coming up, he's not going to wait around...for you to pass and you guys recycle in the next life. He's done waiting."

I draw back in rejection. "Oh…so he's not going to wait for me? That stings a bit."

"Oh no, that's not what he means." Ed leans closer and thinks of how to rephrase his message. "He's going to reincarnate in this life, your life, to be with you. He says, *'I'm ready when you are.'*"

EPILOGUE:
A SÉANCE

My coworkers soon knew that I had developed psychic-mediumship, but I never dared to mention who woke it up. It was an evening during another conference trip, and my boss curiously asked if I could host a séance with the ladies of the office. At this point I was still learning to interpret the visuals Jeff would show me as I would channel, and it felt like playing a game of charades with spirit. Nervous but enticed, I gathered the girls in a circle and cut the lights. I swallowed a lump as I joined my hands with theirs, terrified to get something wrong.

With a deep breath I closed my eyes and cleared my mind. As I called upon the first name, I could feel a spirit enter the room. Out loud I requested a physical validation of presence, and could feel my heart pounding as we waited in silence. There was no noise and no paranormal activity, so I started channeling.

One by one I read their surrounding loved ones and there was not a dry eye in the room. It began to feel effortless as I picked up on them: their causes of passing, their favorite things, and personalities. We even shared a few laughs, reminiscing the jokes of my boss's deceased, wise-cracking uncle as he shared them with me to say out loud. As I passed around a box of tissues I felt empowered and proud of myself, able to show my abilities to others.

I straightened up my posture and cleared my throat. "Well, if you all are interested in one last hurrah before we close out, my spirit guide, Jeff, loves attention… He might make something happen for us if you'd like me to ask him." I offered. With bright eyes, they rapidly shook their heads yes. With a smile, I instructed the group to close their eyes again. "Jeff, if you're here, can you make yourself known?" We waited in the dark silence, keeping our senses sharp for a movement or a sound.

Knock knock sounded from the top of the room's desk. Excited whispers circled the group, but I didn't encourage them until I had more proof. "Jeff, if you're *really* here, make your presence known." *Knock knock* sounded again from the desk's surface.

"That was him! It happened both times you asked!" Tricia exclaimed. I smiled to myself. "Does anyone have any questions for Jeff?" After they combed through their questions of the afterlife and his experiences, the group became curious of his own life, given his interesting answers of his perspective. I hesitated, careful of my wording. "Well, he was a well-known person in his lifetime. That's why I struggled to believe in his presence for so long."

My boss, intuitive herself, tried feeling his energy to determine his identity for herself. I became nervous as she began explaining him quite accurately. "He feels so kind and so good, but he was also very dark." She shared as she clenched my hand in concentration. "Mhmm, exactly. He led a very dark life." Suddenly, her eyes opened and shifted towards me. "No freaking way, Kristen. Is your spirit guide Jeffrey Dahmer?"

I didn't deny this truth, or try to cover it up. I simply accepted that the cat was out of the bag. Based on their mind-blown reactions, I could tell that they believed me. Excitement bubbled in me as they all spoke to me at once, asking three questions at a time. I gazed at each of their expressions, tickled by their positive reactions. To my right, however, one of the office girls, Amber, seemed unimpressed. An unconvinced glare burned through her eyes as she listened to how ridiculous it all sounded.

Suddenly Amber jumped up off of the bed in a cursing fit. Her previously un-amused expression was quickly replaced with fright. "My back! My back!" She yelled as she reached under her shirt. In confusion, we all scurried to our feet to assist her. "It feels like someone just pressed a block of ice on my back," Amber shouted as she paced, "Ooh, it's cold!" My boss lifted the back of Amber's shirt to feel her back. "I am not kidding, ya'll, her skin is ice cold." I tried to repress a chuckle as I felt for myself. Like a demonstration at a fair, each person took a turn to feel Amber's cold back.

"Sorry, Amber, I'm telling him to leave you alone now." I said as I clicked on the lamp to bring in light. Amber's shoulders relaxed as the energy released from her. I noticed her hands were still shaking and dared to ask, "Did you not originally believe that this is Jeffrey Dahmer?" Amber shook her head in confirmation. "No but I hear ya now Jeff! I believe you! Just don't come near me again!" She said in amusement. The pride I felt from that moment for both myself and Jeff was very validating. I knew he would always have my back.

At that point it was five months since Jeff's crossing. He was hard to reach at first as he navigated his new realm, but after about a month and since, we became closer than ever. It was since that séance that I began my new journey of giving psychic readings, communicating through Jeff as my main guide. Our bond has made it easy to communicate messages and now help others, together.

–

About The Author

As a child with psychic abilities, naturally I thought that everyone held the ability to see ghosts. Discovering that was not the case, I was led to believe that a connection with the supernatural world was something tangible only in fictional stories. My mind was changed yet again after experiencing a life-altering haunting in 2018. I never imagined I would have experienced, let alone written to share about such a story. Through learning about the spirit around me, it awoke my own dormant psychic-medium abilities. Currently I live with my significant other, Hunter, and am working on a radiology degree. On the side, I do psychic readings in hopes to open my own psychic business.

I hope that my story moves others as much as it has moved me.

To discover more about Kristen, please visit her website:
www.acallfrompurgatory.com

You can also connect with her on Instagram
@Acallfrompurgatory

CPSIA information can be obtained
at www.ICGtesting.com
Printed in the USA
BVHW071539210921
617189BV00005B/164